Technician Unit 17

IMPLEMENTING AUDIT PROCEDURES

For assessments in December 2003
and June 2004

Interactive Text

In this May 2003 new edition

- For assessments under the new standards

- Layout designed to be easier on the eye – and easy to use

- Clear language and presentation

- Lots of diagrams and flowcharts

- Activities checklist to tie in each activity to specific knowledge and understanding, performance criteria and/or range statement

- Thorough reliable updating of material to 1 April 2003

FOR 2003 AND 2004 SKILLS BASED ASSESSMENTS

PROFESSIONAL EDUCATION

First edition May 2003

ISBN 0 7517 1136 5

British Library Cataloguing-in-Publication Data
A catalogue record for this book
is available from the British Library

Published by

BPP Professional Education
Aldine House, Aldine Place
London W12 8AW

www.bpp.com

Printed in Great Britain by WM Print
Frederick Street
Walsall
West Midlands
WS2 9NE

We are grateful to the Lead Body for Accounting for
permission to reproduce extracts from the Standards
of Competence for Accounting, and to the AAT for
permission to reproduce extracts from the mapping
and Guidance Notes.

Contents

Introduction

How to use this Interactive Text – Technician qualification structure –
Unit 17 Standards of competence – Assessment strategy – Building your portfolio

		Page	Answers to activities
PART A	**Introduction to auditing**		
1	What is an audit?	3	341
2	How is audit regulated?	21	343
3	To whom are the auditors liable?	33	344
4	What are auditors responsible for?	45	346
PART B	**Planning an audit assignment**		
5	Knowledge of the business and its systems	63	348
6	Audit plan	93	351
7	Audit staff	109	352
8	Audit documents	119	353
9	Audit evidence and procedures	131	354
PART C	**Conduction an audit assignment**		
10	Tests of controls	153	356
11	Substantive tests	173	360
12	Stocks	191	364
13	Fixed assets	209	367
14	Debtors and cash	225	369
15	Liabilities, share capital, reserves and statutory books	245	373
16	Audit completion	269	376
17	Group audits	295	–

Page   Answers
to activities

PART **D**   Preparing draft reports

18   Reports to management 307 379
19   The external audit opinion 319 381

Answers to activities 341

Glossary 387

Index 391

Order form

Review form & free prize draw

Introduction

How to use this Interactive Text

Aims of this Interactive Text

To provide the knowledge and practice to help you succeed in the assessment for Technician Unit 17 *Implementing Audit Procedures.*

To pass the assessment successfully you need a thorough understanding in all areas covered by the standards of competence.

To tie in with the other components of the BPP Effective Study Package to ensure you have the best possible chance of success.

Interactive Text

This covers all you need to know for the skills based assessment for Unit 17 *Implementing Audit Procedures.* Numerous activities throughout the text help you practise what you have just learnt.

Assessment Kit

When you have understood and practised the material in the Interactive Text, you will have the knowledge and experience to tackle the Assessment Kit for Unit 17 *Implementing Audit Procedures.* This aims to get you through the assessment, whether in the form of the AAT simulation or in the workplace.

Passcards

These short memorable notes are focused on key topics for the Unit, designed to remind you of what the Interactive Text has taught you.

Recommended approach to this Interactive Text

(a)   To achieve competence in Unit 17 you need to be able to do **everything** specified by the standards. Study the Interactive Text carefully and do not skip any of it.

(b)   Learning is an **active** process. Do **all** the activities as you work through the Interactive Text so you can be sure you really understand what you have read.

(c)   After you have covered the material in the Interactive Text, work through the **Assessment Kit**.

(d)   Before you take the assessment, check that you still remember the material using the following quick revision plan for each chapter.

    (i)   Read and learn the **key learning points**, which are a summary of the chapter. This includes key terms and shows the sort of things likely to come up in an assessment. Are there any gaps in your knowledge? If so, study the section again.

    (ii)   Do the **quick quiz** again. If you know what you're doing, it shouldn't take long.

    (iii)   Go through the **Passcards** as often as you can in the weeks leading up to your assessment.

This approach is only a suggestion. Your college may well adapt it to suit your needs.

Quick quizzes

These include multiple choice questions, true/false and other formats not used by the AAT. However, these types of questions are usually very familiar to students and are used to help students adjust to otherwise unfamiliar material.

Remember this is a **practical** course.

(a)   Try to relate the material to your experience in the workplace or any other work experience you may have had.

(b)   Try to make as many links as you can to your study of the other Units at Technician level.

(c)   Keep this text, (hopefully) you will find it invaluable in your everyday work too!

BPP
PROFESSIONAL EDUCATION

Technician qualification structure

The competence-based Education and Training Scheme of the Association of Accounting Technicians is based on an analysis of the work of accounting staff in a wide range of industries and types of organisation. The Standards of Competence for Accounting which students are expected to meet are based on this analysis.

The AAT issued new standards of competence in 2002, which take effect from 1 July 2003. This Text reflects the **new standards.**

The Standards identify the key purpose of the accounting occupation, which is to operate, maintain and improve systems to record, plan, monitor and report on the financial activities of an organisation, and a number of key roles of the occupation. Each key role is subdivided into units of competence, which are further divided into elements of competences. By successfully completing assessments in specified units of competence, students can gain qualifications at NVQ/SVQ levels 2, 3 and 4, which correspond to the AAT Foundation, Intermediate and Technician stages of competence respectively.

Whether you are competent in a Unit is demonstrated by means of:

- *Either* an Exam Based Assessment (set and marked by AAT assessors)

- *Or* a Skills Based Assessment (where competence is judged by an Approved Assessment Centre to whom responsibility for this is devolved)

- Or *both* Exam *and* Skills Based Assessment

Below we set out the overall structure of the Technician (NVQ/SVQ Level 4) stage, indicating how competence in each Unit is assessed. In the next section there is more detail about the Skills Based Assessments for Unit 17.

Unit 17 is assessed by skills based assessment.

NVQ/SVQ Level 4

Group 1 Core Units – All units are mandatory.

Unit 8 Contributing to the Management of Performance and the Enhancement of Value	Element 8.1 Collect, analyse and disseminate information about costs
	Element 8.2 Make recommendations and make recommendations to enhance value

Unit 9 Contributing to the Planning and Control of Resources	Element 9.1 Prepare forecasts of income and expenditure
	Element 9.2 Produce draft budget proposals
	Element 9.3 Monitor the performance of responsibility centres against budgets

Unit 10 Managing Systems and People in the Accounting Environment	Element 10.1 Manage people within the accounting environment
	Element 10.2 Identify opportunities for improving the effectiveness of an accounting system

Unit 22 Contribute to the Maintenance of a Healthy, Safe and Productive Working Environment	Element 22.1 Contribute to the maintenance of a healthy, safe and productive working environment
	Element 22.2 Monitor and maintain an effective and efficient working environment

BPP)))
PROFESSIONAL EDUCATION

NVQ/SVQ Level 4, continued

Group 2 Optional Units – Choose **one** of the following **four** units.

Unit 11 Drafting Financial Statements (Accounting Practice, Industry and Commerce)	Element 11.1 Draft limited company financial statements
	Element 11.2 Interpret limited company financial statements

Unit 12 Drafting Financial Statements (Central Government)	Element 12.1 Draft Central Government financial statements
	Element 12.2 Interpret Central Government financial statements

Unit 13 Drafting Financial Statements (Local Government)	Element 13.1 Draft Local Authority financial statements
	Element 13.2 Interpret Local Authority financial statements

Unit 14 Drafting Financial Statements (National Health Service)	Element 14.1 Draft NHS accounting statements and returns
	Element 14.2 Interpret NHS accounting statements and returns

NVQ/SVQ Level 4, continued

Group 3 Optional Units – Choose **two** of the following **four** units.

Unit 15 Operating a Cash Management and Credit Control System	Element 15.1 Monitor and control cash receipts and payments
	Element 15.2 Manage cash balances
	Element 15.3 Grant credit
	Element 15.4 Monitor and control the collection of debts

Unit 17 Implementing Audit Procedures	Element 17.1 Contribute to the planning of an audit assignment
	Element 17.2 Contribute to the conduct of an audit assignment
	Element 17.3 Prepare related draft reports

Unit 18 Preparing Business Taxation Computations	Element 18.1 Prepare capital allowances computations
	Element 18.2 Compute assessable business income
	Element 18.3 Prepare capital gains computations
	Element 18.4 Prepare Corporation Tax computations

Unit 19 Preparing Personal Taxation Computations	Element 19.1 Calculate income from employment
	Element 19.2 Calculate property and investment income
	Element 19.3 Prepare Income Tax computations
	Element 19.4 Prepare Capital Gains Tax computations

Unit 17 Standards of competence

The structure of the Standards for Unit 17

The Unit commences with a statement of the **knowledge and understanding** which underpin competence in the Unit's elements.

The Unit is then divided into **elements of competence** describing activities which the individual should be able to perform.

Each element includes:

(a) A set of **performance criteria**. This defines what constitutes competent performance.

(b) A **range statement**. This defines the situations, contexts, methods etc in which competence should be displayed.

(c) **Evidence requirements**. These state that competence must be demonstrated consistently, over an appropriate time scale with evidence of performance being provided from the appropriate sources.

(d) **Sources of evidence**. These are suggestions of ways in which you can find evidence to demonstrate that competence. These fall under the heading: 'observed performance; work produced by candidate; authenticated testimonies from relevant witnesses; personal account of competence; other sources of evidence.' They are reproduced in full in our Assessment Kit for Unit 17.

The elements of competence for Unit 17 *Implementing Audit Procedures* are set out below. Knowledge and understanding required for the unit as a whole are listed first, followed by the performance criteria and range statements for each element. Performance criteria are cross-referenced below to chapters in this Unit 17 *Implementing Audit Procedures* Interactive Text.

Unit 17: Implementing Audit Procedures

What is the unit about?

This unit relates to the **internal** and **external auditing process** and requires the candidate to be involved from planning through to the reporting stage. The candidate is responsible for the identification of control objectives and their assessment, the selection of a sample and tests, drawing appropriate conclusions from the tests and drafting the reports which give preliminary conclusions and recommendations. The unit requires the candidate to be supervised in the work.

Knowledge and understanding

To perform this unit effectively you will need to know and understand:

The business environment	Chapters in this Text
1 A general understanding of the legal duties of auditors: the content of reports; the definition of proper records (Elements 17.1, 17.2 & 17.3)	1,16
2 A general understanding of the liability of auditors under contract and negligence including liability to third parties (Elements 17.1, 17.2 & 17.3)	3
3 Relevant legislation, relevant Statements of Auditing Standards (Elements 17.1, 17.2 & 17.3)	2,3,4
Auditing techniques	
4 Types of audit: relationship between internal and external audit (Elements 17.1, 17.2 & 17.3)	1
5 Recording and evaluating systems: conventional symbols; flowcharts; Internal Control Questionnaires (ICQs); checklists (Elements 17.1 & 17.2)	5
6 Verification techniques: physical examination; reperformance; third party confirmation; vouching; documentary evidence; identification of unusual items (Elements 17.1 & 17.2)	9
7 Basic sampling techniques in auditing: confidence levels; selection techniques (random numbers, interval sampling, stratified sampling) (Elements 17.1 & 17.2)	9
8 The use of audit files and working papers (Elements 17.1, 17.2 & 17.3)	8
9 Auditing techniques in an IT environment (Elements 17.1 & 17.2)	9
10 Types of tests: tests of control; substantive (Elements 17.1 & 17.2)	10,11
11 Management letters which include systems weaknesses, clerical/accounting mistakes, disagreement re. accounting policies or treatment (Element 17.3)	18
Auditing principles and theory	
12 Principles of control: separation of functions; need for authorisation; recording custody; vouching; verification (Elements 17.1, 17.2 & 17.3)	5
13 Materiality (Elements 17.1, 17.2 & 17.3)	6
14 Audit risk (Elements 17.1 & 17.2)	6
The organisation	
15 Understanding that the accounting systems of an organisation are affected by its organisational structure, its administrative systems and procedures and the nature of its business transactions (Elements 17.1, 17.2 & 17.3)	1,5
16 An understanding of the organisation's systems and knowledge of specific auditing procedures (Elements 17.1, 17.2 & 17.3)	10

Element 17.1 Contribute to the planning of an audit assignment

Performance criteria		Chapters in this Text
A	Ascertain **accounting systems** under review and record them clearly on appropriate working papers	5
B	Identify control objectives correctly	5,10
C	Assess risks accurately	6
D	Record significant weaknesses in control correctly	18
E	Identify account balances to be verified and the associated risks	6,11
F	Select an appropriate sample	9
G	Select or devise appropriate **tests** in accordance with the organisation's procedures	9,10,11,12,13,14,15
H	Follow confidentiality and security procedures	2
I	Formulate the proposed audit plan clearly and in consultation with appropriate personnel	7
J	Submit the proposed audit plan to the appropriate person for approval	7

Range statement

1   **Accounting systems relating to:**
   - Purchases
   - Sales
   - Stock
   - Expenses
   - Balance sheet items
   - Payroll

2   **Accounting systems that are:**
   - Manual
   - Computerised

3   **Tests**
   - Tests of control
   - Substantive

Element 17.2 Contribute to the conduct of an audit assignment

Performance criteria		Chapters in this Text
A	Conduct **tests** correctly and as specified in the audit plan, record test results properly and draw valid conclusions from them	12,13,14,15
B	Establish the existence, completeness, ownership, valuation and description of assets and liabilities and gather appropriate evidence to support these findings	11,12,13,14,15
C	Identify all matters of an unusual nature and refer them promptly to the audit supervisor	11,12,13,14,15,16
D	Identify and record material and significant errors, deficiencies or other variations from standard and report them to the audit supervisor	12,13,14,15,16
E	Examine the IT environment and assess it for security	5
F	Conduct discussions with staff operating the system to be audited in a manner which promotes professional relationships between auditing and operational staff	
G	Follow confidentiality and security procedures	2

Range statement

1 **Tests**
- Tests of control
- Substantive

Element 17.3 Prepare related draft reports

Performance criteria		Chapters in this Text
A	Prepare clear and concise **draft reports** relating to the audit assignment and submit them for review and approval in line with organisational procedures	18,19
B	Draw valid conclusions and provide evidence to support them	18,19
C	Make constructive and practicable recommendations	18,19
D	Discuss and agree your preliminary conclusions and recommendations with the audit supervisor	16
E	Follow confidentiality and security procedures	2

Range statement

1 **Draft reports relating to:**
- A manual system

Assessment strategy

Unit 17 is assessed by **skills based assessment**.

Skills Based assessment is a means of collecting evidence of your ability to carry out practical activities and to **operate effectively in the conditions of the workplace** to the standards required. Evidence may be collected at your place of work or at an Approved Assessment Centre by means of simulations of workplace activity, or by a combination of these methods.

If the Approved Assessment Centre is a **workplace** you may be observed carrying out accounting activities as part of your normal work routine. You should collect documentary evidence of the work you have done, or contributed, in an **accounting portfolio**. Evidence collected in a portfolio can be assessed in addition to observed performance or where it is not possible to assess by observation.

Where the Approved Assessment Centre is a **college or training organisation**, devolved assessment will be by means of a combination of the following.

(a) Documentary evidence of activities carried out at the workplace, collected by you in an **accounting portfolio**

(b) Realistic **simulations** of workplace activities; these simulations may take the form of case studies and in-tray exercises and involve the use of primary documents and reference sources

(c) **Projects and assignments** designed to assess the Standards of Competence

If you are unable to provide workplace evidence, you will be able to complete the assessment requirements by the alternative methods listed above.

Building your portfolio

What is a portfolio?

A portfolio is a collection of work that demonstrates what the owner can do. In AAT language the portfolio demonstrates **competence**.

A painter will have a collection of his paintings to exhibit in a gallery, an advertising executive will have a range of advertisements and ideas that she has produced to show to a prospective client. Both the collection of paintings and the advertisements form the portfolio of that artist or advertising executive.

Your portfolio will be unique to you just as the portfolio of the artist will be unique because no one will paint the same range of pictures in the same way. It is a very personal collection of your work and should be treated as a **confidential** record.

What evidence should a portfolio include?

No two portfolios will be the same but by following some simple guidelines you can decide which of the following suggestions will be appropriate in your case.

(a) **Your current CV**

This should be at the front. It will give your personal details as well as brief descriptions of posts you have held with the most recent one shown first.

(b) **References and testimonials**

References from previous employers may be included especially those of which you are particularly proud.

(c) **Your current job description**

You should emphasise financial **responsibilities and duties**.

(d) **Your student record sheets**

These should be supplied by AAT when you begin your studies, and your training provider should also have some if necessary.

(e) **Evidence from your current workplace**

This could take many forms including **letters, memos, reports** you have written, **copies of accounts** or **reconciliations** you have prepared, **discrepancies** you have investigated etc. Remember to obtain permission to include the evidence from your line manager because some records may be sensitive. Discuss the performance criteria that are listed in your Student Record Sheets with your training provider and employer, and think of other evidence that could be appropriate to you.

(f) **Evidence from your social activities**

For example you may be the treasurer of a club in which case examples of your cash and banking records could be appropriate.

(g) **Evidence from your studies**

Few students are able to satisfy all the requirements of competence by workplace evidence alone. They therefore rely on simulations to provide the remaining evidence to complete a unit. If you are not working or not working in a relevant post, then you may need to rely more heavily on simulations as a source of evidence.

(h) **Additional work**

Your training provider may give you work that specifically targets one or a group of performance criteria in order to complete a unit. It could take the form of questions, presentations or demonstrations. Each training provider will approach this in a different way.

(i) **Evidence from a previous workplace**

This evidence may be difficult to obtain and should be used with caution because it must satisfy the 'rules' of evidence, that is it must be current. Only rely on this as evidence if you have changed jobs recently.

(j) **Prior achievements**

For example you may have already completed the health and safety unit during a previous course of study, and therefore there is no need to repeat this work. Advise your training provider who will check to ensure that it is the same unit and record it as complete if appropriate.

How should it be presented?

As you assemble the evidence remember to **make a note** of it on your Student Record Sheet in the space provided and **cross reference** it. In this way it is easy to check to see if your evidence is **appropriate**. Remember one piece of evidence may satisfy a number of performance criteria so remember to check this thoroughly and discuss it with your training provider if in doubt.

To keep all your evidence together a ring binder or lever arch file is a good means of storage.

When should evidence be assembled?

You should begin to assemble evidence **as soon as you have registered as a student**. **Don't leave it all** until the last few weeks of your studies, because you may miss vital deadlines and your resulting certificate sent by the AAT may not include all the units you have completed. Give yourself and your training provider time to examine your portfolio and report your results to AAT at regular intervals. In this way the task of assembling the portfolio will be spread out over a longer period of time and will be presented in a more professional manner.

What are the key criteria that the portfolio must fulfil?

As you assemble your evidence bear in mind that it must be:

- **Valid**. It must relate to the Standards.
- **Authentic**. It must be your own work.
- **Current**. It must refer to your current or most recent job.
- **Sufficient**. It must meet all the performance criteria by the time you have completed your portfolio.

What are the most important elements in a portfolio that covers Unit 17?

You should remember that the unit is about **audit procedures**. Therefore you need to produce evidence that you can carry out certain tasks and procedures.

For Element 17.1 *Contribute to the planning of an audit assignment* you need to demonstrate that you have done so, by including a copy of an audit memorandum you have prepared. To indicate that you have correctly consulted with senior audit staff the memorandum should have been reviewed (and evidenced as reviewed) by senior staff.

The main evidence you need for Element 17.2 *Contribute to the conduct of an audit assignment* is working papers you have compiled while carrying out audit assignments in the relevant areas.

For Element 17.3 *Prepare draft related reports* the best sources of evidence might be management letters you have drafted or memorandums to managers and partners in which you draw conclusions from the audit work you have carried out.

Remember that it is important in Unit 17 that you follow **confidentiality** and **security** procedures as this is vitally important in auditing. You should therefore consult with your manager before including any working papers in your portfolio and also ensure that any client details (including details such as major customers and suppliers) are deleted from working papers included, so that the client is not identifiable.

Finally

Remember that the portfolio is **your property** and **your responsibility**. Not only could it be presented to the external verifier before your award can be confirmed; it could be used when you are seeking **promotion** or applying for a more senior and better paid post elsewhere. How your portfolio is presented can say as much about you as the evidence inside.

For further information on portfolio building, see the BPP Text *Building Your Portfolio*. This can be ordered using the form at the back of this Text or via the Internet: www.bpp.com/aat

P A R T   A

Introduction to auditing

chapter 1

What is an audit?

Contents

1 The problem
2 The solution
3 The company and the law
4 The financial statements
5 The appointment of auditors
6 The audit
7 A different problem
8 The solution

Knowledge and understanding

1   A general understanding of the legal duties of auditors: the content of reports; the definition of proper records

4   Types of audit: relationship between internal and external audit

15   Understanding that the accounting systems of an organisation are affected by its organisational structure, its administrative systems and procedures and the nature of its business transactions.

1 The problem

Anton has **set up in business** selling paper. For two years all goes well. The paper sells steadily and Anton gets some income from the business.

Anton feels that the business could make more money if he invested in some printing equipment and if he employed an assistant to design patterns to print on some of the paper to sell. He needs more money to do this. **He decides to ask his rich friend Jane to invest** in the business.

Jane wants to invest but she does not wish to work for the business or take on any risk for the business debts.

Jane suggests to Anton that he converts the business into a **company**. This will mean that if the company becomes insolvent, she will only lose at maximum the amount she has invested in the company. Anton agrees. Jane buys 95% of the shares and Anton buys 5%. They both agree that Anton is to be paid a reasonable salary as managing director of the business.

At the end of the first year of trading as a limited company, **Jane receives a copy of the accounts. Profits are lower than she expected**. This means that her return from the company (in dividends) will not be as high as she had hoped.

Jane contacts Anton for an explanation. He tells her that the accounts are accurate. Jane knows that Anton gets paid a salary regardless of what the profits are. She is concerned that this means he is not as worried about profit levels as she is.

Jane feels she needs further assurance on the accounts, but she does not know a great deal about financial matters. How can she obtain the assurance she wants?

2 The solution

The assurance Jane is seeking can be given by an **audit** of the financial statements. An auditor can provide the two things Jane requires.

- A **knowledgeable review** of the company's business and of the accounts
- An **impartial view** since Anton's view may be partial

The following diagram shows the process of investing in a company and receiving the benefit of an audit.

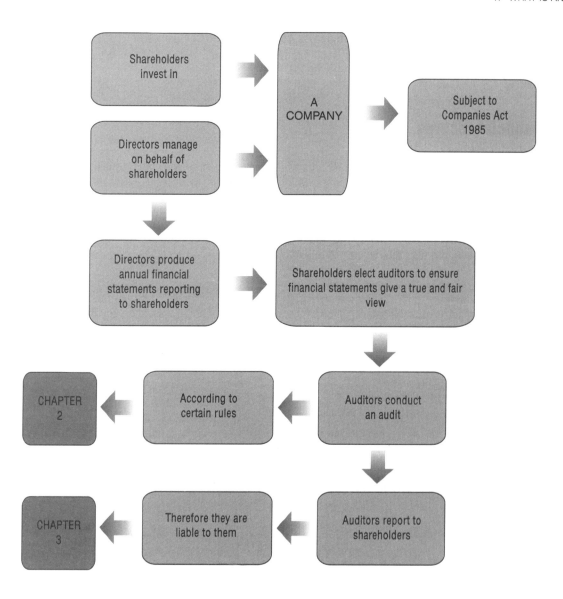

3 The company and the law

3.1 The Companies Act 1985

Jane obtains certain benefits from investing in a company rather than a different form of business vehicle. The key **benefit** is that she will only ever be liable for the cost of her shares. **Creditors of the company** can **never sue Jane for any company debts**.

This **advantage is offset** by the fact that companies are required to conform to a number of **regulations**, some of which require companies to **publish information** about themselves for the benefit of the public and people who deal with the company, for example, suppliers, customers, lenders.

The key law for companies in the UK is the **Companies Act 1985** and the Companies Act 1989. We are going to look at what these Acts require companies to keep in relation to financial records and regulations in connection with audit and auditors.

3.2 Financial records

> 'Every company shall keep accounting records which are sufficient to show and explain the company's transactions and are such as to
>
> (a)   disclose with reasonable accuracy, at any time, the financial position of the company at that time, and
>
> (b)   enable the directors to ensure that any balance sheet and profit and loss account prepared under this Part complies with the requirements of this Act.'
>
> Companies Act 1985

In other words, the records must be detailed enough that an accountant could walk in on any day and be able to prepare a balance sheet and profit and loss account.

The Act then gives details of what this means in practice. Accounting records must contain:

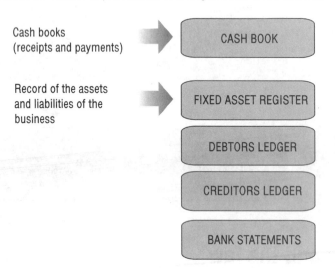

Cash books (receipts and payments) → CASH BOOK

Record of the assets and liabilities of the business → FIXED ASSET REGISTER

DEBTORS LEDGER

CREDITORS LEDGER

BANK STATEMENTS

If the company deals in goods, they are also required to keep:

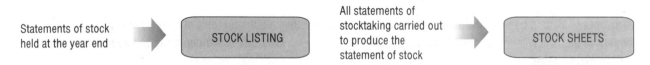

Statements of stock held at the year end → STOCK LISTING

All statements of stocktaking carried out to produce the statement of stock → STOCK SHEETS

Where it is not a normal retail trade, statements of all goods sold and purchased showing enough details of the goods and buyers and sellers that they can all be identified, must be retained.

If the company does not keep these records, the directors and officers of the company may be found guilty of an offence and be imprisoned and/or fined. These records must be kept at the office registered with the Registrar of Companies (a government department) or somewhere else that the directors think is fit.

The law also requires that these accounting records are kept for a certain period of time:

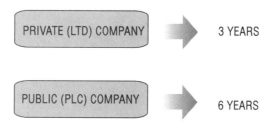

You should be aware from your other AAT studies that in practice, the detail of the accounting records which a company keeps will vary according to the nature of the business. We can see above that the law only requires a company to keep stock records if it has stock. Similarly, if it only makes cash sales, it will not need to keep debtors' records.

3.3 Audit requirement and exemptions

The Companies Act 1985 **requires companies to have an audit**. Some other entities, such as building societies, trade unions, housing associations and large charities are also required to have audits under different laws.

Certain companies are allowed not to have an audit (they are exempt from the audit requirement):

- Small companies
- Small charities that are companies
- Dormant companies

3.3.1 Small companies

A company is small for this purpose if:

- Turnover $\leq$ £1 million
- Balance sheet total $\leq$ £1.4 million
- It is a private limited company
- It is not a banking or insurance company
- It is not part of a larger group of companies

Key
$\leq$ = smaller or equal to

3.3.2 Small charities that are companies

A charity which is a company is small if:

- Gross income $\leq$ £250,000
- Balance sheet $\leq$ £1.4 million

3.3.3 Dormant companies

The shareholders of a dormant company may choose not to have an audit (75% of them must vote in favour). A company is dormant if:

- It has never carried out a transaction which required entering in financial records, or

- It has not carried out a transaction which required entering in financial records during the year under review
- It is not a public company
- It is not a banking or insurance company

3.4 Auditors

3.4.1 Appointment

Auditors should usually be appointed by shareholders at a shareholders' annual general meeting. In unusual circumstances they may be appointed by directors. Auditors are usually re-elected annually, but a private (Ltd) company may pass a resolution which deems that the existing auditors are automatically re-elected annually.

3.4.2 Report

The Companies Act requires auditors to produce a report for company members (shareholders). This should state whether the financial statements show a **true and fair view** of the **state of affairs** at the year end and the **profit and loss** for the year. They shall also consider whether the **report** which the **directors** make as part of the annual statement is **consistent** with the accounts.

As part of their audit, the auditors must check whether the company has **kept adequate accounting records** (as discussed above) and whether each geographical **branch** of the business has given **sufficient information** for the audit, and that the **underlying records match** the financial statements the directors have prepared.

The law **does not** state what form the report should take, but auditors usually use one like the one shown on the next page, due to professional requirements.

The law states that the report must give the auditors' name, the date of the report and their signature. This has been highlighted on the report overleaf.

There are several other things the Companies Act requires auditors to identify in their report, if necessary:

- Proper accounting records have not been kept
- Proper returns have not been received from branches
- The financial statements do not agree with underlying records
- Information and explanations required by the auditors have not been given by the company officials

Obviously, these should only be included if relevant.

Copies of the auditors' report must be:

- Circulated to members of the company (often at the annual general meeting)
- Sent to the Registrar of Companies

Audit Report

INDEPENDENT AUDITORS' REPORT TO THE MEMBERS OF BPP HOLDINGS PLC

We have audited the group's financial statements for the year ended 31 December 2002 which comprise the Group Statement of Total Recognised Gains and Losses, Reconciliation of movements in Shareholders' Funds, Group Profit and Loss Account, Group Balance Sheet, Company Balance Sheet, Group Cash Flow Statement, and the related notes 1 to 30. These financial statements have been prepared on the basis of the accounting policies set out therein. We have also audited the information in the Directors' Remuneration Report that is described as having been audited.

This report is made solely to the company's members, as a body, in accordance with Section 235 of the Companies Act 1985. Our audit work has been undertaken so that we might state to the company's members those matters we are required to state to them in an auditors' report and for no other purpose. To the fullest extent permitted by law, we do not accept or assume responsibility to anyone other than the company and the company's members as a body, for our audit work, for this report, or for the opinions we have formed.

Respective responsibilities of directors and auditors

The directors' responsibilities for preparing the Annual Report, the Directors' Remuneration Report and the financial statements in accordance with applicable United Kingdom law and accounting standards are set out in the Statement of Directors' Responsibilities.

Our responsibility is to audit the financial statements and the part of the Directors' Remuneration Report to be audited in accordance with relevant legal and regulatory requirements, United Kingdom Auditing Standards and the Listing Rules of the Financial Services Authority.

We report to you our opinion as to whether the financial statements give a true and fair view and whether the financial statements and the part of the Directors' Remuneration Report to be audited have been properly prepared in accordance with the Companies Act 1985. We also report to you if, in our opinion, the Directors' Report is not consistent with the financial statements, if the company has not kept proper accounting records, if we have not received all the information and explanations we require for our audit, or if information specified by law or the Listing Rules regarding directors' remuneration and transactions with the group is not disclosed.

We review whether the Corporate Governance Statement reflects the company's compliance with the seven provisions of the Combined Code specified for our review by the Listing Rules, and we report if it does not. We are not required to consider whether the board's statements on internal control cover all risks and controls, or form an opinion on the effectiveness of the group's corporate governance procedures or its risk and control procedures.

We read other information contained in the Annual Report and consider whether it is consistent with the audited financial statements. This other information comprises the Chairman's Statement and Review of Operations, Financial Review, Directors' Report, Corporate Governance Statement and the unaudited part of the Directors' Remuneration Report. We consider the implications for our report if we become aware of any apparent misstatements or material inconsistencies with the financial statements. Our responsibilities do not extend to any other information.

Basis of audit opinion

We conducted our audit in accordance with United Kingdom Auditing Standards issued by the Auditing Practices Board. An audit includes examination, on a test basis, of evidence relevant to the amounts and disclosures in the financial statements and the part of the Directors' Remuneration Report to be audited. It also includes an assessment of the significant estimates and judgements made by the directors in the preparation of the financial statements, and of whether the accounting policies are appropriate to the group's circumstances, consistently applied and adequately disclosed.

We planned and performed our audit so as to obtain all the information and explanations which we considered necessary in order to provide us with sufficient evidence to give reasonable assurance that the financial statements and the part of the Directors' Remuneration Report to be audited are free from material misstatement, whether caused by fraud or other irregularity or error. In forming our opinion we also evaluated the overall adequacy of the presentation of information in the financial statements and the part of the Directors' Remuneration Report to be audited.

Opinion

In our opinion:
- the financial statements give a true and fair view of the state of affairs of the company and of the group as at 31 December 2002 and of the profit of the group for the year then ended; and

- the financial statements and the part of the Directors' Remuneration Report to be audited have been properly prepared in accordance with the Companies Act 1985.

ERNST & YOUNG LLP
Registered Auditor, London
17 March 2003

3.4.3 Rights

The Companies Act gives auditors certain rights, shown in the table.

s 389A(1)	Access to records	A right of access at all times to the books, accounts and vouchers of the company
s 389A(1)	Information and explanations	A right to require from the company's officers such information and explanations as they think necessary for the performance of their duties as auditors
s 390(1)(a) and (b)	Attendance at/notices of general meetings	A right to attend any general meetings of the company and to receive all notices of and communications relating to such meetings which any member of the company is entitled to receive
s 390(1)(c)	Right to speak at general meetings	A right to be heard at general meetings which they attend on any part of the business that concerns them as auditors
s 381B(2)-(4)	Rights in relation to written resolutions	A right to receive a copy of any written resolution proposed
s 253	Right to require laying of accounts	A right to give notice in writing requiring that a general meeting be held for the purpose of laying the accounts and reports before the company (if an elective resolution dispensing with laying of accounts is in force)

4 The financial statements

As you should be aware from your other studies, directors are required to produce financial statements every year.

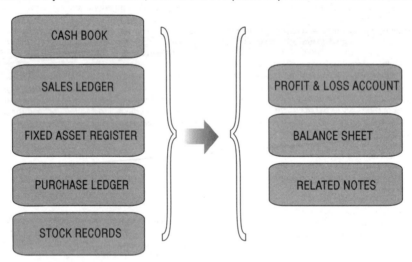

These financial statements are produced for the benefit of shareholders, but many other parties may be interested in them:

- The bank
- Suppliers

- Customers
- Employees
- Tax authorities

These parties have access to the financial statements, a copy of which must be filed for public inspection with the Registrar of Companies. **Most** of these parties will not have access to the underlying records.

5 The appointment of auditors

As was discussed in section 3.4, by **law**, the auditors are appointed by **shareholders**. In **practice**, however, the **directors** will make recommendations to the shareholders. It is usually the directors that will be involved in choosing an audit firm.

5.1 The tender

A company's directors will usually ask several audit firms to **tender** for the audit of the company. In a tender, the audit firm will present a case to the company about why they are the best firm to use. The company will consider factors such as:

- Price (which the **company** has to pay)
- Experience of the audit firm
- Reputation of the audit firm

5.2 What the auditor will do

The auditor will prepare a tender (a report and/or verbal presentation) which addresses the three issues above. It will set out why the firm is right for the job, concentrating on experience and key staff members.

In order to estimate the price of the audit, the auditor must also make a best estimate of what work they will carry out and what it will cost the audit firm to do the work.

5.2.1 Ethical matters

We will discuss ethical matters more in Chapter 2. However, you should be aware that before accepting an appointment, an auditor should ensure that there are no ethical reasons why he should not do so.

This will involve writing to the audit firm that is stopping being the auditor and asking them if there is any such reason. Both audit firms should ask the company for permission to write to each other. If the company says no, the new audit firm should not accept appointment.

The new audit firm should also ensure that the old audit firm has been removed properly, and in accordance with the Companies Act.

5.2.2 Practical issues

The audit firm must consider whether it has time to do the work, whether it can make a profit from the work and whether it has the skills to do the work (if the company is unusual for any reason).

If the audit firm does not already know the client, it should obtain references about it from people who do.

The audit firm is likely to consider whether the audit is high or low risk, that is, the chances of auditors making a mistake and giving the wrong opinion in their report. They will consider things like:

LOW RISK	HIGH RISK
Good long-term prospects	Poor recent or forecast performance
Well-financed	Likely lack of finance
Strong internal controls	Significant control weaknesses
Conservative, prudent accounting policies	Evidence of questionable integrity, doubtful accounting policies
Competent, honest management	Lack of finance director
Few unusual transactions	Significant related party or unexplained transactions

6 The audit

Once auditors have been appointed for the year, they will carry out an audit at the appropriate time.

6.1 Definition of audit

An audit is an exercise that auditors carry out in order to be able to give the legal opinion whether financial statements give a true and fair view.

An audit is a combination of tests and enquiries and judgements made by the auditors. We shall look at these elements in detail in Parts B and C of this Study Text. The purpose of the tests and enquiries and judgements is to give an opinion in a report, which we will look at in more detail in Part D of this Study Text.

6.2 True and fair

The law requires auditors to give an opinion whether financial statements are **true and fair**. However, it does not say what 'true and fair' means. Auditors go by generally accepted meanings:

True: Information is factual and conforms with reality, not false. In addition the information conforms with required standards and law. The accounts have been correctly extracted from the books and records.

Fair: Information is free from discrimination and bias and in compliance with expected standards and rules. The accounts should reflect the commercial substance of the company's underlying transactions.

It is important to understand that true and fair **does not mean absolutely correct**. Auditors cannot say that financial statements are absolutely correct because:

- Financial statements are a combination of fact and **judgement**
- An audit also includes **judgements** made by the auditors
- Auditors do not test every transaction (or audits would be too expensive)
- Company management might tell lies/carry out hidden fraud

6.3 Properly prepared

Auditors also state whether financial statements are properly prepared. This means prepared in accordance with law and accounting standards. You should know about these from your other studies.

6.4 Auditing standards

To ensure that all audits are a good quality, the tests and enquiries and judgements made by auditors have to be carried out in accordance with certain standards. These are discussed in Chapter 2.

6.5 Chronology of audit

The more important duties of the auditors of a limited company were listed in section 3.4

Certain **common elements** form a major part of the auditors' work on any client.

- **Making tests** and enquiries to form an opinion as to the reliability of the accounting records
- **Checking** the **accounts** against the underlying records
- **Reviewing** the **accounts** for compliance with the law and standards

The chart overleaf outlines the main stages of an audit that are **normally** followed.

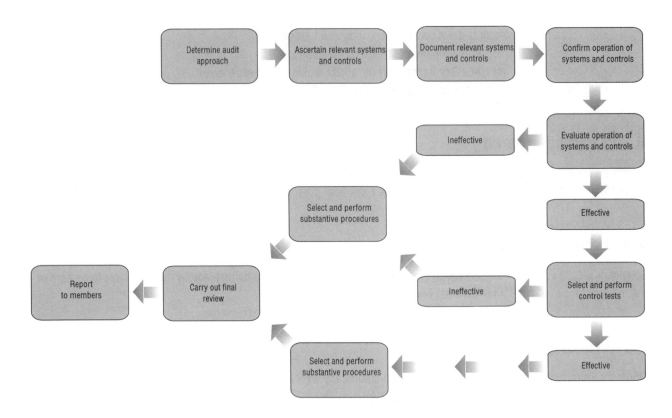

6.5.1 Determine audit approach

Stage 1   The scope of the audit and the auditors' general approach should be determined.

A **letter of engagement** setting out the terms of the audit will be submitted or confirmed before the start of each annual audit. (See Chapter 3)

Auditors must prepare an **audit plan** to be placed on the audit file. (See Chapter 6) The planning aspects of an audit are very important.

6.5.2 Ascertain the accounting system and internal controls

Stage 2   The objective at this stage is to determine the **flow of documents** and **extent of controls** in existence. This is a fact-finding exercise. (See Chapter 5)

Stage 3   The objective here is to prepare a **comprehensive record** for use in evaluation of the systems. (See Chapter 5)

Stage 4   The auditors' objective here is to **confirm** that the **system recorded** is the same as that in **operation**. (See Chapter 5)

6.5.3 Assess the accounting system and internal controls

Stage 5   The purpose of **evaluating** the **systems** is to assess their reliability and formulate a basis for testing their effectiveness in practice.

6.5.4 Test the accounting system and internal controls

Stage 6   If the controls are assessed as effective in theory, tests should be performed to check that they do work in practice. These are called **tests of control**.

    Stage 6 should **only be carried out** if the controls are evaluated at Stage 5 as probably being effective.

    If the auditors know that the controls are ineffective then there is no point in carrying out tests of controls which will merely confirm what is already known. Instead the auditors should go straight on to carry out full substantive procedures (Stage 8).

Stage 7   After evaluating the systems and carrying out tests of controls, auditors normally send management a **report to management** identifying weaknesses and recommending improvements.

6.5.5 Test the financial statements

Stages 8 and 9 These tests are not concerned with the workings of the system. They are concerned with substantiating the figures in the **accounting records**, and eventually, in the final accounts themselves. Hence they are known as **substantive tests.**

6.5.6 Review the financial statements

Stage 10   The aim of the overall review is to determine the **overall reliability** of the accounts by making a critical analysis of content and presentation.

6.5.7 Express an opinion

Stage 11   The **report to the members** (Auditors' report) is the end product of the audit in which the auditors express their opinion of the accounts.

Stage 12   The **report to management** is an additional end product of the audit. Its purpose is to make further suggestions for improvements in the systems and to place on record specific points in connection with the audit and accounts.

All these matters will be looked at in the rest of this Study Text.

7 A different problem

Jane is happier about the financial statements that Anton has sent her now she knows that she can appoint someone to check that they are true and fair.

However, she is worried about some other things. For example, how does she know that the systems Anton has put in place to record transactions on a daily basis work properly? How does she know that Anton won't do business with people that defraud the company and waste her investment? In other words, how does she know that the company is operating efficiently and effectively?

8 The solution

In simple terms, there is no solution to this problem. Jane has invested in Anton's company. She should have considered whether Anton is a good manager before she made that investment, and now she has to **trust** that he will manage it well, as he has a legal duty to do.

However, two things could give her some assurance about this problem too.

8.1 Internal control systems

Directors set up internal control systems to mitigate against risks that the company faces. These systems can be wide-ranging. For example, management might institute controls such as:

- Credit sales will not be made to customers unless references about them have been obtained
- Two directors have to agree before the company buys fixed assets

We will look at internal control systems in more detail in Chapter 5. But if Jane knows there is a system in place, this may give her comfort about the business operating effectively.

8.2 Internal audit

Large companies may employ people who have auditing skills to oversee whether internal control systems operate effectively. These people are known as internal auditors, because they are employed by and are internal to the company.

Internal auditors are **very different** from external auditors, although they use similar skills. The key difference is that internal auditors report to directors, not shareholders. The differences are outlined in the following table.

DIFFERENCES BETWEEN EXTERNAL AND INTERNAL AUDITORS		
	External	**Internal**
Independence	Independent of organisation	Appointed by management
Responsibilities	Fixed by statute	Decided by management
Report to	Members	Management
Scope of work	Express an opinion on truth and fairness of accounts	Consider whatever financial and operational areas management determines

Anton's business is too small to be able to afford to employ an internal audit department. However, if in future the business were to grow, the directors could consider establishing one.

An internal audit department would benefit the company as a whole. It would have no direct benefit to Jane, but she could take comfort from the fact that she knew the internal control systems were being checked to ensure they were operating efficiently and effectively.

Activity 1.1

Anton and Jane have formed a company, AJ (Paper) Ltd. Jane is considering selling some of her shares to her friend, Vikram. Explain to Vikram what an audit is and what rights and duties auditors have.

Activity 1.2

Anton wants to make sure that he is observing the law in relation to accounting records. Explain to Anton what accounting records AJ (Paper) Ltd must keep.

Activity 1.3

Vikram's sister has told him that companies don't have to have external auditors and can have internal auditors instead. Explain the correct position to Vikram.

Key learning points

☑ Companies are subject to law, specifically the Companies Acts 1985 and 1989

☑ The Companies Act 1985 requires companies to:

- Keep accounting records
- Have an annual audit for the benefit of shareholders

☑ The Companies Act 1985 requires auditors to:

- Give an opinion as to whether the accounts give a true and fair view
- Ensure the directors' report is consistent with the accounts
- Be appointed by the shareholders

☑ The Act also gives auditors certain rights, such as to be given information. The auditors must report if information is not given or certain other matters are not complied with.

☑ Directors will recommend audit firms to the shareholders.

☑ Auditors must consider whether they want to accept appointment on practical and ethical grounds.

☑ The aim of an audit is for auditors to report on whether a **true and fair view** is shown by the accounts.

☑ The key stages of an audit are:

- Carry out procedures to obtain sufficient appropriate audit evidence
- Evaluate the presentation of accounts
- Issue a report containing a clear expression of opinion.

☑ The **key** stages of the audit process are:

- Determine audit approach
- Ascertain the accounting system and internal controls
- Assess the accounting system and internal controls
- Test the accounting system and internal controls
- Test the financial statements (substantive testing)
- Review the financial statements
- Express an opinion

☑ **Internal auditors** are employed as part of an organisation's system of controls. Their responsibilities are determined by management and may be wide-ranging.

Quick quiz

1   Auditors normally report on whether accounts give a .... and .... view. Fill in the blanks.

2   What accounting records must be kept by a company?

3   Directors always appoint auditors

TRUE ☐

FALSE ☐

4   Which of the following is not a limitation of auditing?

- The impracticality of examining all items within an account balance or class of transactions
- The impartiality of the auditor
- The possibility of collusion or misrepresentation for fraudulent purposes

5   Which of the following statutes principally governs the audit of limited companies?

- Companies Act 1985
- Financial Services and Markets Act 2000
- Charities Act 1993
- Building Societies Act 1965

6   Walkthrough tests .... auditors' .... of an accounting system. Fill in the blanks.

7   What areas of a company's business would tests of control normally cover?

A   Fixed assets
B   Areas of effective control
C   Areas of weak control
D   Reports

8   What type of test do auditors use to test the financial statements?

Answers to quick quiz

1   Auditors normally report on whether accounts give a **true** and **fair** view.

2   Cash records
Statement of assets and liabilities
If relevant:

- Statements of stockholding at year end
- Any stocktake records

3   False. Shareholders usually appoint auditors.

4   The impartiality of the auditor

5   The Companies Act 1985 governs the audit of limited companies.

6   Walk-through tests **confirm** auditors' **understanding** of an accounting system.

7   B   Tests of control normally cover only those areas subject to effective internal control.

8   Substantive tests are used by auditors to test financial statements.

Activity checklist

This checklist shows which performance criteria, range statement or knowledge and understanding point is covered by each activity in this chapter. Tick off each activity as you complete it.

Activity

1.1   This activity deals with Knowledge & Understanding point 1: A general understanding of the legal duties of auditors; the content of reports; the definition of proper records.

1.2   This activity deals with Knowledge & Understanding point 1: A general understanding of the legal duties of auditors: the content of reports; the definition of proper records.

1.3   This activity deals with Knowledge & Understanding point 4: Types of audit: relation between internal and external audit.

chapter 2

How is
audit regulated?

Contents

1   The problem
2   The solution
3   The structure of the UK accounting and auditing profession
4   Auditing standards
5   Professional ethics

Performance criteria

17.1.H ⎫
17.2.G ⎬ Follow confidentiality and security procedures
17.3.E ⎭

Knowledge and understanding

3   Relevant legislation, relevant Statements of Auditing Standards

1 The problem

Jane has sold some of her shares to Vikram. Vikram has some concerns about the appointment of auditors to the company. Anton has made contact with some firms of auditors and is preparing to accept tenders so that he can make recommendations to Jane and Vikram about who they should appoint.

Jane and Vikram still don't know very much about how auditors work and whether they have to meet specific criteria and conduct their audit in a certain way.

How can Jane and Vikram be sure that the audit conducted on their behalf is good quality and they can rely on it?

2 The solution

As the audit is a tool to check the stewardship of directors in the UK, and is therefore a form of protection to shareholders, it is **highly regulated**. The following levels of regulation exist:

> Law stipulating who may carry out company audits.

> Statements of auditing standards about how to conduct audit work

> Professional ethical standards issued by accountancy bodies

3 The structure of the UK accounting and auditing profession

In the UK there are a large number of different accountancy, or accountancy-related, institutes and associations such as the Association of Accounting Technicians (AAT), Chartered Institute of Management Accountants (CIMA), Chartered Institute of Public Finance and Accountancy (CIPFA).

3.1 Eligibility as auditor

The Companies Act states that auditors must:

- Be a member of a Recognised Supervisory Body (RSB) (discussed below)
- Hold an 'appropriate qualification'

3.2 Ineligibility as auditor

Under the **Companies Act 1985**, a person is **ineligible** for appointment as a company auditor if he or she is:

- An **officer** or **employee** of the company
- A **partner** or **employee** of such a person
- Any partner in a **partnership** in which such a person is a partner
- **Ineligible** by the above for appointment as auditor of any directly connected companies

The legislation does **not** disqualify the following individuals from being an auditor of a limited company.

- A shareholder of the company
- A debtor or creditor of the company
- A close relative (such as a spouse or child) of an officer or employee of the company

However, the regulations of the individual accountancy bodies are stricter than statute in this respect, as we shall discuss in Section 5.

The Companies Act 1985 also states a person may also be ineligible on the grounds of 'lack of independence'. The definition of lack of independence is still to be determined following consultation with the professional bodies.

3.3 Recognised Supervisory Bodies

The EC requires that auditors in the EC are approved by individual member states, including the UK. The authority to give this approval in the UK is delegated to **Recognised Supervisory Bodies** (RSBs).

RSBs are required to have rules to ensure that persons eligible for appointment as a company auditor are either:

- Individuals holding an appropriate qualification, or
- Firms controlled by qualified persons

The following bodies have been designated as Recognised Supervisory Bodies:

- Institute of Chartered Accountants in England and Wales (ICAEW)
- Institute of Chartered Accountants in Scotland (ICAS)
- Institute of Chartered Accountants in Ireland (ICAI)
- Association of Authorised Public Accountants (AAPA)
- Association of Chartered Certified Accountants (ACCA)

Professional qualifications, which will be prerequisites for membership of an RSB, will be offered by Recognised Qualifying Bodies ('RQBs') approved by the Secretary of State.

The AAT is not an RSB, so members of AAT may not be auditors unless they qualify by also being a member of an RSB.

3.4 Supervisory and monitoring roles

RSBs must also implement procedures for inspecting their registered auditors on a regular basis.

Activity 2.1

Who would be ineligible in law for appointment as the auditor of AJ (Paper) Ltd?

4 Auditing standards

4.1 The APB and Statements of Auditing Standards (SASs)

Auditing standards are statements of how audits should be carried out set by the Auditing Practices Board (APB).

The APB issued a document in May 1993 entitled *The scope and authority of APB pronouncements.* The APB makes three categories of pronouncement.

- Statements of Auditing Standards (SASs)
- Practice Notes
- Bulletins

The scope of **SASs** is as follows.

> 'SASs contain basic principles and essential procedures ('Auditing Standards') which are indicated by bold type and with which auditors are required to comply, except where otherwise stated in the SAS concerned, in the conduct of any audit of financial statements.'

Apart from statements in bold type, SASs also contain other material which is not prescriptive but which is designed to help auditors interpret and apply auditing standards.

The authority of SASs is defined as follows.

> 'Auditors who do not comply with Auditing Standards when performing company or other audits in Great Britain make themselves liable to regulatory action by the RSB with whom they are registered and which may include the withdrawal of registration and hence of eligibility to perform company audits.'

Practice Notes are issued 'to assist auditors in applying Auditing Standards of general application to particular circumstances and industries'. **Bulletins** are issued 'to provide auditors with timely guidance on new or emerging issues'. Practice Notes and Bulletins are persuasive guidance.

The APB standards which you should be aware of are discussed through the rest of this Study Text. Remember, you should not rote-learn standards, but learn how to put the guidance into effect.

4.1.1 SAS 240 *Quality control for audit work*

This statement looks at general principles auditors should put into place to ensure audits are of a good quality.

BPP
PROFESSIONAL EDUCATION

It makes points about what auditors should consider when accepting new clients, for example, whether the firm is competent to do the work and whether there are technical barriers to them undertaking the work. We considered such matters in Chapter 1. It also states that should the auditors become aware of any such issues after accepting engagements that, had they known before would have stopped them accepting, they should resign.

The SAS also makes more general points about the set up of the audit firm. For example, it should:

- Put quality control procedures in place in the firm
- Appoint audit partners in charge of each audit the firm does
- Employ staff with suitable skills to carry out audits
- Put a partner in charge of quality control in the firm
- Put a senior partner in charge of reviewing audits carried out by the firm to check they were good quality

We shall look at what this SAS has to say about individual audits in Chapter 7.

Activity 2.2

For Anton's benefit, explain what types of guidance Statements of Auditing Standards (SASs) contain.

5 Professional ethics

There are a number of ethical issues which are of great importance to the client-auditor relationship. The onus is always on the auditors, not only to be ethical, but also to be **seen** to be ethical.

Each RSB issues professional guidance to its members which members should consider when accepting and carrying out audits. Professional guidance often centres around two important concepts, independence and confidentiality.

SAS 100 *Objectives and general principles governing an audit* states that in the conduct of any audit of financial statements auditors should comply with the ethical guidance issued by their professional body.

5.1 Independence

As we mentioned in Chapter 1, it is important that auditors give an **impartial** opinion. It is therefore vital that the auditor is independent of the company.

Professional bodies issue guidelines as to what things constitute a threat to independence. These include:

- Loans to or from clients
- One client representing a high proportion of total fee income
- Having family or other close relationships with client management
- Holding shares in clients (directly or indirectly)
- Providing accountancy services other than audit to audit clients
- Accepting gifts or hospitality from the company/directors
- Having fees outstanding (so that they become like a loan)

Audit firms should put safeguards into place so that these factors do not unduly affect an audit relationship. If any of these threats do exist, audit firms should consider resigning their position, or not accepting the appointment in the first place.

5.2 Confidentiality

Confidentiality is another extremely important concept to the auditor. Auditors are in a position of trust, in that they are external to the company and yet have access to a great deal of **sensitive information**.

Auditors have a duty to keep their client information private. They should not even share information with shareholders beyond the information provided in the audit report.

There are very limited circumstances in which an auditor may disclose confidential client information. They are when:

- The client authorises it
- The law requires disclosure
- There is a professional duty to disclose
- There is a public duty to disclose

5.2.1 Law

Auditors are required to disclose if they know or suspect a client is involved in treason, drug-trafficking or terrorism. Also, under SAS 120 *Consideration of law and regulations*, an auditor must disclose non-compliance with certain regulations when there is a statutory duty to disclose.

5.2.2 Professional duty

It may be necessary to breach confidentiality to give evidence during a trial. Sometimes disclosure will be necessary to reasonably protect a member's interests.

5.2.3 Public duty

Sometimes it will be necessary to make a disclosure in the public interest.

5.3 Security

Security is a matter closely related to confidentiality. **Security procedures** help to **maintain** the **confidentiality** of the client. They tend to be a combination of very practical measures and detailed rules governing the auditor's right to impart information about a client. A typical list of security procedures is as follows.

- **Do not discuss client matters** with any third party, including family and friends, even in a general way.

- **Do not use client information to your own gain**, nor carry on insider dealing by passing price-sensitive information to others.

- **Do not leave audit files unattended** at a client's premises. Lock them up at night.

- **Do not leave audit files** (or computer equipment) in **cars**, even in the boot, or in **unsecured private residences**.

- **Do not take working papers away** from the office or the client **unless strictly necessary**.

5.4 AAT Guidelines on Professional Ethics

In its annual handbook the AAT publishes *Guidelines on Professional Ethics*. These Guidelines state that an essential characteristic of accountants is the development of an ethical approach to the work and to clients acquired by experience and professional supervision under training and safeguarded by a strict disciplinary code.

The *Guidelines* also emphasise the public interest aspects of accountancy and the way accountants recognise and accept their responsibility to the public. Many people, not just clients, rely on the accountant's work.

5.4.1 Fundamental principles

The fundamental principles are very important indeed to AAT members and students.

'1 **Integrity**

Members should be straightforward and honest in performing professional work.

2 **Objectivity**

Members should be fair and should not allow prejudice or bias or the influence of others to override objectivity.

3 **Professional and Technical Competence**

(a) Members should refrain from undertaking or continuing any assignments which they are not competent to carry out unless advice and assistance is obtained to ensure that the assignment is carried out satisfactorily.

(b) Members also have a continuing duty:

(i) to maintain professional knowledge and skills at a level required to ensure that a client or employer receives the advantage of competent professional service based on up-to-date developments in practice, legislation and techniques;

(ii) to maintain their technical and ethical standards in areas relevant to their work through Continuing Professional Development.

4 **Due Care**

(a) A Member, having accepted an assignment, has an obligation to carry it out with due care and reasonable despatch having regard to the nature and scope of the assignment.

(b) Special care is required where Members undertake assignments for clients who may have little or no knowledge of accounting and taxation matters.

> 5   **Confidentiality**
>
> Members should respect the confidentiality of information acquired during the course of performing professional work and should not use or disclose any such information without proper and specific authority or unless there is a legal or professional right or duty to disclose.
>
> 6   **Professional behaviour**
>
> Members should act in a manner consistent with the good reputation of the profession and refrain from any conduct which might bring discredit to the profession.'

Activity 2.3

Jane has asked Anton how they can be sure that an auditor will keep the company's affairs private. Outline the auditor's duty of confidentiality.

Key learning points

☑ The Companies Act requires auditors to hold an **appropriate qualification** and to be a member of a **recognised supervisory body**.

☑ A person is **ineligible** to act as auditor if he is an **employee** or officer or has various other close connections with the company.

☑ Recognised supervisory bodies must follow a number of procedures to ensure their members are **fit** and **proper** and **competent** and that audit work is conducted **properly**.

☑ The Auditing Practices Board issues:

 – SASs
 – Practice Notes
 – Bulletins

☑ SASs contain **basic principles** and **procedures** with which auditors must comply as well as other material designed to help auditors.

☑ Rules on ethical conduct are laid down by professional bodies.

☑ **Independence** is perhaps the most important characteristic of the auditor.

☑ **Confidentiality** is important. Auditors can only disclose information without client permission to others in very limited circumstances.

Quick quiz

1   Match the APB document to its status.

Statements of Auditing Standards
– bold script

Statement of Auditing Standards
– other materials

Practice notes

Bulletins

| PERSUASIVE |

| PERSUASIVE |

| EXPLANATORY |

| PRESCRIPTIVE |

2   (a)   A person does not have to satisfy membership criteria to become a member of a Recognised Supervisory Body

True

False

(b)   Auditing is regulated by the government in the UK.

True

False

(c)   The Auditing Practices Board issues auditing standards which auditors are required to follow.

True

False

3   What are the fundamental principles given in the AAT Guidelines on Professional Ethics? (word/phrase answers will suffice)

4   Which of the following are legitimate reasons for breach of client confidentiality?

(i)   Auditor **suspects** client has committed treason
(ii)   Disclosure **needed** to protect auditor's own interests
(iii)   Information is **required** for the auditor of another client
(iv)   Auditor **knows** client has committed terrorist offence
(v)   There is a **public duty** to disclose
(vi)   Auditor **considers** there to be non-compliance with law and regulations
(vii)   Auditor **suspects** client has committed fraud

Answers to quick quiz

1   Statements of Auditing Standards
                – bold script

    PRESCRIPTIVE

    Statement of Auditing Standards
                – other materials

    EXPLANATORY

    Practice notes

    PERSUASIVE

    Bulletins

    PERSUASIVE

2   (a)   False. All RSBs have stringent membership requirements.
    (b)   False. It is devolved by the government to be regulated by RSBs.
    (c)   True. Auditors face discipline by their RSB if they do not.

3   Integrity
    Objectivity and independence
    Professional competence and due care
    Confidentiality
    Professional behaviour
    Technical standards

4   (i), (ii), (iv), (v), (vi)

Activity checklist

This checklist shows which performance criteria, range statement or knowledge and understanding point is covered by each activity in this chapter. Tick off each activity as you complete it.

Activity

2.1		This activity deals with Knowledge & Understanding point 3: Relevant legislation, relevant Statements of Auditing Standards.
2.2		This activity deals with Knowledge & Understanding point 3: Relevant legislation, relevant Statements of Auditing Standards.
2.3		This activity deals with Performance Criteria 17.1.H, 17.2.G, 17.3.E: Follow confidentiality and security procedures.

chapter 3

To whom are auditors liable?

Contents

1   The problem
2   The solution
3   The engagement letter
4   Contract law
5   Third parties

Knowledge and understanding

2   A general understanding of the liability of auditors under contract and negligence including liability to third parties

3   Relevant legislation, relevant Statements of Auditing Standards

1 The problem

Jane and Vikram were delighted to hear that audit is regulated. They are sure that this will contribute to the company getting a quality audit. However, they still have some concerns remaining. Anton has told them that the bank manager has told him that the bank will not lend AJ (Paper) Ltd money unless Anton shows them audited accounts.

Jane and Vikram are concerned that the auditors might make a mistake in their audit that would adversely affect the bank. What would this mean to AJ (Paper) Ltd? Would the bank be able to take any action against the company or the auditors?

2 The solution

The law does give certain parties some remedies in the event of the auditors making a mistake. However, available remedies fall into two categories, and a third party such as the bank is less likely to have a successful claim against the auditor.

The key claimant is the company, with whom the auditors have a **contract**.

Note that in this context, the **company** means all the shareholders together. Jane will **not be able** to make an **individual claim** against the auditors and nor will Vikram.

Third parties, such as the bank or Jane or Vikram individually **may** have a claim against the auditors. As they have no contract with the auditors, this may be more difficult to prove.

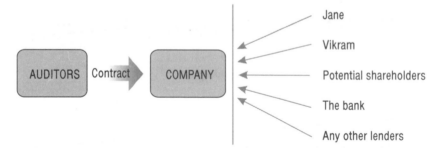

As the auditors have no direct contact with these third parties, the law states that they can only be liable to them if the auditors were aware that the third party **existed AND** that they were going to **rely** on the audited accounts. Even if both these factors are true, the auditor may not be liable to the third party.

In the case of **individual shareholders**, the **reliance** this refers to is **additional reliance** to the usual reliance of seeing how their existing investment has been maintained in the past year. In other words, individual shareholders could only have a case if the auditor was aware that they were using the audited accounts for an **additional purpose**, for example, buying new shares in the company.

3 The engagement letter

When the shareholders (acting as the company itself) agree to engage a firm of auditors and the auditors agree to be engaged, they have a contract.

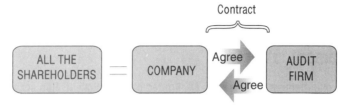

Auditors have a **professional duty** to set out the **terms** of that contract.

They do that in the **engagement letter**.

3.1 SAS 140 *Engagement letters*

This standard states:

> 'The auditors and client should agree on the terms of the engagement, which should be recorded in writing … thereafter auditors should regularly review the terms of engagement and if appropriate agree any updating in writing.'

The auditors must not start an audit assignment if they have not sent an engagement letter to the client.

3.1.1 Contents of the letter

The letter should outline whether the audit firm is going to produce any reports for the benefit of the company **in addition** to the audit report to shareholders required by the law. Such reports might include, for example, reports on the efficiency of internal controls.

The following items **may** be included in the letter:

- **Fees** and billing arrangements

- Procedures where the client has a **complaint** about the service

- Where appropriate, arrangements concerning the **involvement of other auditors and experts** in some aspect of the audit and internal auditors and other staff of the entity

- Arrangements, if any, to be made with the **predecessor auditors**, in the case of an initial audit

- Any **restriction** of the auditors' **liabilities** to the client (when such possibility exists – not possible with limited companies)

- Where appropriate, the country by whose **laws** the engagement is to be governed

- A reference to any **further agreements** between the auditors and the client

- A proposed **timetable** for the engagement
- Ownership and lien of **books and records**
- Action in the event of **unpaid fees**
- The usage of work by **third parties** (including suitable disclaimers)

3.2 Example engagement letter

The following example of an engagement letter is for a UK limited company client. Remember that it is not necessarily comprehensive or appropriate to every audit as each client is different; it must be tailored to meet the specific requirements of the engagement.

AN EXAMPLE OF AN ENGAGEMENT LETTER

To the directors [1] of...

The purpose of this letter is to set out the basis on which we (are to) act as auditors of the company (and its subsidiaries) and the respective areas of responsibility of the directors and of ourselves.

Responsibility of directors and auditors

1   As directors of the above company, you are responsible for ensuring that the company maintains proper accounting records and for preparing financial statements which give a true and fair view and have been prepared in accordance with the Companies Act 1985. You are also responsible for making available to us, as and when required, all the company's accounting records and all other relevant records and related information, including minutes of all management and shareholders' meetings.

2   We have a statutory responsibility [2] to report to the members whether in our opinion the financial statements give a true and fair view of the state of the company's affairs and of the profit or loss for the year and whether they have been properly prepared in accordance with the Companies Act 1985 (or other relevant legislation). In arriving at our opinion, we are required to consider the following matters, and to report on any in respect of which we are not satisfied:

   (a)   whether proper accounting records have been kept by the company and proper returns adequate for our audit have been received from branches not visited by us;

   (b)   whether the company's balance sheet and profit and loss account are in agreement with the accounting records and returns;

   (c)   whether we have obtained all the information and explanations which we think necessary for the purposes of our audit; and

   (d)   whether the information in the directors' report is consistent with the financial statements.

   In addition, there are certain other matters which, according to the circumstances, may need to be dealt with in our report. For example, where the financial statements do not give full details of directors' remuneration or of their transactions with the company, the Companies Act requires us to disclose such matters in our report.

3   We have a professional responsibility [3] to report if the financial statements do not comply in any material respect with applicable accounting standards, unless in our opinion the non-compliance is justified in the circumstances. In determining whether the departure is justified we consider:

(a)   whether the departure is required in order for the financial statements to give a true and fair view; and

(b)   whether adequate disclosure has been made concerning the departure

Our professional responsibilities also include:

(a)   including in our report a description of the directors' responsibilities for the financial statements where the financial statements or accompanying information do not include such a description; and

(b)   considering whether other information in documents containing audited financial statements is consistent with those financial statements.

4   Our audit will be conducted in accordance with the Auditing Standards [4] issued by the Auditing Practices Board, and will include such tests of transactions and of the existence, ownership and valuation of assets and liabilities as we consider necessary. We shall obtain an understanding of the accounting and internal control systems in order to assess their adequacy as a basis for the preparation of the financial statements and to establish whether proper accounting records have been maintained by the company. We shall expect to obtain such appropriate evidence as we consider sufficient to enable us to draw reasonable conclusions therefrom.

5   The nature and extent of our procedures will vary according to our assessment of the company's accounting system and, where we wish to place reliance on it, the internal control system, and may cover any aspect of the business's operations. Our audit is not designed to identify all significant weaknesses [5] in the company's systems but, if such weaknesses come to our notice during the course of our audit which we think should be brought to your attention, we shall report [5] them to you. Any such report may not be provided to third parties without our prior written consent. Such consent will be granted only on the basis that such reports are not prepared with the interests of anyone other than the company in mind and that we accept no duty or responsibility to any other party as concerns the reports.

6   As part of our normal audit procedures, we may request you to provide written confirmation of oral representations [6] which we have received from you during the course of the audit on matters having a material effect on the financial statements. In connection with representations and the supply of information to us generally, we draw your attention to section 389A of the Companies Act 1985 under which it is an offence for an officer of the company to mislead the auditors.

7   In order to assist us with the examination of your financial statements, we shall request sight of all documents or statements, including the chairman's statement, operating and financial review and the directors' report, which are due to be issued with the financial statements. We are also entitled to attend all general meetings of the company and to receive notice of all such meetings.

8   The responsibility for safeguarding the assets of the company and for the prevention and detection of fraud, error and non-compliance with law or regulations [3] rests with yourselves. However, we shall endeavour to plan our audit so that we have a reasonable expectation of detecting material misstatements in the financial statements or accounting records (including those resulting from fraud, error or non-compliance with law or regulations), but our examination should not be relied upon to disclose all such material misstatements or frauds, errors or instances of non-compliance as may exist.

9   (Where appropriate). We shall not be treated as having notice, for the purposes of our audit responsibilities, of information provided to members of our firm other than those engaged on the audit (for example information provided in connection with accounting, taxation and other services).

10   Once we have issued our report we have no further direct responsibility in relation to the financial statements for that financial year. However, we expect that you will inform us of any material event occurring between the date of our report and that of the Annual General Meeting which may affect the financial statements [7].

Other services

11   You have requested that we provide other services in respect of ... . The terms under which we provide these other services are dealt with in a separate letter. We will also agree in a separate letter of engagement the provision of any services relating to investment business advice as defined by the Financial Services Act 1986.

Fees

12   Our fees are computed on the basis of the time spent on your affairs by the partners and our staff and on the levels of skill and responsibility involved. Unless otherwise agreed, our fees will be billed at appropriate intervals during the course of the year and will be due on presentation.

Applicable law

13   This (engagement letter) shall be governed by, and construed in accordance with, (English) law. The Courts of (England) shall have exclusive jurisdiction in relation to any claim, dispute or difference concerning the (engagement letter) and any matter arising from it. Each party irrevocably waives any right it may have to object to an action being brought in those Courts, to claim that the action has been brought in an inconvenient forum, or to claim that those Courts do not have jurisdiction.

14   Once it has been agreed, this letter will remain effective, from one audit appointment to another, until it is replaced [8]. We shall be grateful if you could confirm in writing your agreement to these terms by signing and returning the enclosed copy of this letter, or let us know if they are not in accordance with your understanding of our terms of engagement.

Yours faithfully

Certified Accountants [9]

Key

1   The letter must be addressed to the directors or to the audit committee (division of the board of directors) if one exists.

2   This statutory responsibility was discussed in Chapter 1.

3   We will look at some of the additional professional responsibilities in Chapter 4.

4   We discussed Auditing Standards in Chapter 2.

5   A report on control weakness is the most common 'by product' of a statutory audit. We shall discuss it in Chapter 18.

6   These are 'management representations' which we will discuss in Chapter 16.

7   These are known as 'post balance sheet' or 'subsequent' events, which we shall discuss in Chapter 16.

8   When a new engagement letter is required is discussed in paragraph 3.3.

9   The letter must be signed on behalf of the audit firm. However, the company must also acknowledge that it has been accepted.

3.3 When a new engagement letter is needed

Once it has been agreed by the client, an engagement letter will, if it so provides, remain effective from one audit appointment to another until it is replaced. However, the engagement letter should be **reviewed annually** to ensure that it continues to reflect the client's circumstances. The SAS suggests that the following factors may make the agreement of a new letter appropriate.

- Any indication that the client **misunderstands** the objective and scope of the audit
- A **recent change of management**, board of directors or audit committee
- A **significant change in ownership**, such as a new holding company
- A **significant change** in the **nature or size** of the client's business
- Any **relevant change** in **legal** or **professional requirements**

3.3.1 Changes in the terms of an engagement

There are various reasons why there may be a change in the terms of engagement prior to completion.

- A **change** in **circumstances** affecting the need for the service

- A **misunderstanding** as to the nature of an audit or of the related service originally requested

- A **restriction** on the **scope** of the engagement, whether imposed by management or caused by circumstances

The auditors should consider such a request for change, and the reason for it, very seriously, particularly in terms of any restriction in the scope of the engagement. Auditors may have to withdraw from the engagement.

Activity 3.1

Anton has just received a tender from Khan Associates which mentions an engagement letter. He has asked for clarification. Acting as a trainee at Khan Associates, write some notes for a conversation you will have with Anton:

(a)   Explaining why it is important for auditors to send a letter of engagement to a new client prior to undertaking an audit.

(b)   Describing briefly the main contents of an engagement letter.

4 Contract law

The engagement letter which the company and auditors agree on sets out the **express terms** of the contract.

English law also imposes **implied terms** into contracts.

4.1 Implied terms

Law states that there are certain terms which **always** exist in a contract between the audit firm and the company:

- The auditors have a duty to exercise **reasonable care**.
- The auditors have a duty to carry out the work required with **reasonable expediency**.
- The auditors have a right to **reasonable remuneration**.

4.1.1 What does a duty of reasonable care mean?

There is not a list of things that an auditor must do/not do to prove he has exercised a duty of reasonable care. However, there are several guidelines.

- Auditors should use generally accepted auditing techniques (that is, adhere to auditing standards)

- If auditors' suspicions are aroused, they must carry out investigations until they are satisfied (this is called being 'put on enquiry')

- Auditors must act honestly and carefully when making judgements

4.2 Negligence

If the auditors breach the terms of their contract the **company** will have a claim against them for damages.

If the auditors breach their **implied duty of care** under the contract, the company may be able to sue them for **negligence**.

Three things must exist for the company to bring a successful claim:

(a) **Duty of care**

There existed a duty of care enforceable at law. ⟵ | Under a **contract**, this is always the case. |

(b) **Negligence**

In a situation where a duty of care existed, the auditors were negligent in the performance of that duty, judged by the accepted professional standards of the day.

(c) **Damages**

The client has suffered some monetary loss as a direct consequence of the negligence on the part of the auditors.

5 Third parties

If the auditors have been negligent, it is possible that a third party may also have a claim against the auditors even though they do not have a contract with them.

5.1 Third party negligence claims

The three requirements for a third party negligence claim are the same as they are for the company:

(a) **Duty of care**

There existed a duty of care enforceable at law.

> Without a **contract**, this may not be the case.

(b) **Negligence**

In a situation where a duty of care existed, the auditors were negligent in the performance of that duty, judged by the accepted professional standards of the day.

(c) **Damages**

The client has suffered some monetary loss as a direct consequence of the negligence on the part of the auditors.

5.2 Duty of care

With third party negligence claims, the key issue is whether the auditor owed the third party a duty of care.

The answer to this question can be seen to an extent in the cases that judges have considered in the past.

As a general rule (used in a case known as *Caparo*), it seems that judges **do not think** that **auditors owe third parties a duty of care**. It is only in **exceptional** circumstances that such a duty arises.

The exceptional circumstances which judges have referred to are when an auditor knows that a third party is relying on the audited accounts. For example, if a director tells the auditor that the bank will rely on the audited accounts, or if someone says to the auditor that he will purchase new shares on the strength of the audited accounts.

Remember that the auditor is entitled to try to **disclaim liability** to those people, for example, by writing to them and stating that the audit report is only for the purposes of the shareholders and that they do not admit legal liability to anyone else. If the third party tried to bring a negligence claim, a judge would have to determine whether such a letter had legal effect, given all the facts.

Activity 3.2

For the benefit of Jane and Vikram, explain the legal liability of the audit firm to the company and to third parties.

Key learning points

- ☑ Auditors have a professional duty to set out the terms of their contract with the company in an engagement letter.

- ☑ The engagement letter should be re-issued if the terms of the engagement change or it is clear that the client misunderstands the terms of the engagement.

- ☑ The law also implies terms into the contract between the auditors and the company.

- ☑ A key implied term is that auditors will exercise reasonable care.

- ☑ If the auditors breach their duty of care and it causes loss to the company, the company may sue the audit firm for damages.

- ☑ Third parties (for example banks, individual shareholders) do not have a contract with the audit firm.

- ☑ Therefore, auditors do not automatically owe third parties a duty of care.

- ☑ Third parties may have a claim against auditors for negligence, if they were in a special relationship with the auditor:

  - – If the auditor knows they exist
  - – If the auditor knows they intend to rely on audited financial statements

Quick quiz

1   An engagement letter is only ever sent to a client before the first audit.

    True   [ ]

    False   [ ]

2   Ring the items that are unlikely to be found in an engagement letter.

    (a)   Responsibilities of directors and auditors
    (b)   Detailed audit procedures
    (c)   Other services
    (d)   Agreed fee
    (e)   Reference to applicable law

3   What are the implied terms which the courts will normally impute into a contract entered into by auditors?

4   What three things must a client prove to bring a successful action against auditors in contract?

    1 ....

    2 ....

    3 ....

5   Auditors always owe third parties a duty of care.

    True   [ ]

    False   [ ]

6   List the reasons why an auditor may owe a third party a duty of care.

    1 .... AND

    2 ....

Answers to quick quiz

1   False. It should be re-issued if there is a change in circumstances.

2   (b)

    (d)   Reference will be made to how the fee is set, but no mention of the actual fee will be made as it will fluctuate over time.

3   The implied terms which will normally be imputed are that the auditors have:

    •   A duty to exercise reasonable care
    •   A duty to carry out the work required with reasonable expediency
    •   A right to reasonable remuneration

4   To bring a successful action in contract, a client must prove:

- A duty of care enforceable at law existed.

- The auditors were negligent in performance of that duty, judged by accepted contemporary professional standards.

- The client has suffered monetary loss as a result of auditor negligence.

5   False

6   1   They know the third party exists, AND
     2   They know the third party intends to rely on the audited financial statements

Activity checklist

This checklist shows which performance criteria, range statement or knowledge and understanding point is covered by each activity in this chapter. Tick off each activity as you complete it.

Activity

3.1 ☐   This activity deals with Knowledge & Understanding point 3: relevant legislation, relevant Statements of Auditing Standards.

3.2 ☐   This activity deals with Knowledge & Understanding point 2: a general understanding of the liability of auditors under contract and negligence, including liability to third parties.

chapter 4

What are auditors responsible for?

Contents

1   The problem
2   The solution
3   Statement of directors' responsibilities
4   Other information
5   Fraud and error
6   Law and regulations
7   Going concern
8   Subsequent events
9   Related parties

Knowledge and understanding

3   Relevant legislation, relevant Statements of Auditing Standards

1 The problem

The shareholders of AJ (Paper) Ltd, on the advice of Anton, have accepted the tender of Khan Associates.

Khan Associates have sent AJ (Paper) Ltd an engagement letter for the company to approve. Anton understands the reference in the letter to the auditors' statutory duty. He knows that is the duty to report on the truth and fairness of the financial statements. He is not so sure about the following extracts:

'... Our professional responsibilities also include:

(a)   including in our report a description of the directors' responsibilities for the financial statements ...

(b)   considering whether other information in documents containing audited financial statements is consistent with those financial statements ...

... The responsibility for safeguarding the assets of the company and for the prevention and detection of fraud, error and non-compliance with law and regulations rests with yourselves ...'

What does this all mean? What are the auditors' responsibilities?

2 The solution

The answer to the questions above is that the auditors have two strands of responsibility:

First, they have the **statutory** responsibility of reporting on the truth and fairness of financial statements. As you know from Chapter 1, the **law** imposes other statutory duties on the auditor.

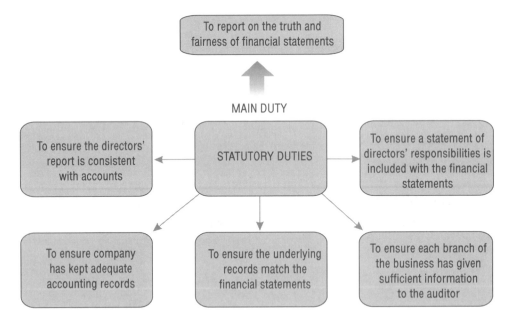

Secondly, auditing standards impose further **professional** responsibilities on the auditors in respect of certain issues:

```
                          ┌─────────────┐
                          │   Related   │
                          │   parties   │
                          └─────────────┘
                                 ▲
                                 │
┌─────────────┐          ┌─────────────┐          ┌─────────────┐
│   Law and   │◄─────────│ PROFESSIONAL │────────►│    Other    │
│ regulations │          │    DUTIES   │          │ information │
└─────────────┘          └─────────────┘          └─────────────┘
       ▲                  ▲    │    ▼                    ▲
       │                  │    │    │                    │
┌─────────────┐    ┌─────────────┐          ┌─────────────┐
│ Subsequent  │    │   Fraud     │          │    Going    │
│   events    │    │  and error  │          │   concern   │
└─────────────┘    └─────────────┘          └─────────────┘
```

Unfortunately the public can sometimes misunderstand the exact nature of these professional responsibilities. That problem will be discussed in more detail in Chapter 19.

Of course, as discussed in Chapter 3, auditors also have a general legal duty to follow auditing standards as part of their duty of care.

3 Statement of directors' responsibilities

As part of the report which they put together to accompany the financial statements, the directors of a company should include a statement of directors' responsibilities, such as:

Company law requires the directors to prepare financial statements for each financial year which give a true and fair view of the state of affairs of the company and of the profit or loss of the company for that period. In preparing those financial statements, the directors are required to:

(a)   Select suitable accounting policies and then apply them consistently
(b)   Make judgements and estimates that are reasonable and prudent
(c)   State whether applicable accounting standards have been followed, subject to any material departures disclosed and explained in the financial statements (large companies only)
(d)   Prepare the financial statements on the going concern basis unless it is inappropriate to presume that the company will continue in business (if not a separate statement on going concern is made by the directors)

The directors are responsible for keeping proper accounting records which disclose with reasonable accuracy at any time the financial position of the company and to enable them to ensure that the financial statements comply with the Companies Act 1985. They are also responsible for safeguarding the assets of the company and hence for taking reasonable steps for the prevention and detection of fraud and other irregularities.

This wording can be adapted to suit the specific situation.

3.1 Auditors' responsibility

If the directors do not include a section of this nature in their annual report, the auditors should include it in the audit report.

4 Other information

SAS 160 *Other information in documents containing financial statements* requires auditors to consider other information that is being published in the same report as the financial statements. This does not apply to information that is released without the auditors' knowledge and consent.

4.1 What information?

A significant amount of financial or non-financial information may be included in an annual report. Much of it will not be the financial statements that the auditors have to report on. The list here does not cover everything that might be included, but gives you some ideas:

- A directors' report (required by statute)
- A chairman's statement
- An operating and financial review
- Financial summaries
- Employment data
- Planned capital expenditures
- Financial ratios
- Selected quarterly data

The auditors **must read all this information**.

4.2 Why do the auditors read it?

The auditors **do not** have to state whether the other information is **fairly stated**. Instead, they must be aware if there are any apparent **misstatements** in it, or whether there are material **inconsistencies** with the financial statements and try to **resolve** these.

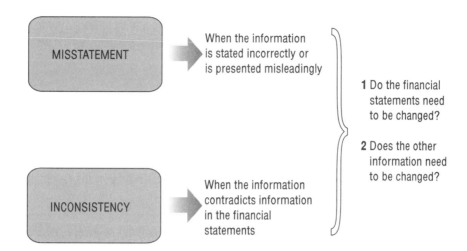

The auditors should **discuss** these issues with the directors and hopefully **resolve the issues**. If the issue is not resolved, that is, the directors have not changed the financial statements or the other information **and** the auditors believe this is necessary to give a true and fair view, the auditors may have to mention this issue in their auditors' report. We will look at how this is done in Chapter 19.

4.2.1 Directors' report

You may remember from Chapter 1 that the auditors have a **statutory** duty to ensure the directors' report is consistent with the accounts.

If it is not consistent, the auditors may have to include a paragraph in their auditors' report explaining why it is not consistent if there is:

(a)   An **inconsistency between amounts or narrative** appearing in the financial statements and the directors' report

(b)   An **inconsistency between the bases of preparation** of related items appearing in the financial statements and the directors' report, where the figures themselves are not directly comparable and the different bases are not disclosed

(c)   An **inconsistency between figures** contained in the financial statements **and a narrative interpretation** of the effect of those figures in the directors' report

5 Fraud and error

Fraud and error, say in recording original transactions when they happen, may cause financial statements to not give a true and fair view.

However, auditors are not at the company on a day to day basis. The type of tests they carry out (which we will look at in Parts B and C) may not discover problems such as these which have occurred during the year.

The **directors** have a **statutory duty** to protect the assets of the company, and this includes a duty to prevent and detect fraud and error. A major way directors try to do this is by having internal control systems, which we mentioned in Chapter 1.

5.1 What is the auditors' responsibility for fraud and error?

This is set out in SAS 110 *Fraud and error.* This states that:

> 'Auditors should plan and perform their audit procedures and evaluate and report the results thereof, recognising that fraud or error may materially affect the financial statements.'

We will talk about **planning** in Chapter 6. The key thing to note is that auditors must be **aware**. Whatever task they are carrying out on an audit, they should be aware that fraud and error might exist. If they are **put on enquiry** by certain factors they notice, they must satisfy themselves as to what those factors indicate.

5.2 What should auditors do if they think fraud or error exists?

Step 1   Carry out extra or different procedures

Step 2   Document their findings

Step 3   Make appropriate reports

Step 4   Consider the impact on the rest of the audit

5.2.1 Reporting

There are three potential sets of people that the auditors could report to:

MANAGEMENT	☑	If they actually discover fraud
	☑	If they suspect fraud
	☑	If they discover substantial error
	☒	If they think the suspected fraud casts doubt on the integrity of the directors
SHAREHOLDERS	☑	**Only** if fraud or error causes the financial statements to not give a true and fair view or there is a fundamental uncertainty – in which case it should be included in the audit report in the usual way (see Chapter 19)
THIRD PARTIES	☑	If the suspected fraud casts doubt on the integrity of the directors, to a proper authority without delay
	☑	If it is in the public interest to report a fraud to the proper authorities and the directors refuse to do so.

5.3 Factors indicating possibility of fraud

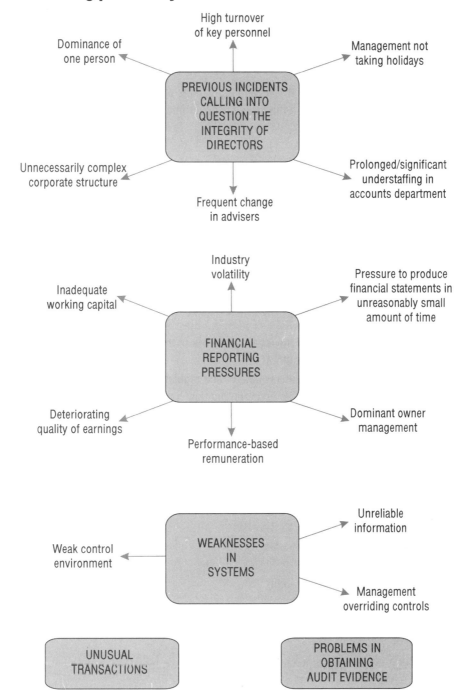

6 Law and regulations

The directors are responsible for ensuring that the company complies with any law and regulations that apply to it. As we have already seen, auditors have **statutory responsibilities** to ensure that companies meet some legal requirements, for example, that they maintain proper accounting records.

However, the company failing to comply with other laws and regulations might have an effect on financial statements. For example, if the company has broken the law, it may owe the government a fine – which should be reflected in the financial statements.

6.1 What is the auditors' responsibility for the company complying with the law?

This is set out in SAS 120 *Consideration of law and regulations*. The provisions are similar to SAS 110.

> 'Auditors should plan and perform their audit procedures, and evaluate and report on the results thereof, recognising that non-compliance by the entity with law or regulations may materially effectively the financial statements.'

Again, notice that auditors must be **aware** of these issues as they carry out their audit. This will involve:

- Getting a general understanding of the legal framework of the company
- Looking at letters from regulatory authorities
- Asking the directors about compliance with laws and regulations
- Getting written confirmation from the directors that they have disclosed all relevant legal issues

6.2 What should auditors do when possible non-compliance with law and regulations is discovered?

Step 1   Get an understanding of the issues and the possible effect on the financial statements

Step 2   Document their findings

Step 3   Make appropriate reports

Step 4   Consider the impact on the rest of the audit

6.2.1 Reporting

Again, there are three potential sets of people that the auditors could report to:

MANAGEMENT	☑	If the auditors suspect non-compliance with law and regulations
	☒	If the suspected non-compliance causes them not to have confidence in the integrity of the directors
SHAREHOLDERS	☑	**Only** if non-compliance causes the financial statements to not give a true and fair view or there is a fundamental uncertainty – in which case it should be included in the audit report in the usual way (see Chapter 19)
THIRD PARTIES	☑	If there is a statutory duty to report: without undue delay
	☑	If it appears to be intentional on the part of management
	☑	If it is in the public interest to report the non-compliance to the proper authorities and the directors refuse to do so

Activity 4.1

Anton has asked his friend, Ali, who is an auditor, how an auditor would handle the following two hypothetical situations.

(a)   A manager submitting false claims for travel expenses and false invoices for non-existent purchases in order to fund his own tastes for expensive cars and his girlfriend's tastes for jewellery and foreign holidays.

(b)   Stores staff acting in collusion to steal significant quantities of stock by claiming that certain stock is damaged or scrap, and has therefore been disposed of for nil value.

Explain what actions an auditor would take to investigate these allegations.

7 Going concern

One of the **assumptions** directors make when putting together financial statements is that the business is a going concern.

7.1 What does 'going concern' mean?

'Going concern' means that the directors expect the business to 'keep going', that is, **be in operation** for the **foreseeable future**. The directors are required to look into the future   not just guessing, but drawing reasoned conclusions based on factors such as:

- Does the company have paying customers?
- Does the company pay its debts?
- Does the company have any reason to stop operating?
- Does the company have long-term strategic aims?

- Has the company prepared budgets for the near and middle future?
- Does the company have sufficient finance to keep operating?

7.2 How does going concern affect true and fair?

If the company expects to stop operating, it would be true and fair to prepare the financial statements on a different assumption or basis – for example, that the company is no longer going to keep its assets to keep operating but will try to sell them. For example:

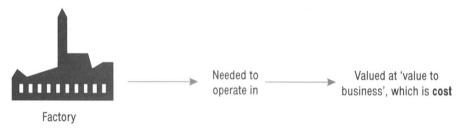

Factory

But, if the company is no longer going to operate, the picture is different:

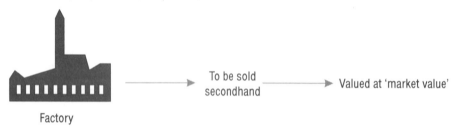

Factory

As we shall see later in Chapters 12-14, auditors check the values of assets to ensure that they are stated in a true and fair way in the balance sheet.

At the outset of their audit, then, auditors should check that the **basis** on which things in the financial statements are valued is correct, or none of these valuations will be correct. We will look at the **tests** that auditors carry out on **going concern** in Chapter 16.

8 Subsequent events

Auditors carry out their audit quite a long time after the date of the financial statements:

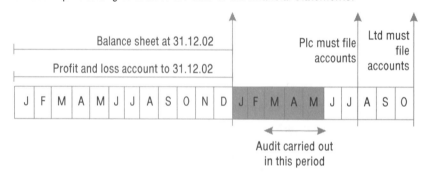

Auditors must ensure that nothing happens between the year end and the day they sign their audit report which would cause the financial statements to no longer be true and fair. For example,

| Debtors owes company money at 31.12.02 | → | 2nd February debtors becomes bankrupt | → | Debt not recoverable |

It would not be true and fair for the company to show in the financial statements that they are owed a debt when they know the debt will never be paid.

We will look at how auditors deal with subsequent events in more detail in Chapter 16.

9 Related parties

The directors are responsible for identifying related party transactions and making appropriate disclosures in financial statements in accordance with accounting standards. You should be aware of what constitutes a related party and a related party transaction under FRS 8 from your previous accounting studies.

9.1 Auditors' responsibilities in relation to related parties

Auditors have similar responsibilities towards related parties as they do in relation to fraud and error and law and regulations. They should plan and perform their audit to obtain sufficient evidence about them.

SAS 460 *Related parties* recognises that an audit cannot be expected to detect all material related party transactions. The risk that undisclosed related party transactions will not be detected by the auditors is especially high when:

(a)   Related party transactions have taken place **without charge.**

(b)   Related party transactions are **not self-evident** to the auditors or management.

(c)   Transactions are with a party that the auditors could **not reasonably be expected to know is a** related party.

(d)   **Active steps** have been taken by directors or management to **conceal** either the full terms of a transaction, or that a transaction is, in substance, with a related party.

Control systems should be instituted by the directors to identify related party transactions. In general, the higher the auditors' assessment of control risk, with respect to related parties, the more emphasis is placed on substantive procedures when developing the audit programme.

The following examples are given of audit procedures

- **Review minutes** of meetings of shareholders and directors and other relevant statutory records such as the register of directors' interests

- **Review accounting records** for large or unusual transactions or balances, in particular transactions recognised at or near the end of the financial period

- **Review confirmations of loans receivable** and payable and confirmations from banks; such a review may indicate the relationship, if any, of guarantors to the entity

- **Review investment transactions**, for example purchase or sale of an interest in a joint venture or other entity

The following substantive procedures are suggested, the extent of which should be determined as a result of tests of controls and the procedures listed above.

- **Enquire of management** and the directors as to whether transactions have taken place with related parties that are required to be disclosed by the disclosure requirements, such as FRS 8, that are applicable to the entity

- **Review prior year working papers** for names of known related parties

- **Enquire** as to the **names** of all pension and other trusts established for the benefit of employees and the names of their management and trustees

- **Enquire** as to the **affiliation** of directors and officers with other entities

- **Review the register of interests in shares** to determine the names of principal shareholders

- **Enquire of other auditors** currently involved in the audit, or predecessor auditors, as to their knowledge of additional related parties

- **Review the entity's tax returns**, listing documents supplied to Stock Exchanges, returns made under companies legislation and other information supplied to regulatory agencies for evidence of the existence of related parties

- **Review invoices and correspondence** from lawyers for indications of the existence of related parties or related party transactions

Auditors should also be alert for undisclosed related party transactions. The following evidence is suggested of the type mentioned in SAS 460.4.

- Transactions which have **abnormal terms of trade**, such as unusual prices, interest rates, guarantees and repayment terms

- Transactions which appear to **lack a logical business reason** for their occurrence

- Transactions in which **substance differs from form**

- Transactions **processed or approved in a non-routine manner** or by personnel who do not ordinarily deal with such transactions

- **Unusual transactions** which are entered into shortly before or after the end of the financial period

The following procedures are suggested when the audit evidence about a related party transaction is limited.

- **Discuss** the **purpose** of **the transaction** with management or the directors

- **Confirm** the **terms** and **amount** of the **transaction** with the related party

- **Corroborate** with the **related party** the **explanation** of the purpose of the transaction and, if necessary, confirm that the transaction is bona-fide

Key learning points

☑ Auditors have statutory duties and professional duties in respect of audits.

☑ The general duty is to follow auditing standards, but certain SASs confer specific professional responsibilities.

☑ The auditors must include a statement of directors' responsibilities in their report if the directors do not elsewhere.

☑ Auditors must read other information in the annual reports and try to reconcile any inconsistencies with the financial statements or misstatements.

☑ In the case of the directors' report, this is a statutory duty.

☑ Auditors must be aware of the possibilities of misstatements in financial statements due to fraud, error or non-compliance with law.

☑ Auditors may have to report to various parties in the event that fraud, error or non-compliance with law is suspected.

☑ Auditors must ensure that the going concern basis used by the directors in the financial statements is reasonable.

☑ Auditors must ensure that events after the year end do not cause the financial statements to no longer show a true and fair view.

☑ Auditors must be aware of the possibility that related parties to the entity exist and should be disclosed in financial statements.

Quick quiz

1   In which two instances might unaudited published information be referred to in the audit report?

1 ....

2 ....

2   An auditor has a duty to detect fraud and error.

True   ☐

False   ☐

3   What audit work should auditors carry out to test client compliance with laws and regulations which are central to the client's ability to conduct its business?

4   List the circumstances in which auditors should report non-compliance with law and regulations to the proper authority.

1 ....

2 ....

Answers to quick quiz

1   Where there is

- An inconsistency between amounts in the financial statements and narratives in the director's report
- An inconsistency between the bases of preparation of related items

2   False. Auditors should seek to have a reasonable expectation of detecting material misstatements arising from fraud or error.

3   Auditors should carry out the following procedures on compliance with laws and regulations:

- Obtain a general understanding of the legal and regulatory framework and the procedures followed to ensure compliance with the framework.

- Inspect correspondence with relevant licensing or regulatory authorities.

- Make enquiries of directors.

- Obtain written confirmation of full disclosure from directors.

4   Auditors should report on non-compliance directly to the proper authority when:

- There is a statutory duty to report.

- They believe it is in the public interest to report, and either the client has not reported non-compliance, or the auditors no longer have confidence in the integrity of the directors.

PROFESSIONAL EDUCATION

Activity checklist

This checklist shows which performance criteria, range statement or knowledge and understanding point is covered by each activity in this chapter. Tick off each activity as you complete it.

Activity

4.1   This activity deals with Knowledge & Understanding point 3: relevant legislation, relevant Statements of Auditing Standards.

P A R T B

Planning an audit
assignment

chapter 5

Knowledge of the

business and its systems

Contents

1   The problem
2   The solution
3   SAS 210 *Knowledge of the business*
4   Accounting and control systems
5   Objectives of internal control systems
6   Recording internal control systems
7   Using the work of internal audit

Performance criteria

17.1.A Ascertain accounting systems under review and record them clearly on appropriate working papers

17.1.B Identify control objectives correctly

17.2.E Examine the IT environment and assess it for security

Range statement

17.1   Accounting systems: purchases; sales; stock; expenses; balance sheet items; payroll

17.1   Accounting systems that are: manual; computerised

17.1   Tests: compliance; substantive

Knowledge and understanding

5   Recording and evaluating systems: conventional symbols; flowcharts; Internal Control Questionnaires (ICQs); checklists

12   Principles of control: separation of functions; need for authorisation; recording custody; vouching; verification

15   Understanding that the accounting systems of an organisation are affected by its organisational structure, its administrative systems and procedures and the nature of its business transactions

1 The problem

Khan Associates has accepted the audit of AJ (Paper) Ltd. It has sent the company an engagement letter as it is required to do and the company have accepted those terms.

Now Khan Associates has to carry out an audit in accordance with auditing standards and which is designed to ensure that the firm does not make a mistake and risk being sued by the company or any interested third parties, as discussed in Chapter 3.

This problem is exacerbated by the fact that at this stage, Khan Associates does not have very much knowledge of the systems of AJ (Paper) Ltd and how the company operates.

2 The solution

The solution for Khan Associates is that the audit team must

1   Obtain a good knowledge of the client
2   Plan their audit in accordance with auditing standards

In this chapter, we are going to look at the first part of this solution.

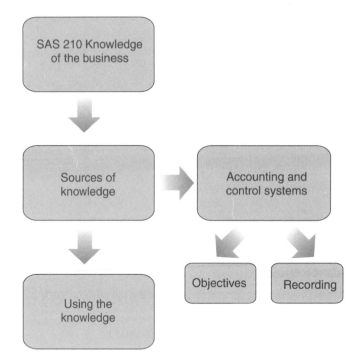

3 SAS 210 *Knowledge of the business*

'Auditors should have or obtain a knowledge of the business of the entity to be audited which is sufficient to enable them to identify and understand the events, transactions and practices that may have a significant effect on the financial statements or the audit thereof.'

Activity 5.1

What are the major areas of business knowledge that an auditor needs when planning an audit?

3.1 Obtaining the knowledge

The SAS stresses that knowledge should continuously be accumulated during the audit.

3.1.1 Sources of knowledge

The sources mentioned by the SAS are as follows.

(a) **Previous experience** of the client and its industry

(b) **Visits** to the client's premises and plant facilities

(c) **Discussion with** the client's **staff** and **directors**

(d) **Discussion with other auditors** and with legal and other advisors who have provided services to the client or within the industry

(e) **Discussion with knowledgeable people outside the client** (for example, economists, industry regulators)

(f) **Publications** related to the industry (for example, government statistics, surveys, texts, trade journals, reports prepared by banks and securities dealers, financial newspapers)

(g) **Legislation** and **regulations** that significantly affect the client

(h) **Documents produced** by the client

- Minutes of meetings
- Material sent to shareholders or filed with regulatory authorities
- Promotional literature
- Prior years' annual and financial reports
- Budgets
- Internal management reports
- Interim financial reports

- Management policy manuals
- Manuals of accounting
- Internal control systems
- Charts of accounts
- Job descriptions
- Marketing and sales plans

(i) **Professional literature** giving industry-specific guidance

As Khan Associates have no previous experience of AJ (Paper) Ltd (although they will have gained some information as part of the tender process) the audit partner will want to have meetings with Anton to find out about the company and how it operates and to see the company in operation. He may well take other members of the audit team with him.

3.2 Matters to consider

It is important to consider what knowledge the auditors require. As we shall discuss in section 4 of this chapter, it is vital that the auditors understand the systems that the directors have in place to capture financial information and to ensure mistakes are not made in recording that information. However, they will also be interested in:

Examples

General economic factors	• Whether there is a recession • What interest rates are like • The government's attitude to business
The industry	• Is activity seasonal? • What are the business risks? • What laws is the industry subject to?
The entity itself	• What is the corporate structure? • What are the attitudes of the owners? • How is the company financed? • Who are the directors and other management?
The business	• What does the company do? • Where is it? • What does it sell and on what terms? • Who buys from it? • Who sells to it?
Information technology	• Does the company use computers? • How do the computer systems work? • How easily available is computerised data?

Examples

Financial performance	• Is the company profitable?
	• Does it have cash flow?
	• What financial commitments does it have?
	• What accounting policies does it use?

Reporting	• Does it have any requirements other than duties under the Companies Act 1985?

The audit partner will want to build up a profile of AJ (Paper) Ltd against the background of the general economic climate. So, for example, we could build up this profile.

AJ (Paper) Ltd

Shareholders:	Jane, Vikram, Anton
Directors:	Anton
Operations:	Buys and sells paper.
	2 divisions – plain paper – printed paper
	The paper is printed in house.
	Activity is not particularly seasonal, although some increase in activity is seen at the beginning of the educational year.
Customers:	Lots of small clients including schools, businesses and stationery shops.
Suppliers:	The main supplier, Forest Paper. There is one other paper supplier, various printing product suppliers and utilities providers.
IT:	The company uses computers in its financial systems but intends to computerise their systems further in the near future.
Financial performance:	The company was recently formed. Prior to incorporation the business was profitable. It has expanded into printing operations and this is also expected to be profitable.
	The company is financed by equity capital injected by Jane and a loan from the bank.
Future plans:	The company intends to expand into purchasing cardboard from its existing supplier and making a range of boxes.

3.3 Using the knowledge

Having obtained the knowledge of the entity discussed above, the auditors must then use it to:

- **Assess risks** and identify problems
- **Plan** and **perform** the audit **effectively** and **efficiently**
- **Evaluate audit evidence**

The audit areas subject to judgement which may be affected by knowledge of the business are given by the SAS as follows.

- **Developing the overall audit plan** and the **audit programme**
- **Considering risks**
- Assessing **inherent risk** and **control risk**
- Determining a **materiality** level
- Considering the complexity of the entity's **information systems**
- Identifying areas where **special audit considerations and skills** may be necessary

> Will be looked at in detail in the rest of Part B

- Assessing **audit evidence** to establish its appropriateness and the validity of the related financial statement assertions
- Evaluating **accounting estimates** and **representations** by the directors
- **Recognising conflicting information** (for example, contradictory representations)
- **Recognising unusual circumstances** (for example, undisclosed related party transactions, possible fraud or non-compliance with law or regulations)
- **Making informed enquiries** and assessing the reasonableness of answers
- **Considering the appropriateness of accounting policies** and accounts disclosures

> Will be looked at in detail in Part C

4 Accounting and control systems

As discussed in Chapter 1, directors of a company put internal control systems into place.

4.1 What are internal control systems?

An **internal control system** comprises the control environment and control procedures. It includes all the policies and procedures (internal controls) adopted by the directors and management to ensure, as far as practicable, the orderly and efficient conduct of its business, including adherence to internal policies, the safeguarding of assets, the prevention and detection of fraud and error, the accuracy and completeness of the accounting records, and the timely preparation of reliable financial information.

Internal control system ——— Control environment + Control procedures

4.1.1 Control environment

Control environment is the framework within which controls operate. The control environment is very much determined by the management of a business. It is the overall **attitude**, **awareness** and **actions of directors and managers** regarding internal controls and their importance in the entity. The control environment encompasses the management style, and corporate culture and values shared by all employees. It provides the background against which the various other controls are operated.

However, a strong control environment does not, by itself, ensure the effectiveness of the overall internal control system. This is a very important point.

The following factors will be reflected in the control environment.

CONTROL ENVIRONMENT	
Philosophy and **operating style** of management	Consider attitude to controls – do management override controls? Do they neglect controls and concentrate solely on results and targets?
Organisation structure and segregation of duties	Consider delegation of authority. Segregation of duties – the principle that no single person should record and process all stages of a transaction – is vital.
Director's methods of imposing controls	Consider extent to which management supervise operations. How do they exercise control? (budgets, management accounts and internal audit)

Segregation of duties is a vital aspect of the control environment. Segregation of duties implies a number of people being involved. Hence it is more difficult for fraudulent transactions to be processed (since a number of people would have to collude in the fraud), and it is also more difficult for accidental errors to be processed (since the more people are involved, the more checking there can be).

4.1.2 Control procedures

Control procedures are those policies and procedures in addition to the control environment which are established to achieve the entity's specific objectives. They include those designed to **prevent** or to **detect** and **correct errors**. As we saw above, segregation of duties is important. Here are some other control procedures:

Specific control procedures	
Approval and control of documents	Transactions should be approved by an appropriate person. For example, overtime should be approved by departmental managers.
Controls over computerised applications	For example, passwords and other programmed controls.
Checking the arithmetical accuracy of records	For example, checking to see if individual invoices have been added up correctly.
Maintaining and reviewing control accounts and trial balances	Control accounts bring together transactions in individual ledgers. Trial balances bring together unusual transactions for the organisation as a whole. Preparing these can highlight unusual transactions or accounts.
Reconciliations	Reconciliations involve comparison of a specific balance in the accounting records with what another source says the balance should be. Differences between the two figures should only be reconciling items. For example, a bank reconciliation.

Specific control procedures	
Comparing the results of cash, security and stock counts with accounting records	For example, a physical count of petty cash. The balance shown in the cash book should be the same amount as is in the tin.
Comparing internal data with external sources of information	For example, comparing records of goods despatched to customers with customers acknowledgement of goods that have been received.
Limiting physical access to assets and records	Only authorised personnel should have access to certain assets (particularly valuable or portable ones). For example, ensuring that the stock store is only open when the store personnel are there and is otherwise locked.

4.2 Why set up internal control systems?

To assess the following:

- **Transactions** are executed in accordance with **proper authorisation**.

- All transactions and other events are **promptly recorded** at the **correct amount**, in the **appropriate accounts** and in the **proper accounting period**.

- **Access to assets** is permitted only in accordance with proper authorisation.

- **Recorded assets** are **compared** with the **existing assets** at reasonable intervals and appropriate action is taken with regard to any differences.

However, any internal control system can only provide the directors with **reasonable assurance** that their objectives are reached, because of **inherent limitations** of control systems.

These inherent limitations include costs of controls not outweighing their benefits, the potential for human error, the possibility of controls being by-passed, and the fact that controls tend to be designed to cope with routine and not non-routine transactions.

Activity 5.2

What objectives should AJ (Paper) Ltd's internal control system aim to fulfil?

4.3 How are internal control systems relevant to auditors?

Auditors are only concerned with assessing policies and procedures which are relevant to assertions made in the financial statements. Auditors try to:

- **Assess the adequacy** of the accounting system as a basis for preparing the accounts

- **Identify** the types of **potential misstatements** that could occur in the accounts
- **Consider factors** that affect the **risk of misstatements**
- **Design appropriate audit procedures**

4.3.1 Accounting system and control environment

Auditors must obtain an **understanding** of the accounting system to enable them to identify and understand:

- **Major classes of transactions** in the entity's operations
- **How such transactions** are initiated
- **Significant accounting records**, supporting documents and accounts
- The **accounting and financial reporting process**

The factors affecting the **nature, timing and extent** of the **procedures** performed in order to understand the systems include:

- **Materiality** considerations
- The **size and complexity** of the entity
- Their **assessment** of **inherent risk**
- The **complexity** of the entity's computer systems
- The **type of internal controls** involved
- The **nature of the entity's documentation** of specific internal controls

> We will look at these things in Chapter 6.

Auditors must also make an assessment of whether accounting records fulfil Companies Act requirements, which we discussed in Chapter 1.

Many company's systems are computerised and auditors need to be computer-literate to assess the controls inherent within the system and also assess whether the system is secure. You should be aware of key security issues in IT from your Unit 21 studies.

Having assessed the accounting system and control environment, the auditors can make a **preliminary assessment** of whether the system is capable of producing reliable financial statements.

5 Objectives of internal control systems

In paragraph 4.2 above, we looked at the general reasons why directors set up systems of internal control. Here we shall look at specific control objectives in the major cycles in a business.

A company's operational cycles will vary according to the type of its business and the demands of its operations. However, most businesses have three major operational cycles linked to three key groups of people: customers, suppliers and employees.

We are going to look at what these cycles are, what the major control objectives are at each point in the cycle, and what types of controls might typically exist.

5.1 The sales system

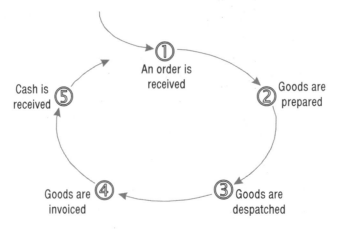

The diagram above shows the five main points of the sales cycle. We shall now consider the key control objectives and potential controls at each point.

Stage	Control objectives	Controls
① Order	Goods only supplied to creditworthy customers	• Authorisation of new customers (credit checks/ references) • Credit limit and current level of debt checked before order accepted
② Preparation	There may be a significant number of operational controls over the quality of products here. These do not have a direct effect on the financial statements.	
③ Despatch	All goods despatched are recorded (ie no theft or error) Customers are sent the right goods	• Goods out note raised • Goods out note checked to order • Checks on sequence of goods out note numbers • Goods sent out checked for quality and quantity • Delivery note signed by customer
④ Invoice	All goods sent out are invoiced correctly All invoices sent out are recorded	• Invoice checked to price lists, order and despatch notes • Calculations on invoices checked • Sequential numbers on invoices checked • Invoices entered into sales day book/ledger
⑤ Cash	Cash is received for invoiced goods	• Regular preparation of debtors statements • Follow up of overdue accounts • Overdue accounts put on 'stop' for future orders

Stage	Control objectives	Controls
	Cash received is recorded	• Restrictions on who receives post • Two people supervise post opening • Amounts received listed • Amounts entered into cash book
	Cash received is safeguarded	• (If cash) agreement of till records to count • Regular banking • Cheques kept in safe when awaiting banking

These are basic controls. You must be able to think about control objectives and controls in any given situation. You should spend a minute thinking about the sales controls you are aware of in your business. Why are they there? How do they achieve that objective?

5.2 The purchases system

The purchases system is often more complex than the sales system. Why? Remember that a business will buy goods for several reasons:

- To use in production (raw materials)
- To resell (in a wholesale business)
- To use for the business (for example, stationery or consumables)

The business will also buy 'utilities' such as electricity and gas, and services, for example cleaners or maintenance firms.

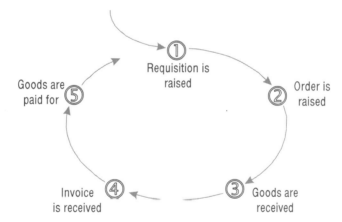

Stage	Control objectives	Controls
① Requisition	Requisitions only raised when they are needed	• Authorised re-order levels • Sequentially numbered requisition notes
② Order	All orders are genuinely for business use and authorised	• Authorisation of purchases • Central policy for choosing suppliers • Pre-numbered order forms • Orders only raised when requisition received • Safeguarding of blank order forms
③ Goods received	Goods are as were ordered Goods received are recorded	• Inspection of goods inwards • Goods received notes • Checking goods received notes to orders
④ Invoice	Liabilities are only recognised for goods and services that have been received Invoices are recorded	• Invoices are checked to goods received notes • Calculations on supplier's invoices checked • Referencing of supplier's invoices • Purchase ledger maintained • Purchase ledger balances reconciled to supplier statements • Correct classification of invoice (expense or asset)
⑤ Payment	The company only pays genuine business expenses	• Cheque requisition supported by payment documentation (eg invoices) • Cheques signed by two authorised personnel • Prompt despatch of cheques • Payment documentation cancelled when paid

You will find it useful to also think through any purchases cycle you are aware of and to ascertain the controls and objectives in it. If you don't know what control systems exist in your business, find out!

5.3 The wages system

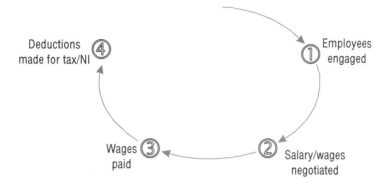

In terms of the financial statements, it is the last two items in the cycle which are important.

Stage	Control objectives	Controls
③ Wage payment	Employees are only paid for work done The correct employees are paid	• Employees use clock cards to punch in and out of work • Authorisation of overtime/holiday • Maintenance of personnel records • Use of automatic bank transfer to pay employees
④ Deductions	Deductions are calculated correctly and authorised	• Comparison of payroll to personnel records • Reconciliation of total pay and deductions • Reconciliation of deductions with total payments to the Inland Revenue

Activity 5.3

What controls would AJ (Paper) Ltd be advised to have over the following circumstances, and why would they want the control in each case? (You should use the headings 'control objective' and 'control' in your answer.)

(a)   Customer returns some goods and requests a credit note.
(b)   Supplier statement refers to an invoice not received by the company.
(c)   The workforce negotiate a pay rise.
(d)   An employee leaves and is replaced.

6 Recording internal control systems

Auditors will keep a record of how the clients' systems work, which will be updated every year for any changes. There are various ways of recording systems. Often a combination of the different methods will be used.

6.1 Narrative notes

Narrative notes have the advantage of being simple to record. However they are awkward to change if written manually. Editing in future years will be easier if they are computerised.

The purpose of the notes is to **describe** and **explain** the **system**, at the same time making any comments or criticisms which will help to demonstrate an intelligent understanding of the system.

For each system notes need to deal with the following questions.

- What functions are performed and by whom?
- What documents are used?
- Where do the documents originate and what is their destination?
- What sequence are retained documents filed in?
- What books are kept and where?

Narrative notes can be used to support flowcharts.

6.2 Flowcharts

There are two methods of flowcharting in regular use.

- Document flowcharts
- Information flowcharts

Document flowcharts are more commonly used because they are relatively easy to prepare.

- **All** documents are followed through from 'cradle to grave'.
- **All** operations and controls are shown.

Information flowcharts are prepared in the reverse direction from the flow: they start with the entry in the accounting records and work back to the actual transaction. They concentrate on significant information flows and key controls and ignore any unimportant documents or copies of documents. These are less common. We shall concentrate on document flowcharts.

Advantages of flowcharts:

(a)   After a little experience they can be **prepared quickly**.

(b)   As the information is presented in a standard form, they are fairly **easy to follow** and to review.

(c)   They generally ensure that the system is **recorded in its entirety**, as all document flows have to be traced from beginning to end. Any 'loose ends' will be apparent from a quick examination.

(d)   They **eliminate** the need for **extensive narrative** and can be of considerable help in highlighting the salient points of control and any weaknesses in the system.

On the other hand, flowcharts do have some **disadvantages**.

(a)   They are **only really suitable for describing standard systems**. Procedures for dealing with unusual transactions will normally have to be recorded using narrative notes.

(b)   They are useful for recording the flow of documents, but once the **records** or the assets to which they relate have **become static** they **can no longer be used for describing the controls** (for example over fixed assets).

(c)   Major **amendment is difficult** without redrawing.

(d)   **Time** can be **wasted** by **charting areas** that are of no **audit significance** (a criticism of **document** not information flowcharts).

Flowcharts should be kept simple, so that the overall structure or flow is clear at first sight.

- There must be **conformity of symbols**, with each symbol representing one and only one thing.
- The direction of the flowchart should be from **top to bottom** and from **left to right**.
- There must be no **loose ends.**
- The main flow should finish at the **bottom right hand corner**, not in the middle of the page.
- Connecting lines should cross **only** where absolutely necessary to preserve the chart's simplicity.

Basic symbols will be used for the charting of all systems, but where the client's system involves mechanised or computerised processing, then further symbols may be required to supplement the basic ones. The basic symbols used are shown below.

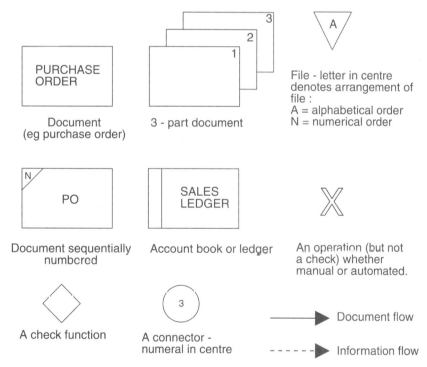

Preparation of a basic flowchart will involve the procedures laid out in the next few paragraphs.

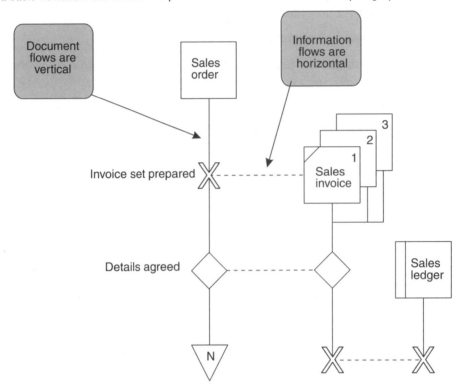

One of the key features of any good system of internal control is that there should be a system of 'internal check'. **Internal check** is the requirement for a segregation of duties amongst the available staff so that one person's work is independently reviewed by another, no one person having complete responsibility for all aspects of a transaction.

This method of flowcharting shows the division of duties. This is achieved by dividing the chart into **vertical columns**. In a **smaller** enterprise there would be one column to show the duties of each **individual**, whereas in a **large** company the vertical columns would show the division of duties amongst the various **departments**.

The following figure shows, in a small company, the division of duties between Mr Major and Mr Minor.

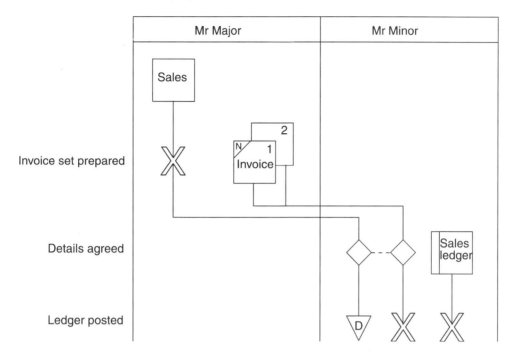

To facilitate ease of reference each operation shown on the chart is numbered in sequence on the chart, a separate column being used for this purpose.

Finally, the chart will be completed by the inclusion of a narrative column which will describe significant operations. Narrative should be kept to a minimum and only included where in fact it is required.

On the following pages you will find two charts which illustrate typical procedures in a company's purchasing system.

- Ordering and receiving of goods
- Approval of invoices

PURCHASES SYSTEM - CHART 1 ORDERING AND RECEIVING OF GOODS

Example Limited

Op. No.	Description
1	Requisition is raised when goods in stock are down to re-order level. A label with purchase requisition attached is removed from box representing re-order level. Order quantity is predetermined. Requisition is a copy of previous purchase order omitting price details.
2	Requisition signed by warehouse manager
3	Buyer checks authorisation of requisition
4	Purchase order prepared using supplier's latest price list
5	
6	
7	Mailed to supplier
8	
9	
10	
11	File of outstanding purchase orders scanned weekly for overdue deliveries. If overdue, follow up with supplier
12	When goods arrive, quantity is checked against the purchase order. Goods are in sealed cartons. If obviously damaged, delivery is refused. If they appear sound, the quantity of cartons is counted - no further inspection
13	Raises goods received note. If goods are short delivered a shortage memo is raised at the same time and cross-referenced to the GRN
14 15	Filed in GRN numerical order / Filed in Shortage Memo numerical order
16	

Warehouse | Buyer | Goods Inwards | P1

To warehouse with goods as next requisition

PURCHASES SYSTEM - CHART 2   APPROVAL OF INVOICES

Example Limited	Op. No.	Goods Inwards	Buyer	Purchase Ledger Clerk	P2

Direct from supplier (via mail room only)

Invoice

GRN

Shortage memo

PO

Debit note

To Supplier

Invoice GRN PO Debit /Shortage memo

Op. No.	Description
17	Matches and checks signature on GRN, quantity and description of goods
18	
19	Invoice given sequential number and stamped with a grid for approvals
20	Invoices filed until goods arrive
21	Invoices matched with GRN and purchase order. If unmatched buyer retains until goods received. Checks quantity, price and discount terms.
22	Enters accounting code and signs approval grid. If price and quantity incorrect notes this on invoice and raises debit note (advising supplier and requesting credit). Debit notes are referenced to supplier invoice.
23	
24	
25	Check all costs and extensions on invoices over £200 and 10% of all invoices under £200
26	Reviews invoices to see that package is complete and approval grid fully signed
27	
28	

6.3 Questionnaires

We can look at two types of questionnaire here, each with a different purpose.

(a)   **Internal Control Questionnaires (ICQs)** are used to ask whether certain controls exist.

(b)   **Internal Control Evaluation Questionnaires (ICEQs)** are used to determine whether whatever controls the system contains fulfil specific objectives or can be relied on to prevent specific weaknesses.

6.3.1 Internal Control Questionnaires (ICQs)

The major question which internal control questionnaires are designed to answer is 'How good is the system of controls?' Although there are many different forms of ICQ in practice, they all conform to certain basic principles.

- They comprise a **list of questions** designed to determine whether desirable controls are present.
- They are formulated so that there is one to cover each of the **major transaction cycles**.

Since it is the primary purpose of an ICQ to evaluate the system rather than describe it, one of the most effective ways of designing the questionnaire is to phrase the questions so that all the answers can be given as 'YES' or 'NO' and a 'NO' answer indicates a weakness in the system. An example would be:

Are purchase invoices checked to goods received
notes before being passed for payment?   YES/NO/Comments

A 'NO' answer to that question clearly indicates a weakness in the company's payment procedures which requires further comment.

The ICQ questions below dealing with goods inward provide additional illustrations of the ICQ approach.

Goods inward

(a)   Are supplies examined on arrival as to quantity and quality?

(b)   Is such an examination evidenced in some way?

(c)   Is the receipt of supplies recorded, perhaps by means of goods inwards notes?

(d)   Are receipt records prepared by a person independent of those responsible for:

(i)   Ordering functions
(ii)   The processing and recording of invoices

(e)   Are goods inwards records controlled to ensure that invoices are obtained for all goods received and to enable the liability for unbilled goods to be determined (by pre-numbering the records and accounting for all serial numbers)?

(f)   (i)   Are goods inward records regularly reviewed for items for which no invoices have been received?
(ii)   Are any such items investigated?

(g)   Are these records reviewed by a person independent of those responsible for the receipt and control of goods?

Each situation must therefore be judged on its own merits and hence, although the ICQs often take the form of a standard pre-printed pack, they should be used with imagination. As using ICQs is a skilled and responsible task, the evaluation should be performed by a senior member of the audit team.

6.3.2 Internal Control Evaluation Questionnaires (ICEQs)

In recent years many auditing firms have developed and implemented an evaluation technique more concerned with assessing whether specific errors (or frauds) are possible rather than establishing whether certain desirable controls are present.

This is achieved by reducing the control criteria for each transaction stream down to a handful of key questions (or control questions). The characteristic of these questions is that they concentrate on criteria that the controls present should fulfil.

The nature of an ICEQ can be illustrated by the following example.

Internal control evaluation questionnaire: control questions

The sales cycle

Is there reasonable assurance that:

(a)   Sales are properly authorised?
(b)   Sales are made to reliable payers?
(c)   All goods despatched are invoiced?
(d)   All invoices are properly prepared?
(e)   All invoices are recorded?
(f)   Invoices are properly supported?
(g)   All credits to customers' accounts are valid?
(h)   Cash and cheques received are properly recorded and deposited?
(i)   Slow payers will be chased and that bad and doubtful debts will be provided against?
(j)   All transactions are properly accounted for?
(k)   Cash sales are properly dealt with?
(l)   Sundry sales are controlled?
(m)   At the period end the system will neither overstate nor understate debtors?

The purchases cycle

Is there reasonable assurance that:

(a)   Goods or services could not be received without a liability being recorded?

(b)   Receipt of goods or services is required in order to establish a liability?

(c)   A liability will be recorded:

• Only for authorised items; and
• At the proper amount?

(d)   All payments are properly authorised?

(e)   All credits due from suppliers are received?

(f)   All transactions are properly accounted for?

(g)   At the period end liabilities are neither overstated nor understated by the system?

(h)   The balance at the bank is properly recorded at all times?

(i)   Unauthorised cash payments could not be made and that the balance of petty cash is correctly stated at all times?

Wages and salaries

Is there reasonable assurance that:

(a)   Employees are only paid for work done?
(b)   Employees are paid the correct amount (gross and net)?
(c)   The right employees actually receive the right amount?
(d)   Accounting for payroll costs and deductions is accurate?

Stock

Is there reasonable assurance that:

(a)   Stock is safeguarded from physical loss (eg fire, theft, deterioration)?
(b)   Stock records are accurate and up to date?
(c)   The recorded stock exists?
(d)   The recorded stock is owned by the company?
(e)   The cut off is reliable?
(f)   The costing system is reliable?
(g)   The stock sheets are accurately compiled?
(h)   The stock valuation is fair?

Fixed tangible assets

Is there reasonable assurance that:

(a)   Recorded assets actually exist and belong to the company?
(b)   Capital expenditure is authorised and reported?
(c)   Disposals of fixed assets are authorised and reported?
(d)   Depreciation is realistic?
(e)   Fixed assets are correctly accounted for?
(f)   Income derived from fixed assets is accounted for?

Investments

Is there reasonable assurance that:

(a)   Recorded investments belong to the company and are safeguarded from loss?

(b)   All income, rights or bonus issues are properly received and accounted for?

(c)   Investment transactions are made only in accordance with company policy and are appropriately authorised and documented?

(d)   The carrying values of investments are reasonably stated?

Management information and general controls

Is the nominal ledger satisfactorily controlled?

Are journal entries adequately controlled?

Does the organisation structure provide a clear definition of the extent and limitation of authority?

Are the systems operated by competent employees, who are adequately supported?

If there is an internal audit function, is it adequate?

Are financial planning procedures adequate?

Are periodic internal reporting procedures adequate?

Each key control question is supported by detailed control points to be considered. For example, the detailed control points to be considered in relation to key control question (b) for the expenditure cycle (Is there reasonable assurance that receipt of goods or services is required to establish a liability?) are as follows.

(1) Is segregation of duties satisfactory?

(2) Are controls over relevant master files satisfactory?

(3) Is there a record that all goods received have been checked for:

- Weight or number?
- Quality and damage?

(4) Are all goods received taken on charge in the detailed stock ledgers:

- By means of the goods received note?

- Or by means of purchase invoices?

- Are there, in a computerised system, sensible control totals (hash totals, money values and so on) to reconcile the stock system input with the creditors system?

(5) Are all invoices initialled to show that:

- Receipt of goods has been checked against the goods received records?
- Receipt of services has been verified by the person using it?
- Quality of goods has been checked against the inspection?

(6) In a computerised invoice approval system are there print-outs (examined by a responsible person) of:

- Cases where order, GRN and invoice are present but they are not equal ('equal' within predetermined tolerances of minor discrepancies)?

- Cases where invoices have been input but there is no corresponding GRN?

(7) Is there adequate control over direct purchases?

(8) Are receiving documents effectively cancelled (for example cross-referenced) to prevent their supporting two invoices?

Alternatively, ICEQ questions can be phrased so that the weakness which should be prevented by a key control is highlighted, such as the following.

Question	Answer	Comments or explanation of 'yes' answer
Can goods be sent to unauthorised suppliers?		

In these cases a 'yes' answer would require an explanation, rather than a 'no' answer.

Advantages	Disadvantages
ICQs	
If drafted thoroughly, they can ensure **all controls** are **considered.** They are **quick** to **prepare.** They are **easy** to **use** and **control**. A manager or partner reviewing the work can easily see what has been done.	The client may be able to **overstate controls.** They may contain a large number of **irrelevant controls.** They can give the impression that all controls are of **equal weight**. In many systems one 'no' answer (for example lack of segregation of duties) may cancel the apparent value of a string of 'yes' answers). They may not include **unusual controls**, which are nevertheless effective in particular circumstances.
ICEQs	
Because they are drafted in terms of **objectives** rather than specific controls, they are easier to apply to a variety of systems than **ICQs**. Answering ICEQs should enable auditors to **identify the most important controls** which they are most likely to test during control testing. ICEQs can **highlight areas of weakness** where extensive substantive testing will be required.	The principal disadvantage is that they can be **drafted vaguely**, hence **misunderstood** and important controls not identified.

7 Using the work of internal audit

As we discussed briefly in Chapter 1, a key role of **internal** audit is testing systems of internal control to ensure that they operate effectively and efficiently.

This means that internal audit may have done a lot of work which is similar in objective to the work the external auditor will do:

- Recording systems
- Evaluating systems
- Testing systems

Auditing standards recognise that external auditors may sometimes want to make use of internal audit work. An effective internal audit function may reduce, modify or alter the timing of external audit procedures, but it can **never** eliminate them entirely. Where the internal audit function is deemed ineffective, it may still be useful to be aware of the internal audit conclusions.

...NAL EDUCATION

In order to use internal audit work, external auditors must do two things:

- Evaluate the internal audit department
- Evaluate the specific work they want to use

7.1 Evaluating the internal audit department

The following important criteria will be considered by the external auditors.

ASSESSMENT OF INTERNAL AUDIT	
Organisational status	Consider **to whom** internal audit **reports** (should be board), whether internal audit has any **operating responsibilities** and constraints or restrictions on the function
Scope of function	Consider **extent** and **nature** of **assignments** performed and the action taken by management as a result of internal audit reports
Technical competence	Consider whether internal auditors have adequate **technical training** and proficiency
Due professional care	Consider whether internal audit is **properly planned**, **supervised**, **reviewed** and **documented**

7.2 Evaluating specific internal audit work

The evaluation here will consider the scope of work and related audit programmes **and** whether the assessment of the internal audit function remains appropriate. This may include consideration of whether:

- The work is performed by persons having **adequate technical training** and **proficiency** as internal auditors

- The work of assistants is properly supervised, reviewed and documented

- Sufficient appropriate audit evidence is obtained to afford a reasonable basis for the conclusions reached

- The conclusions reached are appropriate in the circumstances

- Any reports prepared by internal audit are consistent with the results of the work performed

- Any exceptions or unusual matters disclosed by internal audit are properly resolved

- Amendments to the external audit programme are required as a result of matters identified by internal audit work

- There is a need to test the work of internal audit to confirm its adequacy

If the external auditors decide that the Internal audit work is not adequate, they should extend their procedures in order to obtain appropriate evidence.

Activity 5.4

You are responsible for ascertaining purchases and creditors in AJ (Paper) Ltd. All data is processed through the computer, by full-time computer operators in the creditors section. You are about to start the audit, and want to find out more about the controls operated over processing in the creditors section.

List the main questions you will ask to ascertain what the controls over purchases and creditors are and whether they are effective.

Activity 5.5

During your discussions with Anton he mentions that during the next financial year the company plans to change its computer arrangements, and allow access to a central computer through a number of remote terminals situated throughout the company. Anton is worried about the security arrangements in the new system.

Advise Anton what controls ought to be in operation over access to the new system from remote terminals.

Key learning points

☑   When a new client is acquired the auditors must obtain **knowledge of the business** from various sources.

☑   Important aspects of knowledge of the business are:

–   The industry
–   Directors, managers and ownership
–   Products, markets, suppliers, expenses, operations
–   Financial performance
–   Reporting environment

☑   Knowledge of the business can be used to:

–   Assess risks
–   Develop an effective and efficient audit plan and programme
–   Evaluate audit evidence

☑   The auditors must understand the accounting system and control environment in order to determine the audit approach. They must also assess whether accounting records fulfil Companies Act requirements.

☑   Specific control procedures include the following

–   Approval and control of documents
–   Controls over computerised applications and the information technology environment
–   Checking the arithmetical accuracy of the records
–   Maintaining and reviewing control accounts and trial balances
–   Reconciliations
–   Comparing the results of cash, security and stock counts with accounting records
–   Comparing internal data with external sources of information
–   Limiting direct physical access to assets and records

☑   There are always inherent limitations to internal controls, including cost-benefit requirements and the possibility of controls being by-passed and over-ridden.

☑   Auditors can use a number of methods to record accounting and control systems.

–   Narrative notes
–   Flowcharts
–   ICQs (which ask if various controls exist)
–   ICEQs (which ask if controls fulfil key objectives)

☑   Internal audit can be a very important internal control. It can operate in the following areas.

–   Review of accounting and internal control systems
–   Examination of financial and operating information
–   Review of economy, efficiency and effectiveness
–   Review of compliance
–   Special investigations (fraud)

☑   External auditors may rely on the work of internal audit provided it has been assessed as a reliable internal control. General criteria include:
    – Organisational status
    – Scope of function
    – Technical competence
    – Due professional care

☑   External auditors should also evaluate specific internal work if they wish to use it to reduce the extent of external audit procedures.

Quick quiz

1   What are the main sources of knowledge of the business in SAS 210?

2   What are the main limitations of a system of internal controls?

3   What is the main disadvantage of recording systems by means of manual narrative notes?

4   Flowcharts are suitable for describing unusual systems.

TRUE

FALSE

5   What is the main difference between ICQs and ICEQs?

6   List six factors which the external auditors consider in relation to the work of internal audit

1 ....

2 ....

3 ....

4 ....

5 ....

6 ....

Answers to quick quiz

1   The main sources of knowledge of the business listed in SAS 210 are as follows.

- Previous experience of the client and industry
- Visits to the client
- Discussions with the client's directors and staff
- Discussions with other auditors and legal and other advisers
- Discussions with knowledgeable people outside the client
- Industry publications
- Legislation and regulations that significantly affect the client
- Documents produced by the client
- Professional literature

2   The main limitations of a system of internal controls are:

- Costs of implementing controls may outweigh benefits

- Most internal controls are directed towards routine rather than non-routine transactions

- Mistakes may occur when controls are being operated

- Controls may be bypassed by people acting in collusion

- Controls may be over-ridden

- Changes in conditions or decreased compliance may mean control procedures become inadequate over time

3   The main disadvantage of manual narrative notes is that they can be difficult to change.

4   False.

5   ICQs concentrate on whether specific controls exist, whereas ICEQs concentrate on whether the control system has specific strengths or can prevent specific weaknesses.

6   1   Proficiency and training of staff
      2   Level of supervision, documentation and review of the work
      3   Sufficiency and appropriateness of evidence
      4   Appropriateness of conclusion
      5   Consistency of reports with work performed
      6   Whether work necessitates amendment to original audit plan

Activity checklist

This checklist shows which performance criteria, range statement or knowledge and understanding point is covered by each activity in this chapter. Tick off each activity as you complete it.

Activity

5.1		This activity deals with Performance Criteria 17.1.A: Ascertain accounting systems under review and record them clearly in appropriate working papers.
5.2		This activity deals with Performance Criteria 17.1.B: Identify control objectives correctly.
5.3		This activity deals with Performance Criteria 17.1.B: Identify control objectives correctly.
5.4		This activity deals with Performance Criteria 17.1.B: Identify control objectives correctly.
5.5		This activity deals with Performance Criteria 17.2.E: Examine the IT environment and assess it for security.

chapter 6

Audit plan

Contents

1   The problem (recap)
2   The solution
3   The overall audit plan
4   Risk in the audit process
5   Materiality
6   Analytical procedures

Performance criteria

17.1.C Assess risks accurately

17.1.E Identify account balances to be verified and the associated risks

Range statement

17.1 Accounting systems: purchases; sales; stock; expenses; balance sheet items; payroll

17.1 Accounting systems that are: manual; computerised

17.1 Tests: compliance; substantive

Knowledge and understanding

13 Materiality

14 Audit risk

1 The problem (recap)

As you will remember from Chapter 5, Khan Associates has accepted the audit of AJ (Paper) Ltd. It has sent the company an engagement letter as it is required to do and the company have accepted those terms.

Now Khan Associates has to carry out an audit in accordance with auditing standards which is designed to ensure that the firm does not make a mistake and risk being sued by the company or any interested third parties, as discussed in Chapter 3.

2 The solution

The audit engagement partner at Khan Associates, Tariq Hussain, has held meetings with Anton and has gained some knowledge of the business. An audit team has attended site to ascertain and record the accounting systems before the audit is planned because this is the first year of the audit and this was necessary to obtain sufficient knowledge of the business to put together an audit plan.

In order to comply with auditing standards and conduct a quality audit and to minimise the risk of being sued for negligence, Tariq Hussain must now put together an audit plan.

3 The overall audit plan

Auditors are required by SAS 200 *Planning* to plan audit work to ensure that it is performed in an effective manner.

3.1 Objectives of planning

The key objectives are:

- Ensuring that **appropriate attention is devoted** to different areas of the audit
- Ensuring that **potential problems** are **identified**
- **Facilitating review**

A structured approach to planning will include a number of stages.

- **Updating knowledge of the client**
- **Preparing** the **detailed audit approach**
- Making **administrative decisions** such as staffing and budgets

3.2 Matters to consider

Auditors should develop an overall audit plan setting out the expected scope and conduct of the audit, that is, a general strategy. The auditor should consider the following matters:

Area	Issues
Knowledge of the entity's business	General economic factors and industry conditions
	Important characteristics of the client, (a) business, (b) principal business strategies, (c) financial performance, (d) reporting requirements, including changes since the previous audit
	The operating style and control consciousness of directors and management
	The auditors' cumulative knowledge of the accounting and control systems and any expected changes in the period
Risk and materiality	The setting of materiality for audit planning purposes
	The expected assessments of risks or error and identification of significant audit areas
	Any indication that misstatements that could have a material effect on the financial statements might arise because of fraud or for any other reason
	The identification of complex accounting areas including those involving estimates
Nature, timing and extent of procedures	The relative importance and timing of tests of control and substantive procedures
	The use of information technology by the client or the auditors
	The use made of work of any internal audit function
	Procedures which need to be carried out at or before the year end
	The timing of significant phases of the preparation of the financial statements
	The audit evidence required to reduce detection risk to an acceptably low level.
Co-ordination, direction, supervision and review	The involvement of other auditors
	The involvement of experts, other third parties and internal auditors
	The number of locations
	Staffing requirements
Other matters	Any regulatory requirements arising from the decision to retain the engagement
	The possibility that the going concern basis may be inappropriate
	The terms of the engagement and any statutory responsibilities
	The nature and timing of reports or other communication with the entity that are expected under the engagement

3.3 Changes to the audit work planned

The standard requires that the audit work planned should be reviewed and, if necessary, revised during the course of the audit. An accurate record of changes to the audit plan must be maintained in order to explain the general strategy finally adopted for the audit.

3.4 The audit programme

The general strategy set out in the audit plan should be developed into instructions to the audit team that set out the nature, timing and extent of audit tests that they will carry out. This set of instructions is known as the audit programme.

The audit programme may contain references to matters such as the **audit objectives, timing, sample size** and **basis of selection** for each area. We will discuss in Chapter 9 how auditors design the tests that are included in the audit programme.

4 Risk in the audit process

In Chapter 1, we discussed the fact that auditors do not test everything in financial statements to come to their conclusion. In order to decide what items should be tested, auditors use a 'risk-based approach'.

4.1 Overall audit risk

Overall audit risk is the risk the auditor faces that he may give an inappropriate opinion on the financial statements, that is:

- He may say that the financial statements give a true and fair view when in fact they do not, or

- He may say that the financial statements do not give a true and fair view when in fact they do, or

- He may correctly say that the financial statements do not give a true and fair view, but give the wrong reason for that

Overall audit risk has three elements.

The auditor has no control over inherent and control risks, which are affected by the entity. However, he may control the level of detection risk on an assignment to an extent by carrying out more or fewer audit tests. This means that the auditor can control the level of audit risk he faces in relation to an engagement. However, audit risk can never be eliminated due to the inherent limitations of an audit.

The risk-based approach is shown in the diagram below.

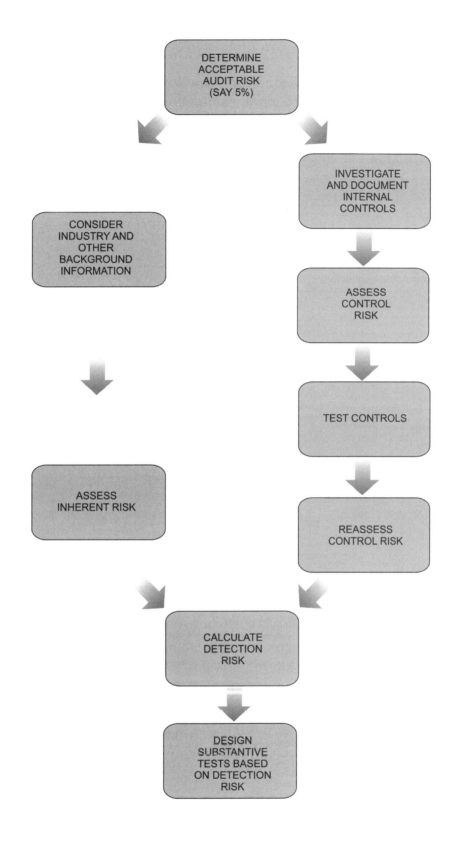

4.2 Inherent risk

Inherent risk is the risk that items will be mis-stated due to **characteristics** of those items, such as the fact that they are estimates or that they are important items in the accounts and hence there is a temptation to mis-state them. The auditors must use their professional **judgement** and all available **knowledge** to assess inherent risk. If no such information or knowledge is available then the inherent risk is **high**.

The results of the assessment must be properly documented and, where inherent risk is assessed as not high, then audit work may be reduced. The relevant factors should be considered under two headings.

FACTORS AFFECTING CLIENT AS A WHOLE	
Integrity and **attitude to risk** of directors and management	Domination by a single individual can cause problems
Management experience and **knowledge**	Changes in management and quality of financial management
Unusual pressures on management	Examples include tight reporting deadlines, or market or financing expectations
Nature of business	Potential problems include technological obsolescence or over-dependence on single product
Industry factors	Competitive conditions, regulatory requirements, technology developments, changes in customer demand
Information technology	Problems include lack of supporting documentation, concentration of expertise in a few people, potential for unauthorised access

FACTORS AFFECTING INDIVIDUAL ACCOUNT BALANCES OR TRANSACTIONS	
Financial statement **accounts prone to misstatement**	Accounts which require adjustment in previous period or require high degree of estimation
Complex accounts	Accounts which require expert valuations or are subjects of current professional discussion
Assets at risk of being **lost or stolen**	Cash, stock, portable fixed assets (computers)
Quality of **accounting systems**	Strength of individual departments (sales, purchases, cash etc)
Unusual transactions	Transactions for large amounts, with unusual names, not settled promptly (particularly important if they occur at period-end)
	Transactions that do not go through the system, that relate to specific clients or processed by certain individuals
Staff	Staff changes or areas of low morale

4.3 Control risk

Control risk is the risk that client controls fail to detect material errors.

As has been discussed in Chapter 5, the auditors ascertain and assess the accounting system and control environment. As a result of this, they should be able to make a preliminary assessment of control risk, that is, the risk that the system will fail to prevent and detect errors.

This assessment will be discussed in more detail in Chapter 10.

4.4 Detection risk

Detection risk is the risk that audit procedures will fail to detect material errors.

Detection risk relates to the inability of the auditors to examine all evidence. Audit evidence is not generally 100% conclusive, and hence some detection risk will almost always be present. What auditors are seeking is to have **reasonable confidence** about the truth and fairness of the accounts.

The auditors' **inherent and control risk assessments** will influence the **nature, timing and extent of tests** on balance sheet and profit and loss account items (substantive procedures) required to reduce detection risk and thereby audit risk.

Substantive procedures can never be abandoned entirely because control and inherent risk can never be assessed at a low enough level. Substantive procedures may though be restricted to analytical procedures if appropriate. (Analytical procedures are discussed later in this chapter.)

When both inherent and control risks are assessed as high, the auditors should consider whether substantive procedures can provide sufficient appropriate audit evidence to reduce detection risk, and therefore audit risk, to an acceptably low level. When auditors determine that detection risk regarding a material financial statement assertion cannot be reduced to an acceptably low level, they should consider the implications for their audit report (discussed further in Chapter 19).

4.5 Changes in risk assessment

Where the auditors' assessment of the components of audit risk changes during the audit, they should modify the planned substantive procedures based on the revised risk levels.

Activity 6.1

Look back to the profile of AJ (Paper) Ltd that Tariq Hussain put together when he visited Anton. You will find this on page 67. Identify any inherent risks you think exist at AJ (Paper) Ltd.

5 Materiality

The concept of 'true and fair' is linked with the fundamental concept of materiality. As we discussed in Chapter 1, the auditors' task is to decide whether accounts show a true and fair view. The auditors are not responsible for establishing whether accounts are correct in every particular for the following reasons.

  (a)   It can take a great deal of time and trouble to check the correctness of even a very small transaction and the resulting benefit may not justify the effort.

  (b)   Financial accounting inevitably involves a degree of estimation which means that financial statements can never be completely precise.

The APB have stated that SASs need only be applied to **material** items.

5.1 What is materiality?

Materiality is an expression of the relative significance or importance of a particular matter in the context of financial statements as a whole, or of individual financial statements. A matter is material if its omission or misstatement would reasonably influence the decisions of an addressee of the auditors' report.

Although the definition refers to the decision of the addressee of the auditors' report (that is, the members of the company), their decisions may well be influenced by how the accounts are used. For example if the accounts are to be used to secure a bank loan, what is significant to the bank will influence the way members act. The views of other users of the accounts must be taken into account.

5.2 SAS 220 *Materiality and the audit*

SAS 220 states that auditors should consider materiality and its relationship with audit risk when conducting an audit.

The SAS goes on:

> 'Auditors plan and perform the audit to be able to provide reasonable assurance that the financial statements are free of material misstatement and give a true and fair view. The assessment of what is material is a matter of professional judgement.'

Small amounts should be considered if there is a risk that they could occur more than once and together add up to an amount which is material in total. Also, qualitative aspects must be considered, for example the inaccurate and therefore misleading description of an accounting policy.

Materiality considerations will differ depending on the aspect of the financial statements being considered.

> 'Materiality is considered at both the overall financial statement level and in relation to individual account balances, classes of transactions and disclosures.'

A good example is directors' pay which make normal materiality considerations irrelevant, because it **must** be disclosed by the auditors if they are not disclosed correctly by the directors in the financial statements.

Materiality considerations during **audit planning** are extremely important. The assessment of materiality when determining the nature, timing and extent of audit procedures should be based on the most recent and reliable financial information and will help to determine an effective and efficient audit approach. Materiality assessment in conjunction with risk assessment will help the auditors to make a number of decisions.

- What items to examine
- Whether to use sampling techniques (see Chapter 9)
- What level of error is likely to lead to an opinion that the accounts do not give a true and fair view

The resulting combination of audit procedures should help to reduce detection risk to an appropriately low level.

5.3 Practical implications

Because many users of accounts are primarily interested in the **profitability** of the company, the level is often expressed as a proportion of its profits before tax. Some argue, however, that materiality should be thought of in terms of the **size** of the business. Hence, if the company remains a fairly constant size, the materiality level should not change; similarly if the business is growing, the level of materiality will increase from year to year.

The **size** of a company can be measured in terms of turnover and total assets before deducting any liabilities (sometimes referred to in legislation as 'the balance sheet total') both of which tend not to be subject to the fluctuations which may affect profit. The auditors will often calculate a range of values, such as those shown below, and then take an average or weighted average of all the figures produced as the materiality level.

Value	%
Profit before tax	5
Gross profit	½ – 1
Turnover	½ – 1
Total assets	1 – 2
Net assets	2 – 5
Profit after tax	5 – 10

The effect of planning materiality on the audit process is shown in the diagram below.

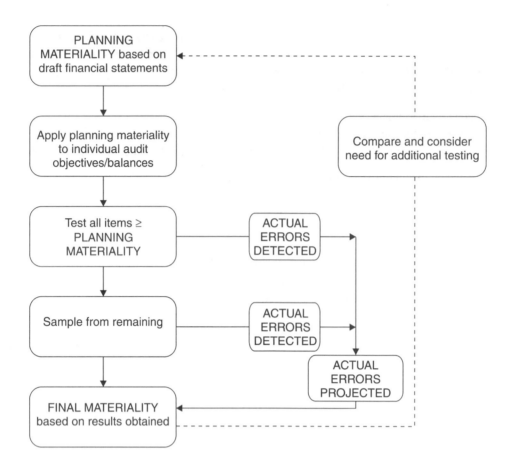

5.4 Changes to the level of materiality

The level of materiality must be reviewed constantly as the audit progresses. Changes to audit procedures may be required for various reasons.

- Draft accounts are altered (due to material error and so on) and therefore overall materiality changes.
- External factors cause changes in the control or inherent risk estimates.
- Changes are caused by errors found during testing.

Activity 6.2

Which measures of the business would Khan Associates use when setting a level of materiality:

(a)   If AJ (Paper) Ltd had a stable asset base, steady turnover over the last few years, but had only made a small pre-tax profit this year owing to a large one-off expense?

(b)   If Jane and Vikram had expressed concern over declining profits over the last few years?

6 Analytical procedures

This is our first mention of analytical procedures (or analytical review). We will cover the topic in depth in Chapter 11. For now you should understand that the purpose of analytical procedures is essentially to **identify figures** that are **not in line with auditor expectations**, and which hence require further investigation.

Analytical review can involve comparisons of current year financial information with

- Past year information
- Budgets
- Predictions by the auditor

It can also involve comparisons between different elements of the current year financial information which are expected to have a **predictable relationship** with each other.

SAS 410 *Analytical procedures* deals with the subject of analytical review. The SAS requires auditors to carry out analytical procedures at the planning stage of each audit, to identify areas of potential audit risk and to help in planning the nature, timing and extent of other audit procedures. We will discuss analytical review at all stages of the audit in greater detail in Chapter 11.

Key learning points

☑   This chapter has covered some very important areas of the planning process.

☑   The auditors will formulate an **overall audit plan** which will be translated into a **detailed audit programme** for audit staff to follow.

☑   In formulating the **audit plan** the auditors will consider:

  –   Knowledge of the entity's business
  –   Risk and materiality
  –   Nature, timing and extent of procedures
  –   Co-ordination, direction, supervision and review of the audit

☑   Any **changes** in the audit approach during the audit should be documented very carefully.

☑   **Audit risk** is the risk that the auditors may give an inappropriate opinion on the financial statements. A risk-based audit will make use of the risk model to determine the amount and extent of audit testing. Audit risk comprises **inherent**, **control** and **detection risk**.

☑   **Materiality** should be calculated at the planning stages of all audits. The calculation or estimation of materiality should be based on experience and judgement. The materiality chosen should be reviewed during the audit.

☑   **Analytical procedures** are very useful at the planning stage, allowing risk areas to be identified.

Quick quiz

1   Fill in the blanks.

   - The audit plan sets out the ....of the audit.
   - The audit programme sets out the ....

2   Complete the definitions.

   .... risk is the risk that .... may give an .... opinion on the financial statements. It has three components.

   .... risk is the .... of an account balance or .... to material ....

3   If control and inherent risk as assessed as sufficiently low, substantive procedures can be abandoned completely.

   True   ☐

   False   ☐

4   Give examples of factors which affect the assessment of inherent risk:

   - For a client as a whole
   - For individual audit areas

5   Match the percentages to the values for a correct calculation of materiality

	%
Profit before tax	5
Gross profit	5-10
Turnover	1-2
Total assets	$1/2$-1
Net assets	2-5
Profit after tax	$1/2$-1

6   What information does an audit programme usually contain?

Answers to quick quiz

1   - The audit plan sets out the **general strategy** of the audit.
     - The audit programme sets out the **detailed work**.

2   Audit, auditors, inappropriate

   Inherent, susceptibility, class of transactions, misstatement

3   False

4   (a)   Factors which affect the inherent risk assessment for the client as a whole include:

- The integrity and attitude to risk of directors and management
- Management experience and knowledge
- Unusual pressures on directors or management
- The nature of the client's business
- Factors affecting the industry

(b)   Factors which affect the inherent risk assessment for individual audit areas include:

- Accounts which are likely to be prone to misstatement
- Complexity of underlying transactions
- Degree of judgement required
- Susceptibility of assets to loss or misappropriation
- Quality of accounting systems
- Unusual transactions around the year-end
- Transactions not subject to ordinary processing
- Areas where there have been significant staff changes

5

	%
Profit before tax	5
Gross profit	½-1
Turnover	½-1
Total assets	1-2
Net assets	2-5
Profit after tax	5-10

6   An audit programme usually contains:

- Audit tests
- Test objectives
- Timing of the tests
- Sample sizes
- Basis of sample selection

Activity checklist

This checklist shows which performance criteria, range statement or knowledge and understanding point is covered by each activity in this chapter. Tick off each activity as you complete it.

Activity

6.1 ☐ This activity deals with Performance Criteria 17.1.C Assess risks accurately.

6.2 ☐ This activity deals with Knowledge & Understanding point 13: Materiality.

Performance Criteria 17.1.E: Identify account balances to be verified and the associated risks will be assessed in Chapter 11.

chapter 7

Audit staff

Contents

1   The problem
2   The solution
3   The audit team
4   Direction, supervision, review
5   Experts

Performance criteria

17.1.I   Formulate the proposed audit plan clearly and in consultation with appropriate personnel

17.1.J   Submit the proposed audit plan to the appropriate person for approval

Range statement

17.1   Accounting systems: purchases; sales; stock; expenses; balance sheet items; payroll

17.1   Accounting systems that are: manual; computerised

17.1   Tests: compliance; substantive

17.3   Draft reports relating to: manual system

1 The problem

Tariq has obtained a good knowledge of the business. The year end is approaching, and it is time to put together the audit plan. However, he has several other clients to attend to, and he is aware that his time is very expensive and that it is not cost effective for him to put together the audit plan.

2 The solution

Tariq must select an audit team for the audit of AJ (Paper) Ltd. He must ensure that in doing so, he complies with the requirements of SAS 240. He must ensure the team is capable of carrying out the audit and that he briefs and directs them properly. It would be appropriate for an audit manager or supervisor to put together the audit plan, but Tariq must review it.

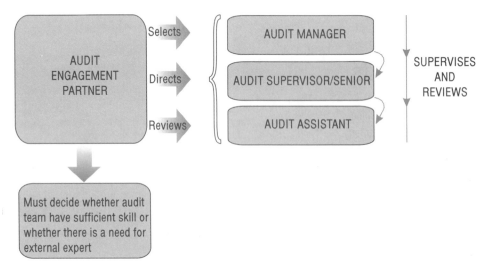

3 The audit team

We saw in Chapter 2 that SAS 240 *Quality control for audit work* deals with the staffing of individual audits. The audit engagement partner (sometimes called the reporting partner, in this case Tariq Hussain) must take responsibility for the quality of the audit to be carried out. He should assign staff with necessary competencies to the audit team.

Some audits are wholly carried out by a sole practitioner (an accountant who practises on his or her own) or a partner. More commonly however the reporting partner will take overall responsibility for the conduct of the audit and will sign the audit report. The reporting partner will however delegate aspects of the audit work such as the detailed testing to the staff of the firm.

The usual hierarchy of staff on an audit assignment is:

When planning the audit, the partner or manager must decide **how many staff** are to be allocated to the assignment, how **experienced** (what grade) and whether any of them will require any **special knowledge, skill or experience**. The partner or manager will review the level of staffing the previous year and consider whether that level of staffing was acceptable.

3.1 Dealing with client staff

An important skill that all staff chosen for the audit assignment should have is the ability to deal with the client staff with whom they come into contact. Discussions with staff operating the system should be conducted in a manner which **promotes professional relationships** between auditing and operational staff.

Relationships with the client will be enhanced if auditors aim to provide a high quality service that caters for the needs of the client. However more specific people skills will also be needed. Negotiation skills and interviewing skills are particularly important.

Auditors should also be trying to understand what managers and staff want from the audit and how hostility to the time they have to spend dealing with auditors can be overcome. This does not mean agreeing with management and staff on every issue, but it does enable the auditors to understand why difficulties have arisen and how those difficulties can be overcome.

4 Direction, supervision, review

Specifically with regard to planning, SAS 240 states that the engagement partner is responsible for ensuring that:

- An appropriate level of professional scepticism is applied by audit staff in the conduct of the audit, and
- There is a proper communication both within the audit team and with the audited entity

Achieving these two objectives is likely to involve the procedures of holding a **planning meeting** with the audit staff on the assignment to discuss the risks anticipated in the audit and appraise them of historical issues on the audit that they should be aware of.

Ensuring communication between client staff and audit staff will be more difficult as the audit engagement partner is unlikely to visit the client site during the audit. However, given that he has a responsibility here, he must take appropriate steps.

What the appropriate steps should be will depend on the individual circumstances of the audit. However, he may have to consider such things as:

- Keeping in **regular contact** with both audit and client staff during the audit to assess the level of communication between them

- **Attending** the site during the audit to facilitate better communication if he feels that it is necessary

- Fostering lines of communication between client staff and audit staff during the period between audits, to ensure a good working relationship is built up between them

Audit engagement partners are also responsible for ensuring that audit work is directed, supervised and reviewed.

4.1 Direction

The SAS states that direction of audit staff involves them being informed of

- Their responsibilities
- The nature of the entity's business
- Accounting or auditing problems that might arise
- The overall audit plan

Clearly a good planning meeting prior to the audit team going on site will achieve all these objectives. The SAS draws particular attention to the needs of junior staff to understand the work that they are undertaking.

Audit partners are responsible for approving the audit plan, promptly, and discussing it with audit staff.

4.2 Supervision

Supervision contains four elements:

- Considering the progress of the audit
- Considering if the audit staff have the competence and understanding to undertake the audit
- Addressing significant accounting and auditing issues arising from the audit
- Identifying matters for further consideration arising from the audit

4.3 Review

Audit work performed by audit staff will be reviewed by more senior staff. SAS 240 outlines a series of things for them to consider when performing a review.

- Whether the work has been performed in accordance with

    ○ Firm procedures
    ○ The overall audit plan

- The work is adequate in the light of results and has been sufficiently documented

- Whether significant matters have been raised for further consideration

- Whether appropriate consultations have taken place and been documented

- Whether the objectives of the audit procedure have been achieved

- Whether the conclusions are consistent with the results of the work performed

When the audit work has been completed and reviewed, the audit engagement partner completes an overall review of the working papers to ensure that he is able to issue his opinion.

4.3.1 Review of audit working papers: practical points

Throughout the audit, a system of review of all working papers will be used. In the case of a large audit, the work of assistants will be reviewed by the senior/supervisor.

Each working paper should be **initialled** (or signed) and **dated** by the person who prepared it.

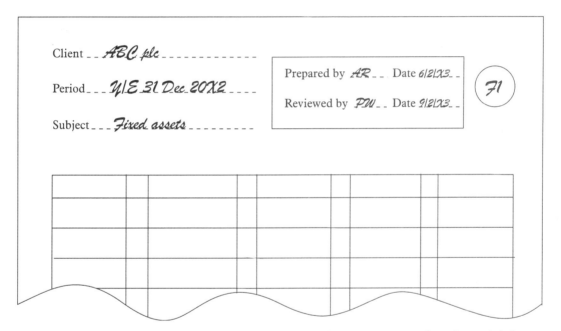

When a review takes place, the reviewer will often use a separate working paper to record queries **and** their answer.

Client _ _ *ABC plc* _ _ _ _ _ _ _ _ _ _ _ _

Period _ _ _ *Y/E 31 Dec 20X2* _ _ _ _

Subject _ _ _ *Manager review* _ _ _ _ _ _

Prepared by *PW* _ _ Date *9/2/X3* _

Reviewed by *TWB* _ Date *11/2/X3* _

$\frac{1}{3}$

			WP Ref	Sign Off
1	*Have the fixed asset balances*	*Yes – see working paper*	*F1*	*PW*
	been agreed to the fixed asset			*TWB*
	register and nominal ledger?			

The need to sign off all working papers and queries acts as an extra check, helping to ensure that all work has been carried out and completed.

After the senior/supervisor has reviewed the work of the assistants there will usually be a **manager review**, which will cover some of the assistants' work, all of the senior/supervisor's work and an overall review of the audit work. Then there will be an **engagement partner review**, which will look at the manager's review, any controversial areas of the audit, the auditors' report and such like.

5 Experts

Professional audit staff are highly trained and educated, but their experience and training is limited to accountancy and audit matters. In certain situations it will be necessary to employ someone else with different expert knowledge.

Auditors have **sole responsibility** for their opinion, but may use the work of an expert. An expert may be engaged by a client to provide specialist advice on a particular matter which affects the financial statements, or by the auditors in order to obtain sufficient audit evidence regarding certain items in the financial statements.

5.1 Determining the need to use the work of an expert

The following list of examples is given by SAS 520 *Using the work of an expert* of the audit evidence which might be obtained from the opinion or valuation of an expert.

- **Valuations of certain types of assets**, for example, land and buildings, plant and machinery
- Determination of quantities or physical condition of assets
- Determination of amounts using specialised techniques or methods
- The measurement of work completed and work in progress on contracts
- Legal opinions

When considering whether to use the work of an expert, the auditors should consider various factors.

- The **importance** of the matter being considered in the context of the accounts
- The **risk of misstatement** based on the nature and complexity of the matter
- The **quantity** and **quality** of other available **relevant audit evidence**

5.2 Competence and objectivity of the expert

The auditors should assess the objectivity and professional qualifications, experience and resources of the expert. This will involve considering the expert's **professional certification**, or membership of an appropriate professional body, and the expert's **experience and reputation** in the field in which the auditors are seeking audit evidence.

The risk that an expert's **objectivity** is **impaired** increases when the expert is **employed** by the entity or **related** in some other manner to the entity, for example having an investment in the entity. If the auditors have **reservations** about the competence or objectivity of the expert they may need to carry out other audit procedures or obtain evidence from another expert. The auditors should then consider the implications for their report.

5.3 The expert's scope of work

The auditors need to obtain evidence that the expert's scope of work is adequate for the purposes of their audit.

Written instructions usually cover the expert's terms of reference and such instructions may cover such matters as follows.

- The **objectives** and **scope** of the expert's work
- A **general outline** as to the specific matters the expert's report is to cover
- The **intended use** of the expert's work
- The **extent** of the **expert's access** to appropriate records and files
- Information regarding the **assumptions and methods intended** to be used

Auditors should assess whether the substance of the expert's findings is properly reflected in the financial statements or supports the financial statement assertions. It will also require consideration of other aspects of the report.

- The source data used

- The **assumptions and methods used**

- **When** the expert carried out the work

- The reasons for any **changes in assumptions and methods** compared with those used in the prior period

- The **results** of the expert's work in the light of the auditors' overall knowledge of the business and the results of other audit procedures

The auditors do **not** have the expertise to judge the assumptions and methods used. These are the responsibility of the expert. However, the auditors should seek to obtain an understanding of these assumptions and methods to consider their reasonableness based on other audit evidence, knowledge of the business and so on.

Where inconsistencies arise between the expert's work and other audit evidence, then the auditors should attempt to resolve them by discussion with both the entity and the expert. Additional procedures (including use of another expert) may be necessary.

Where the audit evidence from the expert is insufficient, and there is no satisfactory alternative source of evidence, then the auditors should consider the implications for their audit report. They **never** refer to the expert in their report however.

Activity 7.1

Tariq has picked an audit team to undertake the audit of AJ (Paper) Ltd for the year ended 31 December 2000:

Audit manager   Sarah Smith
Audit supervisor Shahid Anwar
Audit assistant   Chen Ping

He has asked Shahid to put together the audit plan for the audit year ending 31 December 2000. Explain how Shahid should go about this task, what he should put in the audit plan, where he should get the information and what should happen to the audit plan when he is finished.

Key learning points

☑ Audits should be carried out by staff of **appropriate skills and experience**.

☑ All partners and staff involved on audits have a responsibility to maintain **professional relationships** with clients.

☑ Major components in the quality control of individual audits are:

– Direction
– Supervision
– Review

☑ Direction of audit staff by the partner involves appraising audit staff of their responsibilities, the nature of the business, problems that might arise and the overall audit plan.

☑ Supervision involves considering the progress of the audit and the competence of the staff and addressing and identifying further issues arising from the audit.

☑ All audit work performed will be reviewed by more senior staff.

☑ Auditors may only rely on other **experts** once specific procedures have been carried out.

Quick quiz

1   Can an audit partner delegate responsibility for the audit opinion to his staff?

2   What are the key tasks that should be performed when work is delegated to assistants?

3   The auditor may not use the work of an expert employed by the organisation.

True

False

4   (a)   Why might auditors use the work of an expert?
     (b)   What should auditors consider when deciding whether to use the work of an expert?

Answers to quick quiz

1   No. A partner cannot delegate responsibility for the audit opinion. He can however delegate aspects of the detailed audit work.

2   The audit engagement partner has responsibility for the quality of the audit performed.

     He must ensure that the audit staff approach the job in the correct manner and have proper communication both between themselves and with the client.

     The engagement partner is also responsible for ensuring that the work of other members of the audit team is directed, supervised and reviewed.

3   False

4   (a)   Auditors might use the work of an expert to obtain sufficient audit evidence for certain items in the accounts.

     (b)   When deciding whether to use the work of an expert, auditors should consider:

           (i)   The importance of the audit area
           (ii)   The risks of misstatement
           (iii)   The quantity and quality of other audit evidence

Activity checklist

This checklist shows which performance criteria, range statement or knowledge and understanding point is covered by each activity in this chapter. Tick off each activity as you complete it.

Activity

7.1   This activity deals with Performance Criteria 17.1.I: Formulate the proposed audit plan clearly and in consultation with appropriate personnel and 17.1.J: Submit the proposed audit plan to the appropriate person for approval.

chapter 8

Audit documents

Contents

1 The problem
2 The solution
3 Working papers
4 Audit files

Knowledge and understanding

8 The use of audit files and working papers

1 The problem

Shahid has been busy completing the audit of a different company and has not had a chance to put together the audit plan for AJ (Paper) Ltd yet.

Ping, who is a new trainee, doesn't understand what the problem is. Tariq has given them a briefing about the audit and passed on all the relevant information. Isn't that enough?

2 The solution

The answer to Ping's question is no. It is not sufficient that Tariq has briefed the audit team. Auditing standards require that auditors document the work that they do. This, of course, will be useful if the auditors are sued as a result of their audit, as they will be able to use their working papers as evidence of the quality of the audit they have carried out.

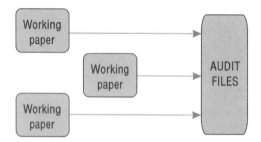

There are two possible solutions to Shahid's immediate problem. Either he must do some overtime to get the audit plan done, or, if he genuinely has been given too much work to do, he should talk to the audit manager, Sarah, and see if she can re-arrange his workload.

3 Working papers

All audit work must be documented: the working papers are the tangible evidence of the work done in support of the audit opinion.

Working papers are the material the auditors prepare or obtain, and retain in connection with the performance of the audit. Working papers may be in the form of data stored on paper, film, electronic media or other media.

Working papers support, amongst other things, the statement in the auditors' report as to the auditors' compliance or otherwise with Auditing Standards to the extent that this is important in supporting their report.

3.1 Form and content of working papers

SAS 210 *Working papers* requires that:

> 'Working papers should record the auditors' planning, the nature, timing and extent of the audit procedures performed, and the conclusions drawn from the audit evidence obtained. Auditors should record in their working papers their reasoning on all significant matters which require the exercise of judgement, and their conclusions thereon.'

Auditors cannot record everything they consider. Therefore judgement must be used as to the extent of working papers, based on:

> 'What would be necessary to provide an experienced auditor, with no previous connection with the audit, with an understanding of the work performed and the basis of the decisions taken.'

The form and content of working papers are affected by various matters.

- Nature of the engagement
- Form of the auditors' report
- Nature and complexity of the entity's business
- Nature and condition of the entity's accounting and internal control systems
- Needs in the particular circumstances for direction, supervision and review of the work of members of the audit team
- Specific methodology and technology the auditors use

The SAS warns against the use of **standardised** working papers, for example, checklists, specimen letters because they:

> 'may improve the efficiency with which such working papers are prepared and reviewed. While they facilitate the delegation of work and provide a means to control its quality, it is never appropriate to follow mechanically a standard approach to the conduct and documentation of the audit without regard to the need to exercise professional judgement.'

While auditors utilise schedules and analyses prepared by the entity, they require evidence that such information is properly prepared.

3.2 Examples of working papers

These include the following.

- Information concerning the legal and organisational structure of the client
- Information concerning the client's industry, economic and legal environment
- Evidence of the planning process
- Evidence of the auditors' understanding of the accounting and internal control systems
- Evidence of inherent and control risk assessments and any revisions

- Analyses of transactions and balances
- Analyses of significant ratios and trends
- A record of the nature, timing, extent and results of auditing procedures
- Copies of communications with other auditors, experts and other third parties
- Copies of correspondence with the client.
- Reports to directors or management
- Notes of discussions with the entity's directors or management
- A summary of the significant aspects of the audit
- Copies of the approved financial statements and auditors' reports

Client: *Example Ltd* ①

Subject: *Creditors* ⑥

Year end: *31 December 20X3* ②

Prepared by	Reviewed by
④ *PC*	⑦ *AD*
	⑧
Date: *16.2.X4* ⑤	Date:... *3.3.X4*

③ *E ³/₁*

⑨ Objective	*To ensure purchase ledger balance fairly stated.*									
⑪ Work done										⑩
	Selected a sample of trade creditors as at 31 December and reconciled the supplier's statement to the									
	year end purchase ledger balance. Vouched any reconciling items to source documentation.									
	⑩									
⑬ Results	*See E ³/₂*									
	One credit note, relating to Woodcutter Ltd, has not been accounted for. An adjustment is required. ⑭									
	DEBIT	*Trade creditors*		*£4,975*						
	CREDIT	*Purchases*			*£4,975 H1/2*					
	One other error was found, which was immaterial, and which was the fault of the supplier.									
	⑭									
	In view of the error found, however, we should recommend that the client management checks									
	supplier statement reconciliations at least on the larger accounts. Management letter point.									
⑮ Conclusion										
	After making the adjustment noted above, purchased ledger balances are fairly stated									
	as at 31 December 20X3.									

Client: _Example Ltd_ _ _ _ _ _ _ _ _ _ _ _ _

Subject: _Creditors_ _ _ _ _ _ _ _ _ _ _ _ _

Year end: _31 December 20X3_ _ _ _ _ _ _ _ _

Prepared by	Reviewed by
PC	AD
Date: 16.2.X4	Date: 3.3.X4

$\mathcal{E}\ ^3/_2$

Client		Purchase ledger £		Supplier statement £		Difference		Agreed		Reconciling item		
A Ltd		⌄ 300	00	300	00	–		✓		–		
B Ltd		⌄ 747	00	732	00	15	00	✗		15	00	Credit note not yet received
				⑫		Key						
						✓ Agreed						
						✗ Not agreed						
						⌃ Adds checked						
						⌄ Agreed to purchase ledger						
		1,047	00									
		⌃										

KEY

① The **name** of the **client**

② The balance sheet **date**

③ The **file reference** of the working paper

④ The **name** of the **person** preparing the working paper

⑤ The **date** the working paper was **prepared**

⑥ The **subject** of the working paper

(7) The **name** of the person **reviewing** the working paper

(8) The **date** of the **review**

(9) The **objective** of the work done

(10) The **sources of information**

(11) The **work done**

(12) A **key** to any audit ticks or symbols

(13) The **results obtained**

(14) **Analysis** of **errors** or other significant observations

(15) The **conclusions drawn**

3.3 Computerised working papers

Automated working paper packages have been developed which can make the documenting of audit work much easier. These are automatically cross referenced and balanced by the computer. Whenever an adjustment is made, the computer will automatically update all the necessary schedules.

The **advantages** of automated working papers are as follows.

(a) The **risk** of **errors** is **reduced**.

(b) The **working papers** will be **neater** and **easier to review**.

(c) The **time saved** will be **substantial** as adjustments can be made easily to all working papers, including working papers summarising the key analytical information.

(d) **Standard** forms **do not have** to be **carried** to audit locations. Forms can be designed to be called up and completed on the computer screen.

(e) **Audit working papers** can be **transmitted** for review via a modem, or fax facilities (if both the sending and receiving computers have fax boards and fax software).

3.4 Confidentiality, safe custody and ownership

SAS 230 states:

> 'Auditors should adopt appropriate procedures for maintaining the confidentiality and safe custody of their working papers.'

Working papers are the property of the auditors. They are not a substitute for, nor part of, the client's accounting records.

Auditors must follow ethical guidance on the confidentiality of audit working papers. They may, at their discretion, release parts of or whole working papers to the client, as long as disclosure does not undermine 'the independence or validity of the audit process'. Information should not be made available to third parties without the permission of the entity.

4 Audit files

For recurring audits, working papers may be split between permanent and current audit files.

(a) **Permanent audit files** are updated with new information of continuing importance such as legal documents, background information and correspondence with the client of relevance for a number of years. The file should also contain a copy of each year's final accounts.

(b) **Current audit files** contain information relating primarily to the audit of a single period.

4.1 Permanent audit files

The following example contents page illustrates the typical contents of a permanent audit file. You should note that there is no one specified way that an audit firm would set up an audit file. This is just an example.

CONTENTS: Example Client Ltd	
Financial statements	A
Correspondence	B
Title deeds	C
Copies of directors' service contracts	D
Background information	E
Product catalogue	F
Accounting systems notes	G
Engagement letter	H

4.2 Current audit files

The current audit 'file' will often consist of several files as it contains all the audit work relating to the audit for a particular year. Again, there is no set composition of a current audit file, but the contents page below should give you an indication of what a current audit file contains.

CONTENTS: Example Client Ltd y/e 31.12.2002

1 Current financial statements

2 Preview financial statements

3 Journals

4 Report to partner

5 Audit plan

6 Partner review

7 Manager review

8 Accounts checklist

9 Sundry other [....]

A Fixed assets

B Stock

C Debtors

D Cash

E Creditors

F Share capital

G Reserves

H Profit and loss account

I Wages

In each audit area (referenced A – I in our example) working papers covering the following should be given:

- Lead schedule including details of figures in the accounts
- Problems encountered and conclusions drawn
- Audit programmes for the specific area
- Risk assessments for that area
- Sampling plans
- Analytical review
- Details of tests undertaken

4.3 Retention of audit files

The law does not state a required time to maintain audit working papers for. However, if the auditor has an ongoing relationship with a client, he may wish to retain files for reference. Some professional bodies recommend keeping all files for a period of seven to ten years.

Remember, as the auditor has a duty of confidentiality to a client, he must be very careful if he does choose to dispose of files.

Activity 8.1

Explain for the benefit of Ping:

(a)   With what details should working papers of audit tests performed be headed?

(b)   What other details should working papers covering audit tests contain?

Key learning points

☑ The **proper completion of working papers** is fundamental to the recording of audits. They should show:

 – When and by whom the audit work was **performed and reviewed**
 – Details of the **client**
 – The **year-end**
 – The **subject** of the paper

☑ Working papers should also show:

 – The objectives of the work done
 – The sources of information
 – How any sample was selected and the sample size determined
 – The work done
 – A key to any audit ticks or symbols
 – Results obtained
 – Errors or other significant observations
 – Conclusions drawn
 – Key points highlighted

☑ Computerised working papers are being used more by auditors. Their main advantages are that they are **neat** and **easy to update** and the **risk of errors** is reduced.

☑ The permanent audit file is the file in which auditors keep items of significance to ongoing audits.

☑ The current audit file is the file where all the audit work for the current year is stored.

Quick quiz

1   The audit programme is a standardised document.

    True [   ]

    False [   ]

2   What is the general rule for documenting the audit process?

3   Give two advantages and one disadvantage of standardised working papers.

    1 ....   1 ....

    2 ....

4   Complete the table, using the working papers given below.

Current audit file	Permanent audit file

engagement letters	new client questionnaire
financial statements	management letter
accounts checklists	audit planning memo
board minutes of continuing relevance	accounting systems notes

Answers to quick quiz

1   False

2   Documentations should include what would be necessary to provide an experienced auditor, with no previous connection with the audit, with an understanding of the work performed and the basis of decisions taken

3   **Advantages**   **Disadvantage**

    1   Facilitate the delegation of work   1   Detracts from proper exercise of
    2   Means to control quality   profession judgement

4

Current audit file	Permanent audit file
financial statements	engagement letters
management letter	new client questionnaire
accounts checklists	board minutes of continuing relevance
audit planning memo	accounting systems notes

Activity checklist

This checklist shows which performance criteria, range statement or knowledge and understanding point is covered by each activity in this chapter. Tick off each activity as you complete it.

Activity

8.1   ☐   This activity deals with Knowledge & Understanding point 8: The use of audit files and working papers.

chapter 9

Audit evidence and procedures

Contents

1 The problem
2 The solution
3 Audit evidence
4 Computer assisted audit techniques (CAATs)
5 Audit sampling

Performance criteria

17.1.F Select an appropriate sample

17.1.G Select or devise appropriate tests in accordance with the organisation's procedures

Range statement

17.1 Accounting systems: purchases; sales; stock; expenses; balance sheet items, payroll

17.1 Accounting systems that are: manual; computerised

17.1 Tests: Tests of control; substantive

Knowledge and understanding

6 Verification techniques: physical examination; reperformance; third party confirmation; vouching; documentary evidence; identification of unusual items

7 Basic sampling techniques in auditing: confidence levels; selection techniques (random numbers, interval sampling, stratified sampling)

9 Auditing techniques in an IT environment

1 The problem

The auditors must carry out tests in order to gain evidence to support the audit option as a result of their risk assessments. But three questions still remain:

- How much and what evidence?
- What tests should they carry out?
- How should they select their sample?

2 The solution

Auditing standards help auditors out with these problems.

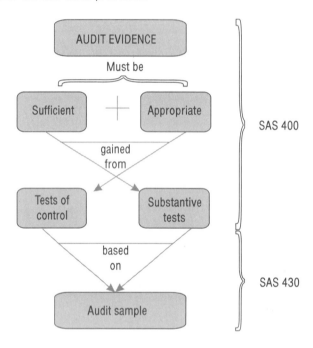

We will look at what these SASs set out as solutions to the above problems in this chapter.

3 Audit evidence

Audit evidence is the information auditors obtain in arriving at the conclusions on which their report is based. In order to reach a position in which they can express a professional opinion, the auditors need to gather evidence from various sources.

3.1 Sufficient appropriate audit evidence

SAS 400 *Audit evidence* requires that auditors obtain sufficient appropriate audit evidence to be able to draw reasonable conclusions on which to base the audit opinion.

'Sufficiency' and 'appropriateness' are interrelated and apply to both tests of controls and substantive procedures.

- **Sufficiency** is the measure of the **quantity** of audit evidence.
- **Appropriateness** is the measure of the **quality** or **reliability** of the audit evidence.

What constitutes sufficient appropriate audit evidence for the different types of audit tests – tests of control and substantive tests – relates to what auditors are trying to assess when carrying out these tests.

Auditors are essentially looking for **enough reliable** audit evidence. Audit evidence usually indicates what is probable rather than what is definite (is usually persuasive rather then conclusive) so different sources are examined by the auditors. Auditors can only give reasonable assurance that the financial statements are free from misstatement, as not **all** sources of evidence will be examined.

The auditors' judgement as to what is sufficient appropriate audit evidence is influenced by various factors.

- Assessment of risk
- The nature of the accounting and internal control systems
- The materiality of the item being examined
- The experience gained during previous audits
- The auditors' knowledge of the business and industry
- The results of audit procedures
- The source and reliability of information available

3.2 Tests of control

SAS 400 states:

> 'In seeking to obtain audit evidence from tests of control, auditors should consider the sufficiency and appropriateness of the audit evidence to support the assessed level of control risk.'

There are two aspects of the relevant parts of the accounting and internal control systems about which auditors should seek to obtain audit evidence.

(a) **Design**: the accounting and internal control systems are designed so as to be capable of preventing or detecting material misstatements.

(b) **Operation**: the systems exist and have operated effectively throughout the relevant period.

3.3 Substantive procedures

SAS 400 states:

> 'In seeking to obtain audit evidence from substantive procedures, auditors should consider the extent to which that evidence together with any evidence from tests of controls supports the relevant financial statement assertions.'

Substantive procedures are designed to obtain evidence about the financial statement assertions which are basically what the accounts say about the assets, liabilities and transactions of the client, and the events that affect the client's accounts.

FINANCIAL STATEMENT ASSERTIONS	
Existence	An asset or liability exists
Rights and obligations	An asset or liability 'belongs' to the client
Occurrence	A transaction or event took place which relates to the client
Completeness	All relevant assets, liabilities, transactions and events are recorded, and there are no undisclosed items
Valuation	An asset or liability is recorded at an appropriate value
Measurement	A transaction or event is measured at a proper amount and allocated to the proper period
Presentation and disclosure	An item is disclosed, classified and described in accordance with the applicable reporting framework

An eighth assertion, **accuracy**, that all assets, liabilities, transactions and events are recorded accurately, is sometimes added.

Audit evidence is usually obtained for assets, liabilities and transactions to support each financial statement assertion and evidence from one does not compensate for failure to obtain evidence for another. However, audit tests may provide audit evidence of more than one assertion.

3.4 Reliability of evidence

The following generalisations may help in assessing the reliability of audit evidence.

(a)   Audit evidence from **external sources** (for example, confirmation received from a third party) is **more reliable** than that obtained from **internal sources** (the client's records).

(b)   Audit evidence obtained from the **entity's records** is more reliable when the related accounting and internal **control system operates effectively**.

(c)   Evidence obtained **directly by auditors** is **more reliable** than that obtained by or **from the client**.

(d)   Evidence in the **form of documents and written representations** is more reliable than **oral representations**.

(e)   **Original documents** are **more reliable** than **photocopies, telexes or faxes**.

Consistency of audit evidence from different sources will have a cumulative effect, making the evidence more persuasive. Auditors must consider the cost-benefit relationship of obtaining evidence **but** any difficulty or expense is not in itself a valid basis for omitting a necessary procedure.

Activity 9.1

Ping has asked you to explain the strength or weakness of the following sources of audit evidence, and the financial statement assertions to which they relate.

(a)   Physical inspection of a fixed asset by an auditor

(b)   Confirmation by a debtor of money owed

(c)   Oral representations by management that all creditors owed money at the year-end have been included in the accounts

3.5 Procedures for obtaining audit evidence

Auditors obtain evidence by one or more of the following procedures.

PROCEDURES	
Inspection of assets	Examining or counting assets that physically exist
	Inspection confirms **existence**, gives evidence of **valuation** but does not confirm ownership
Inspection of documentation	Demonstrates that a transaction **occurs** or a balance **exists**, also that client has **rights** and **obligations** in relation to assets or liabilities
	Can also be used to **compare** documents, and hence test **consistency** of audit evidence, and to **confirm authorisation**
Observation	Involves watching a procedure being performed (eg post opening)
	Of limited use, as only confirms procedure took place when auditor watching
Enquiries	Seeking information from **client staff** or **external sources**
	Strength of evidence depends on knowledge and integrity of source of information
Confirmation	Seeking confirmation from another source of details in client's accounting records eg confirmation from bank of bank balances
Computations	Checking arithmetic of client's records eg adding up ledger account
Analytical procedures	See Chapter 11

4 Computer assisted audit techniques (CAATs)

Computer-based accounting systems allow auditors to use either the client's computer or another computer during their audit work. Techniques performed with computers in this way are known as Computer Assisted Audit Techniques (CAATs).

There is no mystique about using CAATs to help with auditing. You probably use common computer assisted audit techniques all the time in your daily work without realising it.

    (a)   Most modern accounting systems allow data to be manipulated in various ways and extracted into a **report**.

    (b)   Even if reporting capabilities are limited, the data can often be exported directly into a **spreadsheet** package (sometimes using simple Windows-type cut and paste facilities in very modern systems) and then analysed.

    (c)   Most systems have **searching** facilities that are much quicker to use than searching through print-outs by hand.

There are a variety of packages specially designed either to ease the auditing task itself, or to carry out audit interrogations of computerised data automatically. There are also a variety of ways of testing the processing that is carried out. Auditors can use PCs such as laptops that are independent of the organisation's systems when performing CAATs. There are various types of CAAT.

    (a)   **Audit interrogation software** is a computer program used for audit purposes to examine the content of the client's computer files.

    (b)   **Test data** is data used by the auditors for computer processing to test the operation of the client's computer programs.

    (c)   **Embedded audit facilities** are elements set up by the auditor which are included within the client's computer system. They allow the possibility of continuous checking.

4.1 Audit interrogation software

Interrogation software performs the sort of checks on data that auditors might otherwise have to perform by hand. Using it is particularly appropriate during substantive testing of transactions and especially balances. By using audit software, the auditors may scrutinise large volumes of data and concentrate skilled manual resources on the investigation of results, rather than on the extraction of information.

4.2 Test data

An obvious way of seeing whether a system is **processing** data in the way that it should be is to input some test data and see what happens. The expected results can be calculated in advance and then compared with the results that actually arise.

The problem with test data is that any resulting corruption of the data files has to be corrected. This is difficult with modern real-time systems, which often have built in (and highly desirable) controls to ensure that data entered **cannot** easily be removed without leaving a mark. Consequently test data is used less and less as a CAAT.

4.3 Embedded audit facilities

The results of using test data would, in any case, be completely distorted if the programs used to process it were not the ones **normally** used for processing. For example a fraudulent member of the IT department might substitute a version of the program that gave the correct results, purely for the duration of the test, and then replace it with a version that siphoned off the company's funds into his own bank account.

To allow a **continuous** review of the data recorded and the manner in which it is treated by the system, it may be possible to use CAATs referred to as 'embedded audit facilities'. An embedded facility consists of audit modules that are incorporated into the computer element of the enterprise's accounting system.

EXAMPLES OF EMBEDDED AUDIT FACILITIES	
Integrated test facility (ITF)	Creates a **fictitious entity** within the company application, where transactions are posted to it alongside regular transactions, and actual results of fictitious entity compared with what it should have produced
Systems control and review file (SCARF)	Allows auditors to have transactions above a **certain amount** from **specific ledger account** posted to a file for later auditor review

4.4 Simulation

Simulation (or 'parallel simulation') entails the preparation of a separate program that simulates the processing of the organisation's real system. Real data can then be passed not only through the system proper but also through the simulated program. For example the simulation program may be used to re-perform controls such as those used to identify any missing items from a sequence.

4.5 Planning and controlling CAATs

In certain circumstances the auditors will need to use CAATs in order to obtain the evidence they require, whereas in other circumstances they may use CAATs to improve the efficiency or effectiveness of the audit.

In choosing the appropriate combination of CAATs and manual procedures, the auditors will need to take the following points into account.

(a) Computer programs often perform functions of which **no visible evidence** is available. In these circumstances it will frequently not be practicable for the auditors to perform tests manually.

(b) In many audit situations the auditors will have the choice of performing a test either **manually** or with the **assistance of a CAAT**. In making this choice, they will be influenced by the respective efficiency of the alternatives, which is influenced by a number of factors.

- The extent of tests of controls or substantive procedures achieved by both alternatives
- The pattern of cost associated with the CAAT
- The ability to incorporate within the use of the CAAT a number of different audit tests

(c)   Sometimes auditors will need to report within a comparatively **short time-scale**. In such cases it may be more efficient to use CAATs because they are quicker to apply.

(d)   If using a CAAT, auditors should ensure that the **required computer facilities, computer files** and **programs are available**.

(e)   The operation of some CAATs requires **frequent attendance** or access by the auditors.

Where CAATs are used, however, particular attention should be paid to the need to **co-ordinate the work of staff** with specialist computer skills with the work of others engaged on the audit. The **technical work** should be **approved** and **reviewed** by someone with the necessary computer expertise.

The original purpose of an **audit trail** was to preserve details of all stages of processing on **paper**. This meant that transactions could be followed stage-by-stage through a system to ensure that they had been processed correctly.

Traditionally, therefore, it was widely considered that auditors could fulfil their function without having any detailed knowledge of what was going on inside the computer.

The auditors would commonly audit **'round the computer'**, ignoring the procedures which take place within the computer programs and concentrating solely on the input and corresponding output. Audit procedures would include checking authorisation, coding and control totals of input and checking the output with source documents and clerical control totals.

The 'round the computer' approach is now frowned upon. Typical audit problems that arise as audit trails move further away from the hard copy trail include testing computer generated totals when no detailed analysis is available and testing the completeness of output in the absence of control totals.

One of the principal problems facing the auditors is that of acquiring an understanding of the workings of electronic data processing and of the computer itself.

Auditors now customarily audit **'through the computer'**. This involves an examination of the detailed processing routines of the computer to determine whether the controls in the system are adequate to ensure complete and correct processing of all data. In these situations it will often be necessary to employ computer assisted audit techniques.

Activity 9.2

Again, for Ping's benefit, explain:

(a)   What is meant by the term 'loss of audit trail' in the context of computerised accounting procedures.

(b)   How auditors can gain assurance about the operation of computerised accounting procedures given the 'loss of audit trail'.

5 Audit sampling

SAS 430 *Audit sampling* is based on the premise that auditors do not normally examine all the information available to them; it would be impractical to do so and using audit sampling will produce valid conclusions.

Audit sampling is the application of audit procedures to less than 100% of the items within an account balance or class of transactions. It enables auditors to obtain and evaluate evidence about some characteristic of the items selected in order to form a conclusion about the population sampled.

Sampling units are the individual items that make up the population.

Error is an unintentional mistake in the financial statements. **Tolerable error** is the maximum error in the population that the auditors are willing to accept and still conclude that the audit objective has been achieved.

Sampling risk is the risk that the auditors' conclusion, based on a sample, may be different from the conclusion that would be reached if the entire population was subject to the same audit procedure. **Non-sampling risk** is the risk that the auditors might use inappropriate procedures or might misinterpret evidence and thus fail to recognise an error.

The SAS points out that some testing procedures do **not** involve sampling.

(a) Testing 100% of items in a population (this should be obvious)

(b) Testing all items with a certain characteristic (for example, over a certain value) as selection is not representative

The SAS distinguishes between **statistically based sampling**, which involves the use of techniques from which mathematically constructed conclusions about the population can be drawn, and **non-statistical or judgmental methods**, from which auditors draw a judgmental opinion about the population. However, the principles of the SAS apply to both methods.

In practice, the following things will strongly affect the sample that the auditor chooses:

- Materiality
- Risk
- Items that look 'odd' to the auditor

5.1 Design of the sample

Auditors must consider the **specific audit objectives** to be achieved and the audit procedures which are most likely to achieve them. The auditors also need to consider the **nature and characteristics** of the **audit evidence** sought and **possible error conditions**. This will help them to define what constitutes an error and what population to use for sampling.

Furthermore auditors must consider the **level of error** they are prepared to accept and **how confident** they wish to be that the population does not contain an error rate greater than what is acceptable.

Thus for a test of controls auditors may wish to be 95% confident that controls have failed to work on no more than 3 occasions. For a substantive test of fixed assets, they may wish to be 90% confident that fixed assets are not misstated by more than £10,000.

The % confidence auditors wish to have is the **'confidence level'** and it is related to the degree of audit risk auditors are prepared to accept.

The population from which the sample is drawn must be **appropriate** and **complete** for the specific audit objectives.

5.2 Sample size

SAS 430 states:

> 'When determining sample sizes, auditors should consider sampling risk, the amount of error that would be acceptable and the extent to which they expect to find errors.'

Examples of some factors affecting sample size are given in an appendix to the SAS, reproduced here.

Table 1: Some factors influencing sample size for tests of controls	
Factor	*Impact on sample size*
Sampling risk	• The greater the reliance on the results of a test of control using audit sampling, the lower the sampling risk the auditors are willing to accept and, consequently, the larger the sample size.
	• The lower the assessment of control risk, the more likely the auditors are to place reliance on audit evidence from tests of control.
	• A high control risk assessment may result in a decision not to perform tests of control and rely entirely on substantive procedures.
Tolerable error rate	The higher the tolerable error rate the lower the sample size and vice versa.
Expected error rate	• If errors are expected, a larger sample ordinarily needs to be examined to confirm that the actual error rate is less than the tolerable error rate.
	• High expected error rates may result in a decision not to perform tests of control.
Number of items in population	Virtually no effect on sample size unless population is small.

Table 2: Some factors influencing sample size for substantive tests	
Factor	**Impact on sample size**
Inherent risk	• The higher the assessment of inherent risk, the more audit evidence is required to support the auditors' conclusion.
Control risk	• The higher the assessment of control risk, the greater the reliance on audit evidence obtained from substantive procedures.
Detection risk	• Sampling risk for substantive tests is one form of detection risk. The lower the sampling risk the auditors are willing to accept, the larger the sample size. • Other substantive procedures may provide audit evidence regarding the same financial statement assertions and reduce detection risk. This may reduce the extent of the auditors' reliance on the results of a substantive procedure using audit sampling. • The lower the reliance on the results of a substantive procedure using audit sampling, the higher the sampling risk the auditors are willing to accept and, consequently, the smaller the sample size.
Tolerable error rate	The higher the monetary value of the tolerable error rate the smaller the sample size and vice versa.
Expected error rate	If errors are expected, a larger sample ordinarily needs to be examined to confirm that the actual error rate is less than the tolerable error rate.
Population value	The less material the monetary value of the population to the financial statements, the smaller the sample size that may be required.
Numbers of items in population	Virtually no effect on sample size unless population is small.
Stratification	If it is appropriate to stratify the population this may lead to a smaller sample size.

5.2.1 Sampling risk

Sampling risk is encountered by the auditors in both tests of control and substantive procedures. It is the risk of drawing a **wrong conclusion** from audit sampling. It is part of detection risk.

For tests of control, drawing a wrong conclusion means making an **incorrect assessment** (too high or too low) of **control risk**. For substantive procedures it means either stating a population is **materially misstated when it is not**, or stating a population is **not materially misstated when it is**.

The **greater** their reliance on the results of the procedure in question, the **lower** the sampling risk auditors will be willing to accept and the **larger** the sample size needs to bc.

Thus if inherent risk is high, control risk is high and sampling is the only substantive procedure auditors are carrying out, then auditors are placing maximum reliance on sampling. Hence the level of sampling risk auditors will be prepared to accept will be at its minimum, and sample sizes will be high.

5.2.2 Tolerable error

For **tests** of **control,** the tolerable error is the **maximum rate** of **deviation** from a control that auditors are willing to accept in the population and still conclude that the preliminary assessment of control risk is valid. Often this rate will be very low, since the auditor is likely to be concentrating on testing important controls.

Sometimes even a single failure of an important control will cause auditors to reject their assessment of control risk. If, for example, an important control is that all major capital expenditure is approved by the board, failure to approve expenditure on one item may be an unacceptable deviation as far as the auditors are concerned.

For substantive procedures, the **tolerable error** is the **maximum monetary error** in an account balance or class of transactions, that auditors are willing to accept so that when the results of all audit procedures are considered, they are able to conclude with reasonable assurance, that the financial statements are not materially misstated.

Sometimes the tolerable error rate will be the materiality rate. Some accounting firms set tolerable error as being a fixed percentage of materiality, say 50% or 70% for reasons of prudence.

5.2.3 Expected error

Larger samples will be required when errors are expected than would be required if none were expected, in order to conclude that the **actual** error is **less** than the **tolerable** error. If the expected error rate is high then sampling may not be appropriate and auditors may have to examine 100% of a population.

5.3 Selection of the sample

SAS 430 states:

> 'Auditors should select sample items in such a way that the sample can be expected to be representative of the population in respect of the characteristics being tested.'

The SAS makes a very important point.

> 'For a sample to be representative of the population, all items in the population are required to have an equal or known probability of being selected.'

There are a number of selection methods available, but the SAS identifies three that are commonly used.

(a) **Random selection** ensures that all items in the population have an equal chance of selection, for example, by use of random number tables.

(b) **Systematic selection** (or interval sampling) involves selecting items using a constant interval between selections, the first interval having a random start.

   Suppose the auditors decide to pick every 50th item and start at random at item number 11. They will then pick item number 61 (11 + 50), item number 111 (11 + (50 × 2)), item number 161 (11 + (50 × 3)) and so on. Auditors, when using this method, must guard against the risk of errors occurring systematically in such a way as not to be detected by sampling. In our example this would be errors occurring at item number 41, 91, 141, 191 etc.

(c) **Haphazard selection** involves auditors choosing items subjectively without using formal random methods but also avoiding bias. The biggest danger of haphazard selection is that bias does in fact occur. Auditors may for example end up choosing items that are easily located, and these may not be representative. Haphazard selection is more likely to be used when auditors are using judgmental rather than statistical sampling.

In addition the auditors may also consider for certain tests:

(a) **Stratification.** This involves division of the population into a number of parts. Each sampling unit can only belong to one, specifically designed, stratum. The idea is that each stratum will contain items which have significant characteristics in common. This enables the auditors to direct audit effort towards items which, for example, contain the greatest potential monetary error.

(b) **Selection by value** is selecting the largest items within a population. This will only be appropriate if auditors believe that the size of the item is related to the risk of the item being seriously misstated.

(c) **Sequence sampling** may be used to check whether certain items have particular characteristics. For example, an auditor may use a sample of 50 consecutive cheques to check whether cheques are signed by authorised signatories rather than picking 50 single cheques throughout the year. Sequence sampling may however produce samples that are not representative of the population as a whole particularly if errors occurred only during a certain part of the year.

Certain items may be tested because they are considered unusual, for example debit balances on a purchase ledger or a nil balance with a major supplier.

5.3.1 Statistical and judgmental sampling

As mentioned above, auditors need to decide when sampling whether to use statistical or non-statistical methods. Statistical sampling means using statistical theory to measure the impact of sampling risk and evaluate the sample results. Non-statistical sampling relies on judgement to evaluate results.

Whether statistical or non-statistical methods are used, auditors will still have to take account of risk, tolerable and expected error, and population value for substantive tests when deciding on sample sizes.

If these conditions are present, **statistical sampling** normally has the following **advantages**.

(a) At the conclusion of a test the auditors are able to state with a **definite level of confidence** that the whole population conforms to the sample result, within a stated precision limit.

(b) **Sample size** is **objectively determined**, having regard to the degree of risk the auditors are prepared to accept for each application.

(c) The process of fixing required precision and confidence levels compels the auditors to consider and **clarify their audit objectives**.

(d) The **results of tests** can be **expressed** in precise **mathematical terms**.

(e) **Bias is eliminated**.

5.4 Evaluation of sample results

Auditors have to:

- Analyse any errors detected in the sample; and
- Draw inferences for the population as a whole.

5.4.1 Analysis of errors in the sample

To begin with, the auditors must consider whether the items in question are **true errors**, as they defined them before the test, for example, a misposting between customer accounts will not count as an error as far as total debtors are concerned.

Assuming the problems are errors, auditors should consider the **nature and cause** of the error and any possible **effects** the error might have on other parts of the audit.

5.4.2 Inferences to be drawn from the population as a whole

The auditors should project the error results from the sample on to the relevant population. The projection method should be consistent with the method used to select the sampling unit.

The auditors will estimate the **probable error** in the population by extrapolating the errors found in the sample. They will then estimate any **further error** that might not have been detected because of the imprecision of the sampling technique (in addition to consideration of the nature and effects of the errors).

The auditors should then compare the **projected population error** (net of adjustments made by the entity in the case of substantive procedures) to the **tolerable error**, taking account of other audit procedures relevant to the specific control or financial statement assertion.

If the projected population error *exceeds* tolerable error, then the auditors should **re-assess sampling risk**. If it is unacceptable, they should consider **extending auditing procedures** or **performing alternative procedures**, either of which may result in a proposed adjustment to the financial statements.

5.5 Section summary

Key stages in the sampling process are as follows.

- Determining objectives and population
- Determining **sample size**
- **Choosing method** of **sample selection**
- **Analysing** the **results** and **projecting errors**

Activity 9.3

The recorded value of debtors in the sales ledger as at 31 December 2000, was £235,000.

Out of the 314 debtors accounts, your audit assistant, Chen Ping, selected 12 accounts for confirmation as part of the external audit of the company.

In selecting accounts for confirmation Ping picked the 2 largest accounts totalling £2,050 and 10 other accounts selected haphazardly. Her working paper states that she rejected any accounts that were less than £100 as not being worth confirming and accounts with government bodies since she know they never bother replying to confirmation requests.

You are going to review Ping's working papers, and, as this is the first time she has selected a sample of debtors, discuss the outcome with her in detail. You are required to make notes to accompany that discussion, covering Ping's method of selecting items to be confirmed. You should:

(a)   Identify any aspects of her approach that might be considered inconsistent with sampling

(b)   Suggest alternative means of selecting a sample ensuring that the more material balances stand the greatest chance of selection

(c)   Compare and contrast the haphazard method of selection with random selection and systematic selection.

Key learning points

☑ The auditors must be able to evaluate all types of audit evidence in terms of its sufficiency and appropriateness.

☑ Evidence can be in the form of tests of controls or substantive procedures.

☑ Tests of control concentrate on the design and operation of controls.

☑ Substantive testing aims to test all the financial statement assertions.

- Existence
- Rights and obligations (ownership)
- Occurrence
- Completeness
- Valuation
- Measurement
- Presentation and disclosure

☑ The reliability of audit evidence is influenced by its source and by its nature.

☑ Audit evidence can be obtained by the following techniques.

- Inspection
- Observation
- Enquiry and confirmation
- Computation
- Analytical procedures

☑ Auditors may use a number of computer assisted audit techniques including audit interrogation software, test data and embedded audit facilities.

☑ The main stages of audit sampling are:

- Design of the sample
- Selection of the sample
- Evaluation of sample results

☑ Sample sizes for tests of control are influenced by sampling risk, tolerable error rate and expected error rate.

☑ Sample sizes for substantive tests are influenced by inherent, control and detection risk, tolerable error rate, expected error rate, population value and stratification.

☑ Sample sizes can be picked by a variety of means including random selection, systematic selection and haphazard selection.

☑ When evaluating results, auditors should:

- Analyse any errors considering their amount and the reasons why they have occurred
- Draw conclusions for the population as a whole

Quick quiz

1   Auditors should obtain ....audit evidence to be able to draw ....on which to base their opinion.

2   When auditors are testing controls, about which two aspects are they seeking evidence?

3   List the financial statement assertions (single, two or three word descriptions will suffice).

4   Rank the following sources of evidence in terms of reliability:

  • Auditor evidence
  • External evidence
  • Client evidence

5   Of which type of audit procedure are the following examples?

  • Physical check of fixed assets
  • Watching the payment of wages
  • Receiving a letter from the client's bank concerning balances held at the bank by the client
  • Adding up the client's trial balance

6   Name three methods of sample selection

  1 ....

  2 ....

  3 ....

7   Define:

  • Error
  • Tolerable error
  • Sampling risk

8   Summarise the factors that affect sample sizes for substantive tests.

Answers to quick quiz

1   Auditors should obtain **sufficient appropriate** audit evidence to be able to draw **reasonable conclusions** on which to base their opinion.

2   When testing controls, auditors are concentrating on their design and operation.

3   The financial statement assertions are:

  • Existence
  • Rights and obligations
  • Occurrence
  • Completeness
  • Valuation

- Measurement
- Presentation and disclosure

4   General comments that can be made about audit evidence are as follows.

1   Audit evidence from external sources is more reliable than evidence from internal sources.

2   Directly obtained audit evidence is more reliable than evidence obtained from the entity.

3   Evidence obtained form the client's records is more satisfactory if the accounting and internal control system is operating effectively.

5
- Inspection
- Observation
- Confirmation
- Computation

6
- Random
- Haphazard
- Systematic

7   (a)   An error is an unintentional mistake in the financial statements.

(b)   Tolerable error is the maximum error in the population that auditors are willing to accept and still conclude the audit objectives have been achieved.

(c)   Sampling risk is the risk that the auditors' conclusion, based on a sample, may be different from the conclusion that would be reached if the entire population was subject to the audit procedure.

8   Factors that affect the sample sizes for substantive tests are:

- Inherent risk
- Control risk
- Detection risk
- Tolerable error rate
- Expected error rate
- Population value
- Number of items (in small population)

Stratification may also lead to smaller sample sizes.

Activity checklist

This checklist shows which performance criteria, range statement or knowledge and understanding point is covered by each activity in this chapter. Tick off each activity as you complete it.

Activity

9.1		This activity deals with Performance Criteria 17.1.G: Select or devise appropriate tests in accordance with the organisation's procedures.
9.2		This activity deals with Knowledge & Understanding point 9: Auditing techniques in an IT environment.
9.3		This activity deals with Performance Criteria 17.1.F: Select an appropriate sample.

P A R T   C

Conducting an audit assignment

chapter 10

Tests of control

Contents

1   The problem
2   The solution
3   Confirmation of the system
4   Tests of control
5   Sales system
6   Purchases system
7   Wages system

Performance criteria

17.1.B Identify control objectives properly

17.1.G Select or devise appropriate tests in accordance with the organisation's procedures

Range statement

17.1   Accounting systems: purchases; sales; stock; expenses; balance sheet items; payroll

17.1   Accounting systems that are: manual; computerised

17.1   Tests: Tests of control; substantive

Knowledge and understanding

10   Types of tests; substantive

16   Understanding of the organisation's systems and knowledge of specific auditing procedures

1 The problem

The auditors have to obtain sufficient, appropriate evidence on which to base the audit opinion. They may do so using a mixture of tests of control and substantive tests.

How do they know what level of controls testing to undertake?

2 The solution

In Chapter 6, we referred briefly to **assessment of control risk**. The solution to this problem lies in this assessment.

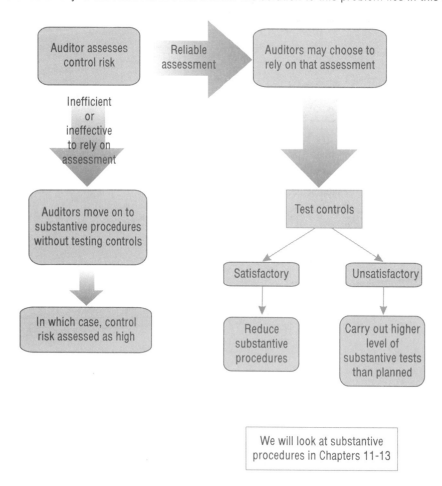

In this chapter we will look at what tests of control are, and at specific tests of controls in the major accounting cycles.

3 Confirmation of the system

One thing auditors must do before making an assessment of control risk is to confirm that the system operates as they believe that it does. We mentioned in Chapter 5 the work auditors do to ascertain the system. They will do this as part of every audit, even for existing clients, as the systems may have changed during the year.

Auditors ascertain the system largely by making enquiries of the personnel who operate it. When they have finished doing this, they will carry out a **walk-through test** on the transaction going through the system to confirm that it operates as they have been told.

This will involve starting at the initial point (usually the order in either the sales or purchases system) and tracing that transaction through all the other documentation to the general ledger.

4 Tests of control

Tests of controls are used to confirm auditors' assessments of the **design and operation** of control systems, and to support the auditors' assessment of control risk. They are tests to obtain audit evidence about the effective operation of the accounting and internal control systems, that is, that properly designed controls identified in the preliminary assessment of control risk exist in fact and have operated effectively throughout the relevant period.

Tests of control may include the following.

(a) **Enquiries** about, and observation of, internal control functions

(b) **Inspection of documents** supporting controls or events to gain audit evidence that internal controls have operated properly, for example verifying that a transaction has been authorised or a reconciliation approved

(c) **Examination** of evidence of **management views**, for example minutes of management meetings

(d) **Reperformance** of control procedures, for example reconciliation of bank accounts, to ensure they were correctly performed by the entity

(e) **Testing** of the internal controls operating on **computerised systems**

(f) **Observation of controls,** considering the manner in which the control is being operated

Auditors should consider how controls were **applied**, the **consistency** with which they were applied during the period and **by whom** they were applied.

Changes in the **operation** of controls (such as those caused by change of staff) may increase control risk and tests of control may need to be modified to confirm effective operation during and after any change. Radical changes in controls, including a periodic breakdown in controls, should be considered as **separate periods** by the auditors.

4.1 Interim testing

As auditors will want to test that controls have existed and operated properly throughout the period under review, they may carry out some of their controls testing before the year end, in what is known as an 'interim audit'.

SAS 300 states:

> 'If intending to rely on tests of control performed in advance of the period end, auditors should obtain sufficient appropriate audit evidence as to the nature and extent of any changes in design or operation of the entity's accounting and internal control systems within the accounting period since such procedures were performed.'

4.2 Final assessment of control risk

SAS 300 *Accounting and internal control systems* states that:

> 'Having undertaken tests of control, auditors should evaluate whether the preliminary assessment of control risk is supported.'

Failures of controls to operate should be investigated, but in such cases the preliminary assessment may still be supported if the failure is isolated. More frequent failures may require the level of control risk to be revised. In such cases the nature, timing and extent of the auditors' planned substantive procedures should be modified.

We shall now look at specific tests of control in the key accounting cycles. Look back at these in Chapter 5 to refresh your memory.

5 Sales system

Remember back to the control objectives we identified in Chapter 5. Tests of control are seeking to observe whether the control meets the objective and that it has operated effectively throughout the period.

5.1 Ordering and credit control

The key objective over ordering was that goods were only sold to customers who were likely to pay. This is strongly linked to the objective that customers pay promptly, as it is often past customers who make orders.

Obviously, auditors can only test the controls that are in place, but given the types of control we mentioned in Chapter 5, they could conduct the following.

5.1.1 Tests of control

- Check that references are being obtained for all new customers
- Check that all new accounts on the sales ledger have been authorised by senior staff
- Check that orders are only accepted from customers who are within their credit terms and credit limits
- Check that customer orders are being matched with production orders and despatch notes
- Check that debtor statements are prepared and sent out regularly
- Check that overdue accounts have been followed up
- Check that all bad debts written off have been authorised by management
- Check that despatches of goods free of charge or on special terms have been authorised by management

5.2 Despatches and invoices

Key objectives were that despatches were recorded properly and invoiced correctly.

5.2.1 Tests of control

- Verify details of **trade sales** or goods despatched notes with **sales invoices checking:**

  - Quantities
  - Prices charged with official price lists
  - Trade discounts have been properly dealt with
  - Calculations and additions
  - Entries in sales day book are correctly analysed
  - VAT, where chargeable, has been properly dealt with
  - Postings to sales ledger

- Verify details of trade sales with entries in stock records.

- Verify non-routine sales (for example, scrap or fixed assets) with:

  - Appropriate supporting evidence
  - Approval by authorised officials
  - Entries in plant register etc

- Verify **credit notes** with:

  - **Correspondence** or other supporting evidence
  - **Approval** by authorised officials
  - **Entries** in **stock records**
  - **Entries** in **goods returned records**
  - **Calculations** and **additions**
  - **Entries** in **day book**, checking these are correctly analysed
  - **Postings** to **sales ledger**

- Test **numerical sequence of despatch notes** and enquire into missing numbers.

- Test **numerical sequence of invoices** and credit notes, enquire into missing numbers and inspect copies of those cancelled.

- **Test numerical sequence** of **order forms** and enquire into missing numbers.

5.3 Recording and accounting

Key objectives were that invoices were recorded and made to the correct sales ledger accounts.

5.3.1 Tests of control

Sales day book

- Check entries with invoices and credit notes respectively
- Check additions and cross casts
- Check postings to sales ledger control account
- Check postings to sales ledger

Sales ledger

- **Check** entries in a **sample of accounts** to sales day book
- Check additions and balances carried down
- Note and enquire into contra entries
- Check that control accounts have been regularly reconciled to total of sales ledger balances
- Scrutinise accounts to see if credit limits have been observed

5.4 Cash receipts

Auditors will carry out the following tests to ensure receipts are being recorded. Note that as well as testing controls over receipts, auditors are also obtaining evidence to support the assertion that sales and receipts are **completely** recorded.

5.4.1 Receipts received by post

- Observe procedures for post opening are being followed.

- **Observe** that **cheques** received by post are immediately **crossed** in the company's favour.

- For items entered in the rough cash book (or other record of cash or cheques received by post), **trace entries** to:
    - Cash book
    - Paying-in book
    - Counterfoil or carbon copy receipts

- **Verify amounts entered** as **received** with remittance advices or other supporting evidence.

5.4.2 Cash sales, branch takings

- For a sample of cash sales summaries/branch summaries from different locations:
    - **Verify with till rolls** or copy cash sale notes
    - **Check to paying-in slip** date-stamped and initialled by the bank
    - **Verify that takings** are banked intact daily
    - **Vouch expenditure** out of takings

5.4.3 Collections

- For a sample of items from the original collection records:

    ○ **Trace amounts** to **cash book** via collectors' cash sheets or other collection records

    ○ **Check entries** on **cash sheets** or collection records with collectors' receipt books

    ○ **Verify** that **goods delivered** to travellers/salesmen have been regularly **reconciled** with sales and stocks in hand

    ○ **Check numerical sequence** of collection records

5.4.4 Receipts cash book

- For cash receipts for several days throughout the period:

    ○ **Check to entries in rough cash book**, receipts, branch returns or other records

    ○ **Check to paying-in slips** obtained direct from the bank, observing that there is no delay in banking monies received. Check additions of paying-in slips

    ○ **Check additions of cash book**

    ○ **Check postings to the sales ledger**

    ○ **Check postings to the general ledger**, including control accounts

- Scrutinise the cash book and investigate items of a special or unusual nature

6 Purchases system

As we mentioned before, a company will purchase stock or fixed assets as well as pay bills. We shall consider any extra tests of control which may be carried out in these areas in this section too.

6.1 Ordering

A key objective was that orders were for authorised goods or services.

6.1.1 Tests of control

A most important test of controls is for auditors to check that all **invoices** are **supported** by authorised **purchase invoices** and **purchase orders**. The officials who approve the invoices should be operating within laid-down **authority limits**.

6.2 Receipt of goods and services

All goods and services received should be recorded and liabilities duly recognised when goods and services have been received.

6.2.1 Tests of control

- Check invoices for goods, raw materials are:

  ○ Supported by goods received notes and inspection notes
  ○ Entered in stock records
  ○ Priced correctly by checking to quotations, price lists to see the price is in order
  ○ Properly referenced with a number and supplier code
  ○ Correctly coded by type of expenditure

- **Trace entry** in **record of goods returned** and see credit note duly received from the supplier, for invoices not passed due to defects or discrepancy

- For invoices of all types:

  ○ Check calculations and additions
  ○ Check entries in purchase day book and verify that they are correctly analysed
  ○ Check posting to purchase ledger

- For credit notes:

  ○ **Verify** the **correctness** of credit received with correspondence
  ○ **Check entries** in **stock records**
  ○ **Check entries** in **record of returns**
  ○ **Check entries** in **purchase day book** and verify that they are correctly analysed
  ○ **Check postings** to **purchase ledger**

- Check for **returns** that **credit notes** are duly **received** from the suppliers

- Test **numerical sequence** and enquire into missing numbers of:

  ○ Purchase requisitions
  ○ Purchase orders
  ○ Goods received notes
  ○ Goods returned notes
  ○ Suppliers' invoices

- **Obtain explanations** for **items** which have been **outstanding** for a long time

  ○ Unmatched purchase requisitions
  ○ Purchase orders
  ○ Goods received notes (if invoices not received)
  ○ Unprocessed invoices

6.3 Recording of expenditure

Ensuring all expenditure is properly recorded.

6.3.1 Tests of control

Purchase day book

- Verify that invoices and credit notes recorded in the purchase day book are:
    - **Initialled** for prices, calculations and extensions
    - **Cross-referenced** to purchase orders, goods received notes
    - **Authorised** for payment

- **Check additions**

- **Check postings** to general ledger accounts and control account

- **Check postings** of entries to purchase ledger

Purchase ledger

- For a sample of accounts recorded in the purchase ledger:
    - **Test check entries** back into books of prime entry
    - **Test check additions** and **balances** forward
    - **Note** and **enquire** into all contra entries

- Confirm **control account balancing** has been regularly carried out during the year

- **Examine control account** for unusual entries

- Recording stock or fixed assets correctly

6.4 Cash payments

Auditors will be concerned with whether **payments** have been **authorised** and are to the **correct payee**.

6.4.1 Tests of controls

- For a sample of payments in the cash book:
    - **Compare** with paid cheques to ensure payee agrees

    - **Check** that **cheques** are **signed** by the **persons authorised** to do so within their authority limits

    - **Check** to **suppliers' invoices** for goods and services. Verify that supporting documents are signed as having been **checked** and **passed for payment** and have been stamped 'paid'

    - **Check** supplier details and amounts to **suppliers' statements**

- ○ **Check** details to **other documentary evidence**, as appropriate (agreements, authorised expense vouchers, wages/salaries records, petty cash books etc)

- When checking the **recording** of **payments**, auditors will carry out the following tests.

  - ○ Check the sequence of cheque numbers and enquire into missing numbers

  - ○ Trace transfers to other bank accounts, petty cash books or other records, as appropriate

  - ○ Check additions, including extensions, and balances forward at the beginning and end of the months covering the periods chosen

  - ○ Check postings to the purchase ledger

  - ○ Check postings to the general ledger, including the control accounts

When checking that bank and cash are **secured** auditors should consider the security arrangements over bank cheques and cash. Bank reconciliations are also a very important control and auditors should carry out the following tests on these.

- Verify that reconciliations have been prepared and reviewed at regular intervals throughout the year
- Scrutinise reconciliations for unusual items

The following tests should be carried out on petty cash.

- For a sample of payments:

  - ○ **Check** to supporting vouchers
  - ○ **Check** whether they are properly **approved**
  - ○ **See** that **vouchers** have been **marked and initialled** by the cashier to prevent their re-use

- For a sample of weeks:

  - ○ Trace amounts received to cash books
  - ○ Check additions and balances carried forward
  - ○ Check postings to the nominal ledger

6.5 Stock

Most of the testing relating to stock has been covered in the purchase and sales testing. Auditors will thereafter be concerned with ensuring that the business keeps **track of stock**. To confirm this, checks must be made on how stock **movements** are **recorded** and how **stock** is **secured**.

6.5.1 Tests of control

- Select a sample of **stock movements records** and **agree** to **goods received** and **goods despatched notes**, confirming that movements have been **authorised** as appropriate

- Select a sample of **goods received** and **goods despatched notes** and **agree to stock movement records**

- Check **sequence** of stock records

Other tests that auditors are likely to perform include:

- **Test** check **stock counts** carried out from time to time (eg monthly) during the period and confirm:

    ○ **All discrepancies** between **book** and **actual** figures have been fully investigated

    ○ **All discrepancies** have been **signed off** by a senior manager

    ○ **Obsolete, damaged or slow-moving goods** have been **marked accordingly** and written down to NRV

- Observe security arrangements for stocks

- Consider environment in which stocks are held

6.6 Fixed assets

A key concern of auditors will be proper controls over **movements** during the year, that is acquisitions and disposals.

6.6.1 Tests of control

- For a sample of fixed asset purchases during the year in the general ledger:

    ○ **Check authorisation** (and board approval if necessary)
    ○ **Vouch purchase price** to invoice and cash book
    ○ **Check** asset has been **recorded** in the **fixed asset register**
    ○ **Check correct depreciation** rates applied

- For a sample of fixed asset disposals during the year:

    ○ Check disposal authorised by senior official
    ○ Check invoice issued for any proceeds
    ○ Agree recording of proceeds in the cash books
    ○ Check asset has been removed from fixed asset register
    ○ Check calculations of profit or loss on disposal

Auditors should also carry out some testing on **security, maintenance** and **recording** of fixed assets.

- For a sample of fixed assets from the fixed asset register:

    ○ Check physical existence of asset
    ○ Ensure asset in good condition
    ○ Consider whether asset value should be written down

- Check whether fixed asset register has been **reconoiled to general ledger**.

- For a sample of fixed assets of all varieties:

    ○ **Agree existence** to fixed asset register
    ○ **Consider whether write down required**

Activity 10.1

AJ (Paper) Ltd operates a computerised purchase system. Invoices and credit notes are posted to the purchase ledger by the purchase ledger department. The computer subsequently raises a cheque when the invoice has to be paid.

List the controls that should be in operation:

(a)   Over the addition, amendment and deletion of suppliers, ensuring that the file of suppliers' data only includes suppliers from the company's list of authorised suppliers

(b)   Over purchase invoices and credit notes, to ensure only authorised purchase invoices and credit notes are posted to the purchase ledger.

Activity 10.2

Describe the main controls that the business should implement in order to ensure safe custody of:

(a)   Stock
(b)   Tangible fixed assets

7 Wages system

7.1 Setting of wages and salaries

Auditors should check that the **wages** and **salary summary** is approved for payment. They should confirm that procedures are operating for **authorising changes** in **rates of pay**, overtime, and holiday pay.

Joiners and leavers are of particular concern. Auditors will need to obtain evidence that staff only start being paid when they join the company, and are removed from the payroll when they leave the company. They should check that the **engagement** of **new employees** and **discharges** have been **confirmed in writing**.

Auditors will also wish to check calculations of wages and salaries. This test should be designed to check that the client is carrying out **checks** on **calculations** and also to provide substantive assurance that **wages** and **salaries** are being **calculated correctly**.

For wages, this will involve checking **calculation** of **gross pay** with:

- Authorised rates of pay
- Production records, seeing that production bonuses have been authorised and properly calculated
- Clock cards, time sheets or other evidence of hours worked. Verify that overtime has been authorised

For salaries, auditors should **verify that gross salaries and bonuses are in accordance with personnel records** or **letters of engagement** and that increases in pay have been properly authorised.

7.2 Payment of wages and salaries

If wages are paid in cash, auditors should carry out the following procedures.

- **Arrange to attend** the **pay-out** of wages to confirm that the official procedures are being followed
- **Examine receipts** given by employees; **trace unclaimed wages** to unclaimed wages book
- **Check entries** in the **unclaimed wages book** with the entries on the wages sheets
- **Check that unclaimed wages** are **banked regularly**
- **Check** that unclaimed wages books shows **reasons** why wages are unclaimed
- For holiday pay, verify a sample of payments with the underlying records and check the calculation of the amounts paid

For salaries, auditors should check that comparisons are being made between payment records and they should themselves **examine paid cheques** or a **certified copy** of the **bank list** for employees paid by cheque of banks transfer.

7.3 Recording of wages and salaries

A key control auditors will be concerned with will be the reconciliation of wages and salaries.

For wages, there should have been reconciliations with:

- The **previous week's payroll**
- Clock cards/time sheets/job cards
- Costing analyses, production budgets

The total of **salaries** should be **reconciled** with the **previous week/month** or the **standard payroll.**

In addition auditors should confirm that important calculations have been checked by the clients and re-perform those calculations.

These include for wages, checking for a number of weeks:

- Additions of payroll sheets
- **Totals** of **wages sheets** selected to summary
- **Additions** and **cross-casts** of summary
- **Postings** of **summary** to **general ledger** (including control accounts)
- **Casts** of **net cash column** to cash book

For salaries, they include checking for a number of weeks/months:

- Additions of payroll sheets
- Totals of salaries sheets to summary
- Additions and cross-casts of summary
- Postings of summary to general ledger (including control accounts)
- Total of net pay column to cash book

7.4 Deductions

Auditors should **check** the **calculations** of **PAYE, National Insurance** and **non-statutory deductions.** For PAYE and NI they should carry out the following tests.

- Scrutinise the control accounts maintained to see appropriate deductions have been made
- Check to see that the employer's contribution for national insurance has been correctly calculated
- Check that the payments to the Inland Revenue and other bodies are correct

They should **check other deductions to appropriate records. For voluntary deductions, they should see** the **authority completed** by the relevant employees.

Activity 10.3

The following questions have been selected from an internal control questionnaire for wages and salaries.

Internal control questionnaire – wages and salaries

		Yes	No

1   Does an appropriate official authorise rates of pay?

2   Are written notices required for employing and terminating employment?

3   Are formal records such as time cards used for time keeping?

4   Does anyone verify rates of pay, overtime hours and computations of gross pay before the wage payments are made?

5   Does the accounting system ensure the proper recording of payroll costs in the financial records?

Tasks

(a)   Describe the internal control objective being fulfilled if the controls set out in the above questions are in effect.

(b)   Describe the audit tests which would test the effectiveness of each control and help determine any potential material error.

(c)   Identify the potential consequences for the company if the above controls were not in place.

You may answer in columnar form under the headings:

ICQ question	Internal control objective	Audit tests	Consequences of lack of control

Key learning points

☑ Auditors will either choose to rely on an assessment of control risk, in which case they will test controls, or not, in which case they will automatically assess control risk as high and go on to substantive testing.

☑ Tests of control must cover the whole accounting period.

☑ The sales and purchases systems will be the most important components of most company accounting systems.

☑ The tests of controls of the sales system will be based around:

- Selling (authorisation)
- Goods outwards (custody)
- Accounting (recording)

☑ Similarly, the purchases systems tests will be based around:

- Buying (authorisation)
- Goods inwards (custody)
- Accounting (recording)

☑ Important tests of control by auditors include:

- Checking documentation for correct details, calculations and authorisation
- Comparing documents
- Checking completeness of documentation sequences

☑ Controls over cash receipts and payments should prevent fraud or theft.

☑ Key controls over receipts include:

- Proper post-opening arrangements
- Prompt recording
- Prompt banking
- Reconciliation of records of cash received and banked

☑ Key controls over payments include:

- Restriction of access to cash and cheques
- Procedures for preparation and authorisation of payments

☑ A further important control is regular independent bank reconciliations.

☑ Stock controls are designed to ensure safe custody. These include:

- Restriction of access to stock
- Documentation and authorisation of movements

☑ Other important controls over stock include regular independent stock-taking and review of stock condition.

☑ Important controls over tangible fixed assets include physical custody and authorisation of purchases and disposals.

☑ Tangible fixed assets should be recorded in a fixed asset register.

☑ Controls over investments should include maintenance of an investment register and investment control account and custody of documents of title.

☑ Obviously, most manufacturing companies will have a large payroll. Wages and salaries are usually dealt with in very different ways, but they are often grouped together for audit testing purposes.

☑ Key controls over wages cover:

- Documentation and authorisation of staff changes
- Calculation of wages and salaries
- Payment of wages and salaries
- Authorisation of deductions

Quick quiz

1   What are the key elements in authorisation of credit terms to customers?

2   Which of the following should the auditors check when reviewing sales invoices?

- Correct calculation of discounts
- Customer exists
- Prices charged with price lists
- Quantities
- Invoices have been correctly entered and analysed in the sales day book
- VAT has been properly dealt with
- Credit limit not exceeded
- National insurance contributions
- Calculations and additions
- Invoices have been posted to the sales ledger

3   How can a company ensure that quantities of goods ordered do not exceed those that are required?

4   How frequently should cashiers bank money received?

5   Which of the following checks should be carried out on invoices from suppliers?

- Check price correct
- Agree to purchase order
- Ensure credit limit not exceeded
- Agree quantities
- Agree to goods outward note
- Check calculations

6   What tests should auditors carry out on credit notes received?

7   (a)   Name four examples of purchase documentation on which numerical sequence should be checked.

   1   ....

   2   ....

   3   ....

   4   ....

   (b)   Why is numerical sequence checked?

8   What are the key controls over a system of cheque requisitions?

9   What are the most important controls over the signing of cheques?

10   Three important controls over the protection of stocks are:

- Restriction of access to stocks

- Regular stocktaking

- Reconciliation of book stock to physical stock

True ☐

False ☐

11 What controls should businesses exercise over stock levels?

12 Which of the following tests would auditors normally carry out on controls over fixed asset purchases?

- The asset has been recorded in the cash book and fixed asset register.
- Check posting to purchase ledger
- The purchase price can be confirmed to supporting documentation.
- Fixed asset purchases have been authorised.
- Check the sequence of cheque numbers
- Review condition of stock
- An appropriate depreciation rate has been chosen and has been applied correctly to the asset.

13 What are the most important authorisation controls over amounts to be paid to employees?

14 How should auditors confirm that wages have been paid at the correct rate to individual employees?

Answers to quick quiz

1 References and credit checks should be obtained before customers are given credit. Credit limits should be authorised by senior staff and should be regularly reviewed.

2 When checking sales invoices, auditors should check:

- Quantities
- Prices charged with price lists
- Correct calculation of discounts
- Calculations and additions
- Invoices have been correctly entered and analysed in the sales day book
- VAT has been properly dealt with
- Invoices have been posted to the sales ledger

3 A company can ensure goods ordered do not exceed requirements by setting re-order quantities and re-order limits.

4 Cash receipts should ideally be banked every day.

5 Invoices from suppliers should be checked for correctness of prices and quantities and accuracy of calculation. They should be compared with purchase orders and goods received notes.

6 Auditors should:

- Verify the correctness of credit notes with previous correspondence.
- Confirm by reviewing stock records and records of returns that goods have been returned.
- Check credit notes have been correctly accounted for by checking entries in the purchase day book and purchase ledger.

7 (a) 1 purchase requisitions
     2 purchase orders
     3 goods received notes
     4 goods returned notes
     5 suppliers' invoices

 (b) Sequence provides a control that purchases are complete. Missing documents should be explained, or cancelled copies available.

8 The key controls over a system of cheque requisition are as follows.

- Requisitions should be supported by appropriate documentation.

- Requisitions should be approved by appropriate staff, who should not be the same as the staff authorised to sign cheques.

- Requisitions should be presented to the cheque signatories.

- Once a cheque has been drawn, requisitions should be cancelled and marked with the cheque number.

9 The most important controls over the signing of cheques are as follows.

- Signatories should not also approve cheque requisitions.
- All cheques/cheques for larger amounts should be signed by more than one person.
- Signatories should be restricted to signing cheques for a prescribed maximum amount.
- Documentation supporting cheques should be cancelled once the cheque has been signed.
- The signing of blank cheques should be prohibited.

10 True

11 Clients should set maximum and minimum stock levels, also stock levels at which stock should be ordered and the normal re-order quantities.

12 Auditors should normally check that:

- Fixed asset purchases have been authorised.
- The purchase price can be confirmed to supporting documentation.
- The asset has been recorded in the cash book and fixed asset register.
- An appropriate depreciation rate has been chosen and has been applied correctly to the asset.

13 The most important authorisation controls over wages and salaries are controls over:

- Engagement and discharge of employees
- Changes in pay rates
- Overtime
- Non-statutory deductions
- Advances of pay

14 Auditors should confirm that wages have been paid at the correct rate by checking calculation of gross pay to:

- Authorised rates of pay
- Production records
- Clock cards, time sheets or other evidence of hours worked

Activity checklist

This checklist shows which performance criteria, range statement or knowledge and understanding point is covered by each activity in this chapter. Tick off each activity as you complete it.

Activity

10.1		This activity deals with Performance Criteria 17.1.B: Identify control objectives properly.
10.2		This activity deals with Performance Criteria 17.1.B: Identify control objectives properly.
10.3		This activity deals with Performance Criteria 17.1.B: Identify control objectives properly and Performance Criteria 17.1.G: Select or devise appropriate tests in accordance with the organisation's procedures.

BPP
PROFESSIONAL EDUCATION

chapter 11

Substantive tests

Contents

1   The problem
2   The solution
3   Designing substantive tests
4   Analytical procedures
5   Testing estimates
6   Opening balances and comparatives

Performance criteria

17.1.E Identify account balances to be verified and the associated risks

17.1.G Select or devise appropriate tests in accordance with the organisation's procedures

17.2.B Establish the existence, completeness, ownership, valuation and description of assets and liabilities and gather appropriate evidence to support these findings

17.2.C Identify all matters of an unusual nature and refer them promptly to the audit supervisor

Range statement

17.1/2 Accounting systems: purchases; sales; stock; expenses; balance sheet items; payroll

17.1/2 Accounting systems that are: manual; computerised

17.1/2 Tests: Tests of control; substantive

Knowledge and understanding

•   Types of test: tests of control; substantive

1 The problem

Auditors must carry out substantive procedures. Even if they carry out tests of controls which find the operation of controls to be satisfactory, they cannot eliminate substantive procedures.

So, what are substantive procedures? How are they designed? What tests must be carried out as part of a substantive audit?

2 The solution

As discussed in Chapter 9, substantive tests are designed to prove financial statement assertions.

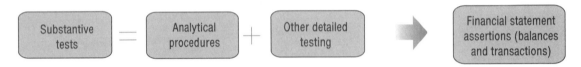

The types of test included in 'detailed testing' were discussed in Chapter 9, for example, vouching figures or transactions to third party evidence such as invoices or supplier statements, or inspection of assets or re-calculations.

Complications arise if **estimates** have been used in the financial statements, when the auditors will have to assess judgements made by directors.

If auditors are undertaking a highly-substantive audit they will commonly adopt a balance-sheet approach, as this is an efficient method. This involves testing year-end balances in detail and assessing transactions in the year in less detail, for example, by analytical review. When undertaking a balance-sheet approach, auditors must be sure that the **opening position** is also correctly stated.

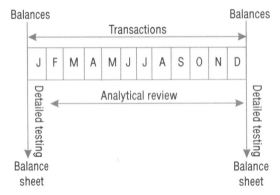

3 Designing substantive tests

Substantive tests are designed to confirm the **completeness**, **accuracy** and **validity** of the items in the accounts or the accounting records. Tests are also carried out to confirm that there are **no material omissions** in the accounts or accounting records. Substantive tests will always be required even if all risks are assessed as low. Substantive tests are designed to obtain evidence relating to the financial statement assertions. Look back at the financial statement assertions in Chapter 9 on page 134.

Some of the financial statement assertions relate to assets and liabilities, some to transactions. In practice also some balance sheet assertions are more important for specific balance sheet items than others. We also discussed in Chapter 9 the different types of tests auditors can use to obtain evidence. Auditors need to consider how different tests can give the required level of assurance, either by themselves or in combination with other tests.

Auditors should also consider the need to test individual items. **Sampling**, testing of a representative selection of individual items, is one way of doing this but it is not the only way. Auditors may in certain circumstances, be able to gain the assurance they require, by testing **all items over a certain amount**, or **testing key items**, items which are particularly prone to error.

Auditors should in any event **scrutinise all** areas of the accounts and the accounting records and investigate all unusual or suspicious items. This is a key test in particular in the areas of fraud and error, compliance with laws and regulations and related party transactions.

Activity 11.1

Complete the following table showing possible audit tests for each balance sheet objective.

Audit objective	Typical audit tests
Completeness	
Rights and obligations	
Valuation	
Existence	
Disclosure	

4 Analytical procedures

Analytical procedures are a key type of substantive procedure. They are the analysis of relationships:

(a) Between items of financial data, or between items of financial and non-financial data, deriving from the same period, or

(b) Between comparable financial information deriving from different periods to identify consistencies and predicted patterns or significant fluctuations and unexpected relationships, and the results of investigation thereof.

4.1 Nature and purpose of analytical procedures

SAS 410 *Analytical procedures* states that they include:

(a) The **consideration of comparisons** of this year's financial information with:

   (i) Similar information for prior periods

   (ii) Anticipated results of the client

   (iii) Predictions prepared by the auditors

   (iv) Industry information, such as a comparison of the client's ratio of sales to trade debtors with industry averages, or with the ratios relating to other entities of comparable size in the same industry

(b) Those between **elements of financial information** that are **expected to conform** to a predicted pattern based on experience, such as the relationship of gross profit to sales

(c) Those between **financial information** and **relevant non-financial information**, such as the relationship of payroll costs to number of employees

A variety of methods can be used to perform the procedures discussed above, ranging from **simple comparisons** to **complex analysis** using statistics, on a company level, branch level or individual account level. The choice of procedures is a matter for the auditors' professional judgement.

4.2 Using analytical procedures

We saw in Chapter 6 that auditors are required to use analytical procedures as part of the planning stage of the audit, to:

- Identify risk areas
- Determine the nature, timing and extent of procedures

The auditor may also use analytical procedures as substantive procedures. SAS 410 states that auditors must decide whether using analytical procedures as substantive procedures will be effective and efficient in reducing **detection risk** for specific financial statement assertions. Auditors may efficiently use analytical data produced by the entity itself, provided they are satisfied that it has been properly prepared.

The SAS lists a number of factors which the auditors should consider when deciding whether to use analytical procedures as substantive procedures.

Factors to consider	Example
Plausibility and predictability of the relationships	The strong relationship between certain selling expenses and turnover in businesses where the sales force is paid by commission
Objectives of analytical procedures and extent to which their results are reliable	
Degree to which information can be **disaggregated**	Analytical procedures may be more effective when applied to financial information on individual sections of an operation such as individual factories or shops
Availability of information	Financial: budgets or forecasts Non-financial: eg the number of units produced or sold
Relevance of available information	Whether budgets are established as results to be expected rather than as tough targets (which may well not be achieved)
Comparability of available information	Comparisons with average performance in an industry may be of little value if a large number of businesses differ significantly from the average.
Knowledge gained during previous audits	The effectiveness of the accounting and internal control systems The types of problems giving rise to accounting adjustments in prior periods

4.2.1 Reliance on analytical procedures

From our earlier coverage of audit evidence we can see that the information used in analytical procedures will be more reliable if it comes from sources independent from, rather than internal to, the client. Information produced independently outside the accounting function is more reliable than that originating from within it.

The results of **other audit procedures** will help to determine the reliability of the information used in analytical procedures, as will the importance of the results of the procedure for the auditors' opinion.

The SAS identifies other factors which should be considered when determining the reliance that the auditors should place on the results of substantive analytical procedures.

Reliability factors	Example
Other audit procedures directed towards the same financial statements assertions	Other procedures auditors undertake in reviewing the collectability of debtors, such as the review of subsequent cash receipts, may confirm or dispel questions arising from the application of analytical procedures to a profile of customers' accounts which lists for how long monies have been owed
The **accuracy** with which the expected results of analytical procedures can be predicted	Auditors normally expect greater consistency in comparing the relationship of gross profit to sales from one period to another than in comparing expenditure which may or may not be made within a period, such as research or advertising
The **frequency** with which a relationship is observed	A pattern repeated monthly as opposed to annually

Reliance on the results of analytical procedures depends on the auditors' assessment of the **risk** that the procedures may identify relationships (between data) do exist, whereas a material misstatement exists (that is, the relationships, in fact, do not exist).

Reliance also depends on the **results of investigations** that auditors have made if substantive analytical procedures have highlighted significant fluctuations or unexpected relationships (see below).

SAS 410 goes on to look at analytical procedures as part of the overall review when completing the audit. The key aim of procedures is to see whether the overall accounts appear reasonable.

The conclusions from these analytical procedures should be consistent with the conclusions formed from other audit procedures on parts of the financial statements. However, these analytical procedures may highlight areas which require further investigation and audit. We will look more at audit completion in Chapter 16.

4.3 Investigating significant fluctuations or unexpected relationships

When analytical procedures identify significant fluctuations or unexpected relationships that are inconsistent with other relevant information or that deviate from predicted patterns, auditors should investigate and obtain adequate explanations and appropriate corroborative evidence.

Investigations will start with **enquiries** to management and then **confirmation** of management's responses.

(a) By **comparing them** with the auditors' knowledge of the entity's business and with other evidence obtained during the course of the audit

(b) By **carrying out additional audit procedures** where appropriate to confirm the explanations received

If explanations cannot be given by management, or if they are insufficient, the auditors must determine which further audit procedures to undertake to explain the fluctuation or relationship.

4.4 Practical techniques

When carrying out analytical procedures, auditors should remember that every industry is different and each company within an industry differs in certain respects.

Significant items
Creditors and purchases
Stocks and cost of sales
Fixed assets and depreciation, repairs and maintenance expense
Intangible assets and amortisation
Loans and interest expense
Investments and investment income
Debtors and bad debt expense
Debtors and sales

Important accounting ratios

$$\text{Gross profit margin} = \frac{\text{Gross profit}}{\text{Turnover}} \times 100\%$$

This should be calculated in total and by product, area and month/quarter if possible.

$$\text{Debtors turnover period} = \frac{\text{Debtors}}{\text{Sales}} \times 365$$

$$\text{Stock turnover ratio} = \frac{\text{Cost of sales}}{\text{Stock}}$$

$$\text{Current ratio} = \frac{\text{Current assets}}{\text{Current liabilities}}$$

$$\text{Quick or acid test ratio} = \frac{\text{Current assets (excluding stock)}}{\text{Current liabilities}}$$

$$\text{Gearing ratio} = \frac{\text{Loans}}{\text{Share capital and reserves}} \times 100\%$$

$$\text{Return on capital employed} = \frac{\text{Profit before tax}}{\text{Total assets - current - liabilities}}$$

Ratios mean very little when used in isolation. They should be **calculated for previous periods** and for **comparable companies**. The permanent file should contain a section with summarised accounts and the chosen ratios for prior years. In addition to looking at the more usual ratios the auditors should consider examining **other ratios** that may be **relevant** to the particular **clients' business**, such as revenue per passenger mile for an airline operator client, or fees per partner for a professional office.

One further important technique is to examine **important related accounts** in conjunction with each other. It is often the case that revenue and expense accounts are related to balance sheet accounts and comparisons should be made to ensure that the relationships are reasonable.

Other areas that might be investigated as part of the analytical procedures include the following.

- Examine changes in products, customers and levels of returns

- Assess the effect of price and mix changes on the cost of sales

- Consider the effect of inflation, industrial disputes, changes in production methods and changes in activity on the charge for wages

- Obtain explanations for all major variances analysed using a standard costing system. Particular attention should be paid to those relating to the over or under absorption of overheads since these may, amongst other things, affect stock valuations

- Compare trends in production and sales and assess the effect on any provisions for obsolete stocks

- Ensure that changes in the percentage labour or overhead content of production costs are also reflected in the stock valuation

- Review other profit and loss expenditure, comparing:

  ○ Rent with annual rent per rental agreement

- ○ Rates with previous year and known rates increases

- ○ Interest payable on loans with outstanding balance and interest rate per loan agreement

- ○ Hire or leasing charges with annual rate per agreements

- ○ Vehicle running expenses to vehicles

- ○ Other items related to activity level with general price increase and change in relevant level of activity (for example, telephone expenditure will increase disproportionately if export or import business increases)

- ○ Other items not related to activity level with general price increases (or specific increases if known)

- **Review** profit and loss account for **items** which may have been **omitted** (for example, scrap sales, training levy, special contributions to pension fund or provisions for dilapidation).

- **Ensure expected variations** arising from the following have occurred:

  - ○ Industry or local trends

  - ○ Known disturbances of the trading pattern (for example, strikes, depot closures, failure of suppliers)

Certain of the comparisons and ratios measuring liquidity and longer-term capital structure will assist in evaluating whether the company is a **going concern**, in addition to contributing to the overall view of the accounts. We will look at detailed tests on going concern in Chapter 16.

The working papers must contain the completed results of analytical procedures. They should include:

- The outline programme of the work
- The summary of significant figures and relationships for the period
- A summary of comparisons made with budgets and with previous years
- Details of all significant fluctuations or unexpected relationships considered
- Details of the results of investigations into such fluctuations/relationships
- The audit conclusions reached
- Information considered necessary for assisting in the planning of subsequent audits

Activity 11.2

You are Shahid. Anton passed on a draft profit and loss account to you when you were carrying out the audit planning exercise. The comparative figures are for the unincorporated business last year. The business was incorporated on 1 January 2000. The draft profit and loss account is set out below.

Perform analytical review on the profit and loss account figures, comparing 2000 to 1999 on a percentage basis, gross and net profit percentages between the two years and each category of expense (for example, administration and establishment charges). Highlight significant variations which will require further investigation during the audit. You should prepare a working paper, giving the test objective, the work done, the results and the conclusions drawn. You should also set out any areas where you believe you should take further action.

Draft profit and loss account

	2000 £	1999 £
Turnover	1,536,088	978,045
Cost of sales	(1,245,930)	(903,487)
Gross profit	290,158	74,558
Administration and establishment charges		
Salaries and wages	103,279	58,224
Computer charges	602	598
Incidental expenses	54	20
Insurance	4,725	3,928
Legal and other professional fees	24,949	629
Printing, postage and stationery	10,430	2,794
Repairs and renewals	2,226	1,237
Telephone	4,829	944
Depreciation	4,836	632
	155,930	69,006
Finance charges		
Audit	468	-
Accountancy	2,049	1,031
Bank charges	1,625	625
Loan interest	2,495	2,495
Bad debts	967	62
	7,604	4,213
Selling and distribution charges		
Travelling and entertainment expenses	5,327	411
Motor expenses	927	317
Advertising	6,417	297
	12,671	1,025
	113,953	314

5 Testing estimates

An **accounting estimate** is an approximation of the amount of an item in the absence of a precise means of measurement. SAS 420 *Audits of accounting estimates* gives these examples.

- Allowances to reduce stocks and debtors to their estimated realisable value
- Depreciation provisions
- Accrued revenue
- Provision for a loss from a lawsuit
- Profits or losses on construction contracts in progress
- Provision to meet warranty claims

Directors and management are responsible for making accounting estimates included in the financial statements. These estimates are often made in conditions of **uncertainty** regarding the outcome of events and involve the use of judgement. The risk of a material misstatement therefore increases when accounting estimates are involved (and thus inherent risk is higher). **Audit evidence** supporting accounting estimates is generally less than conclusive and so auditors need to exercise **significant judgement**.

Accounting estimates may be produced as part of the routine operations of the accounting system, or may be a non-routine procedure at the period end. Where, as is frequently the case, a **formula** based on past experience is used to calculate the estimate, it should be reviewed regularly by management (for example, actual vs estimate in prior periods).

Examples: nature of accounting estimates

From a routine operation: a warranty provision calculated automatically as a percentage of sales revenue.

From a non-routine operation: a provision for legal costs and damages payable in an impending legal dispute.

Using a standard formula: the use of standard rates for depreciating each category of fixed assets.

5.1 Audit procedures

SAS 420 states:

> 'Auditors should obtain sufficient appropriate evidence as to whether an accounting estimate is reasonable in the circumstances and, when required, is appropriately disclosed.'

The auditors should gain an understanding of the procedures and methods used by management to make accounting estimates. This will aid the auditors' planning of their own procedures. Auditors must carry out one or a mixture of the following procedures.

Procedure 1   Review and testing the process

The auditors will

- Evaluate the data and consider the assumptions on which the estimate is based
- Test the calculations involved in the estimate

- Compare estimates made for prior periods with actual results of those periods
- Consider management's/directors' review and approval procedures

Procedure 2   Use of an independent estimate

Such an estimate (made or obtained by the auditors) may be compared with the accounting estimate. The auditors should **evaluate** the **data**, **consider** the **assumptions** and **test the calculation** procedures used to develop the independent estimate. Prior period independent assessments and actual results could also be compared.

Procedure 3   Review of subsequent events

The auditors should review transactions or events after the period end which may reduce or even remove the need to test accounting estimates. For example, if directors have estimated a bad debt provision, but all debt existing at the balance sheet date has been paid by the date of the audit report, this provision will no longer be required.

5.2 Evaluation of results of audit procedures

SAS 420 says:

> 'Auditors should make a final assessment of the reasonableness of the accounting estimate based on their knowledge of the business and whether the estimate is consistent with other audit evidence obtained during the audit.'

Auditors must assess the differences between the amount of an estimate supported by evidence and the estimate calculated by management. If the auditors believe that the difference is unreasonable then an adjustment should be made. If the directors or management refuse to revise the estimate, then the difference is considered a misstatement and will be treated as such.

6 Opening balances and comparatives

Note that the preceding period accounts, when new auditors are appointed, may have been reported on by the predecessor auditors or they may have been **unaudited**.

6.1 Opening balances

Opening balances are those account balances that exist at the beginning of the period. Opening balances are based upon the closing balances of the preceding period and reflect the effect of transactions of preceding periods and accounting policies applied in the preceding period.

SAS 450 *Opening balances and comparatives* looks at opening balances from the point of view of both **continuing auditors** and **incoming auditors**. It states:

> 'Auditors should obtain sufficient appropriate audit evidence that:
>
> (a)   opening balances have been appropriately brought forward;

> (b) opening balances do not contain errors or misstatements which materially affect the current period's financial statements; and
>
> (c) appropriate accounting policies are consistently applied or changes in accounting policies have been properly accounted for and adequately disclosed.'

6.1.1 Continuing auditors

Continuing auditors are the auditors who audited and reported on the preceding period's financial statements and continue as the auditors for the current period.

Audit procedures need not extend beyond ensuring that opening balances have been **appropriately brought forward** and the current accounting policies have been **consistently applied**, if:

- The continuing auditors issued an **unqualified report** on the preceding period's financial statements.

- The audit of the current period does not reveal any matters which cast **doubt** on those financial statements.

If a **qualified audit report** was issued on the preceding period's financial statements then the auditors should consider whether the matter which gave rise to the qualification has been **adequately resolved** and properly dealt with in the **current period's financial statements**. This is in addition to the procedures above.

6.1.2 Incoming auditors

Incoming auditors are the auditors who are auditing and reporting on the current period's financial statements, not having audited and reported on those for the preceding period. **Predecessor auditors** are the auditors who previously audited and reported on the financial statements of an entity, and who have been replaced by the incoming auditors.

This situation is obviously more difficult. Appropriate and sufficient audit evidence is required on the opening balances and this depends on matters such as the following.

- The **accounting policies** followed by the entity

- Whether the **preceding period's financial statements were audited** and, if so, whether the auditors' report was **qualified**

- The **nature of the opening balances**, including the risk of their misstatement

- The **materiality of the opening balances** relative to the current period's financial statements

The **procedures given** above for continuing auditors should be carried out. Other procedures suggested by the SAS are as follows.

- **Consultations with management** and review of records, working papers and accounting and control procedures for the preceding period

- **Substantive testing of any opening balances** in respect of which the results of other procedures are considered unsatisfactory

Consultations with predecessor auditors will not normally be necessary as the above procedures will be sufficient. Predecessor auditors have no legal or ethical duty to provide information and would not normally be expected to release relevant working papers. However:

> 'they are expected to cooperate with incoming auditors to provide clarification of, or information on, specific accounting matters where this is necessary to resolve any particular difficulties.'

6.2 Comparatives

Opening balances will, in the current year's financial statements, become comparative figures which must be disclosed. The profit and loss account will also contain comparatives for income and expenses for the preceding period.

> 'Auditors should obtain sufficient appropriate audit evidence that:
>
> (a)   the accounting policies used for the comparatives are consistent with those of the current period and appropriate adjustments and disclosures have been made where this is not the case;
>
> (b)   the comparatives agree with the amounts and other disclosures presented in the preceding period and are free from errors in the context of the financial statements of the current period; and
>
> (c)   where comparatives have been adjusted as required by relevant legislation and accounting standards, appropriate disclosures have been made.'

> 'The comparatives form part of the financial statements on which the auditors express an opinion, although they are not required to express an opinion on the comparatives as such. Their responsibility is to establish whether the comparatives are the amounts which appeared in the preceding period's financial statements or, where appropriate, have been restated.'

6.2.1 Continuing auditors

The extent of audit procedures for comparatives will be significantly less then those for current year balances; normally they will be limited to a **check that balances have been brought forward correctly**. Materiality of any misstatements should be considered in relationship to **current** period figures.

The auditors' report on the previous period financial statements may have been qualified. Where the qualification matter is still **unresolved**, two situations may apply.

(a)   If the matter is material in the context of the current period's opening balances as well as comparatives, the report on the current period's financial statements should be **qualified regarding opening balances and comparatives**.

(b)   If the matter does not affect opening balances but is material in the context of the current period's financial statements, the report on the current period's financial statements should **refer to the comparatives**.

    (i)   If comparatives are **required by law or regulation**, the reference will be in the form of a **qualification on the grounds of non-compliance** with that requirement.

    (ii)   If comparatives are presented solely as **good practice**, the reference should be in the form of an **explanatory paragraph**.

6.2.2 Incoming auditors: audited comparatives

In this situation, the preceding period's financial statements have been audited by other auditors. The incoming auditors only bear audit responsibility for the comparatives in the context of the financial statements as a whole. The incoming auditors will use the knowledge gained in the current audit to decide whether the previous period's financial statements have been properly reflected as comparatives in the current period's financial statements.

The procedures below should be considered should such a situation arise.

6.2.3 Incoming auditors: unaudited comparatives

In this situation (for example, where the company took advantage of the small company audit exemption in the previous period) the auditors should check that there is clear **disclosure** in the current financial statements that the comparatives are unaudited. They must still undertake the duties mentioned above as far as is appropriate. If there is not sufficient appropriate evidence, or if disclosure is inadequate, the auditors should consider the implications for their reports.

Activity 11.3

As AJ (Paper) Ltd has only recently been incorporated it has not previously been subject to an audit.

Plan the work that should be carried out on the opening balances and comparatives for the first audit.

Key learning points

☑ Substantive tests may include testing of individual items and analytical procedures. Scrutiny tests should always be carried out.

☑ Analytical procedures cover comparisons of financial data with other financial or non-financial data of the same or previous periods, also comparisons of financial data with expected data.

☑ Analytical procedures aim to identify inconsistencies or significant fluctuations.

☑ Analytical procedures must be undertaken at the planning stage of audits.

☑ Analytical procedures can be used as substantive procedures, depending on the available information and the plausibility and predictability of the relationships.

☑ Analytical review should be undertaken at the final stage of an audit on the final accounts.

☑ Significant fluctuations and unexpected variations should be investigated by enquiries of management, comparisons with other evidence and further audit procedures as required.

☑ Accounts may contain accounting estimates in a number of areas.

☑ Auditors can test accounting estimates by:

    – Reviewing and testing the management process
    – Using an independent estimate
    – Reviewing subsequent events

☑ Specific procedures must be applied to opening balances at a new audit client.

☑ The auditors' responsibilities for comparatives relate mainly to consistency, although comparatives and opening balances can have an impact on current results.

Quick quiz

1   Name four sources of analytical information which can be used at the planning stage of the audit.

   1   ....

   2   ....

   3   ....

   4   ....

2   Identify the significant relationships in the list of items below

   (a)   creditors   (b)   interest   (c)   purchases   (d)   sales

   (e)   amortisation   (f)   loans   (g)   debtors   (h)   intangibles

3   Complete the definition.

   An accounting estimate is an .... of the .... of an item in the absence of a .... of measurement.

4   Give three examples of an accounting estimate.

   1   ....

   2   ....

   3   ....

5   What are:

   •   The current ratio
   •   The acid test ratio
   •   The return on capital employed

6   Auditors are responsible for making accounting estimates to be used in the accounts.

   True   [   ]

   False [   ]

7   What checks should continuing auditors carry out on opening balances if their report on the previous year's accounts was unqualified?

8   The audit report covers the comparatives as well as the current year figures

   True   [   ]

   False [   ]

Answers to quick quiz

1   Any of:

   - Interim financial information
   - Budgets
   - Management accounts
   - Non-financial information
   - Bank and cash records
   - VAT returns
   - Board minutes
   - Discussions or correspondence with the client at the year end

2   (a)   (c)
     (b)   (f)
     (d)   (g)
     (e)   (h)

3   approximation, amount, precise means

4   Any of

   - Allowances to reduce stock or debtors to their estimated realisable value
   - Depreciation provisions
   - Accrued revenue
   - Provision for a loss from a lawsuit
   - Profits or losses on construction contracts in process
   - Provision to meet warranty claims

5   (a) $\text{Current ratio} = \dfrac{\text{Current assets}}{\text{Current liabilities}}$

     (b) $\text{Acid test ratio} = \dfrac{\text{Current assets (excluding stock)}}{\text{Current liabilities}}$

     (c) $\text{Return on capital employed} = \dfrac{\text{Profit before tax}}{\text{Total assets less current liabilities}}$

6   False

7   Continuing auditors should check opening balances have been appropriately brought forward and the current accounting policies consistently applied.

8   True

Activity checklist

This checklist shows which performance criteria, range statement or knowledge and understanding point is covered by each activity in this chapter. Tick off each activity as you complete it.

Activity

11.1 [ ] This activity deals with Performance Criteria 17.1.G: Select or devise appropriate tests in accordance with the organisation's procedures and 17.2.B: Establish the existence, completeness, ownership, valuation and description of assets and liabilities and gather appropriate evidence to support these findings.

11.2 [ ] This activity deals with Performance Criteria 17.1.E: Identify account balances to be verified and the associated risks and 17.2.C: Identify all matters of an unusual nature and refer them promptly to the audit supervisor.

11.3 [ ] This activity deals with Performance Criteria 17.1.G: Select or devise appropriate tests in accordance with the organisation's procedures.

chapter 12

Stocks

Contents

1   The problem
2   The solution
3   Accounting for stock
4   The stocktake
5   Stock cut-off
6   Valuation of stock

Performance criteria

17.1.G   Select or devise appropriate tests in accordance with organisation's procedures

17.2.A   Conduct tests correctly and as specified in the audit plan, record tests properly and draw valid conclusions from them

17.2.B   Establish the existence, completeness, ownership, valuation and description of assets and liabilities and gather appropriate evidence to support these findings

17.2.C   Identify all matters of an unusual nature and refer them promptly to the audit supervisor

17.2.D   Identify and record material and significant errors, deficiencies or other variations from standard and report them to the audit supervisor

Range statement

17.1   Accounting systems: purchases; sales; stock; expenses; balance sheet items;

17.1   Accounting systems that are: manual; computerised

17.1   Tests: Tests of control; substantive

1 The problem

It is now 2003. Khan Associates are about to start the third audit of AJ (Paper) Ltd.

The audit team is:
Partner	Tariq Hussain
Manager	Sarah Smith
Supervisor	Chen Ping
Senior	Andrew Walker
Assistant	Chantal Bishop

AJ (Paper) Ltd has grown significantly over the last three years. It now manufactures a large range of printed paper and cardboard products, ranging from cartons to ornaments. It has a workforce of 40 employees. It has employed a full-time accountant, Arun Khanna.

Note: From this point on, for the purposes of assignments in this Text, you are Andrew.

Stock causes more problems for auditors than any other audit area. Closing stock appears on both the profit and loss account and balance sheet and often has a material effect on both. Also, stock does not form part of the double entry. It is not possible to find errors in stock as a result of finding errors in other areas. Stock errors can arise for a number of reasons.

Stock often is very portable and easy to steal. Companies face problems controlling stock because stock is often held in a number of different locations or is held by third parties.

If a company sells a large number of different products, then stock will be made up of a large number of **diverse items** with **different unit values**. **Different stock valuation methods** are allowed by the Companies Act and by SSAP 9 *Stocks and long term contracts* although they must be applied consistently.

Stock does get damaged. Some stock may be difficult to sell because fashions change or technology has moved on. The Companies Act requires stock to be written down to its ultimate selling price if that price is below the cost of the stock. However identifying stock which has selling price below cost is a **subjective** process and can prove difficult.

Valuing work in progress can also be **difficult**. Its valuation depends on the state of completion it has reached. This may be quite difficult to gauge. For both stock and work in progress, valuation will include overheads, production overheads and other overheads attributable to bringing the product or service to its present location or condition. Which overheads constitute **overheads attributable** is again a **subjective** decision.

How, then, should auditors audit stock?

2 The solution

The auditors must understand how stock is **accounted for** under the relevant provisions of the Companies Act and SSAP 9.

In order to test **existence** of stock the central audit procedure in auditing stock is **attending the stocktake.** Most companies carry out a stocktake at the year-end and auditors should aim to attend the stocktake. The reason for this is that it can provide evidence of completeness, existence, ownership and valuation (by observing the condition of stock).

Much audit time after the stocktake will be taken up checking the **valuation** of stock. This has several aspects. Partly it involves checking costs to invoices, and it also involves review of the absorption of overheads. Auditors may also have seen at the stocktake stock which appeared to be old or in poor condition, and will follow this up by reviewing post year end sales. General analytical procedures on stock are also important.

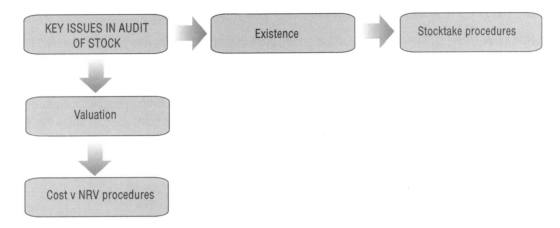

3 Accounting for stock

The rules surrounding the audit of stocks and the related reporting requirements come from three sources:

- Companies Act 1985 (disclosure and basis of valuation)
- SSAP 9 *Stocks and long-term contracts* (disclosure and valuation)
- The auditing standards and guidelines relating to the audit of stock (audit approach and valuation)

3.1 Companies Act 1985

The Companies Act 1985 lays out the format of the balance sheet. The following headings must be used under stock in current assets.

1   Raw materials and consumables
2   Work in progress
3   Finished goods and goods for resale
4   Payments on account

In terms of valuation, the Act states that all current assets should be stated at the lower of their **purchase price** or production cost and their **net realisable value**. 'Purchase price' can be interpreted as 'fair value'. 'Production cost' is determined according to the provision of SSAP 9.

CA 1985 allows certain methods of identifying cost, because it recognises that it is impossible to identify cost for each item individually. The methods allowed are:

- First in first out (FIFO)
- Last in first out (LIFO)
- Weighted average cost
- Other similar methods

SSAP 9 does not allow last in first out (LIFO) as a method of valuation except on rare occasions.

3.2 SSAP 9 *Stocks and long-term contracts*

SSAP 9 states that stocks must be valued at the lower of cost and net realisable value.

Net realisable value (NRV) is the estimated or actual selling price (net of trade discounts but before settlement discounts) less all further costs to completion and all costs to be incurred in marketing, selling and distributing the good or service.

Cost is that expenditure which has been incurred in the normal course of business in bringing the product or service to its present location and condition. This includes the purchase price plus production costs appropriate to the location and condition of the stock.

Production costs (costs of conversion) include:

- Costs specifically attributable to units of production
- Production overheads
- Other overheads attributable to bringing the product or service to its present location and condition

4 The stocktake

RESPONSIBILITIES IN RELATION TO STOCK	
Management	Ensure stock figure in accounts: • Represents stock that exists • Includes all stock owned Ensure accounting records include stocktaking statements
Auditors	Obtain sufficient audit evidence about stock figure from: • Stock records • Stock control systems • Results of stocktaking • Test counts by auditors Attend stocktaking if stock is material and evidence of existence is provided by management stocktake

4.1 Methods of stocktaking

A business may take stock by one or a combination of the following methods.

(a)   Stocktaking at the year-end

From the viewpoint of the auditor, often the best method

(b) **Stocktaking before or after the year-end**

Provides audit evidence of varying reliability depending on:

- The **length of time** between the stocktake and the year-end; the greater the time period, the less the value of the stocktake as audit evidence

- The business's system of **internal controls**

- The **quality of records** of stock movements in the period between the stocktake and the year-end

(c) **Continuous stocktaking** where management has a programme of stock-counting throughout the year

If continuous stocktaking is used, auditors will check that:

(a) Management maintains **adequate stock records** that are kept up-to-date.

(b) The client has **satisfactory procedures** for **stocktaking** and **test-counting**. Auditors should confirm the stocktaking instructions are as rigorous as those for a year-end stock-take. Crucially the auditors should confirm that all stock lines are counted at least once a year.

(c) The client **investigates** and **corrects** all **material differences**.

Auditors should **attend one** of the **stock counts** (to observe and confirm that instructions are being adhered to). They should also **review** the **year's stock counts** to confirm the extent of counting, the treatment of discrepancies and the overall accuracy of records. If matters are not satisfactory, auditors will only be able to gain sufficient assurance by a full count at the year-end.

Evidence of the existence of work-in-progress should be obtained by **attending** a **stocktake**, or **reviewing management controls** over completeness and accuracy of accounting records and inspection of work-in-progress. (These procedures will be required if the nature of work-in-progress means that a stocktake is impractical.)

The auditors need to do this to gain assurance that the stock-checking system as a whole is effective in maintaining accurate stock records from which the amount of stocks in the financial statements can be derived.

4.2 The main stocktaking procedures

PLANNING STOCKTAKE	
Gain knowledge	**Review** previous year's **arrangements**
	Discuss with **management stock-taking arrangements** and **significant changes**
Assess key factors	The **nature and volume** of the **stocks**
	The **identification** of **high value items**
	Method of accounting for stocks
	Location of stock and how it affects stock control and recording
	Internal control and **accounting systems** to identify potential areas of difficulty

PLANNING STOCKTAKE	
Plan procedures	**Ensure** a **representative selection** of **locations, stocks** and **procedures** are covered
	Ensure sufficient attention is given to **high value items**
	Arrange to obtain from **third parties confirmation** of stocks they hold
	Consider the need for **expert help**

REVIEW OF STOCKTAKING INSTRUCTIONS	
Organisation of count	**Supervision** by senior staff including senior staff not normally involved with stock
	Tidying and **marking** stock to help counting
	Restriction and **control** of the production process and stock movements during the count
	Identification of damaged, obsolete, slow-moving, third party and **returnable** stock
Counting	**Systematic counting** to ensure all stock is counted
	Teams of **two counters,** with one counting and the other checking or two **independent counts**
Recording	**Serial numbering, control** and **return** of all stock sheets
	Stock sheets being **completed** in **ink** and **signed**
	Information to be recorded on the **count records** (location and identity, count units, quantity counted, conditions of items, stage reached in production process)
	Recording of **quantity, conditions** and **stage of production** of **work-in-progress**
	Recording of last numbers of **goods inwards** and **outwards** records and of internal transfer records
	Reconciliation with **stock records** and **investigation** and correction of any **differences**

4.2.1 During the stocktaking

Key tasks during the stocktake are as follows.

- **Check** the **client's staff** are following instructions

- **Make test counts** to ensure procedures and internal controls are working properly

- Ensure that the **procedures** for **identifying damaged, obsolete** and **slow-moving** stock operate properly. The auditors should **obtain information** about the stocks' **condition, age, usage** and in the case of work in progress, its **stage of completion**

- Confirm that **stock held** on behalf of **third parties** is separately identified and accounted for

- Ensure that **proper account** is taken of **stock movements** during the stocktake, and noting the last numbers of stock documentation for cut-off purposes (see below)

- Conclude whether the **stocktaking** has been **properly carried out** and is sufficiently reliable as a basis for determining the existence of stocks

- Consider whether any **amendment** is necessary to subsequent **audit procedures**

When carrying out test counts the auditors should select items from the count records and from the physical stocks and check in both directions, to confirm the accuracy of the count records. The auditors should concentrate on high value stock. If the results of the test counts are not satisfactory, the auditors may request stock be recounted.

The auditors should conclude by trying to gain an **overall impression** of the levels and values of stocks held so that they may, in due course, judge whether the figure for stocks appearing in the financial statements is reasonable.

The auditors' working papers should include:

- Details of their **observations** and **tests**

- The manner in which **points** that are **relevant** and **material** to the stocks being counted or measured have been dealt with by the client

- Instances where the **client's procedures** have **not been satisfactorily carried out**

- **Items for subsequent testing**, such as photocopies of rough stocksheets

- **Details** of the **sequence** of **stocksheets**

- The **auditors' conclusions**

4.2.2 After the stocktaking

After the stocktaking, the matters recorded in the auditors' working papers at the time of the count or measurement should be followed up.

Key tests include the following.

- **Trace items** that were **test counted** during the stocktake to final stocksheets

- **Check all count** records have been **included** in final stocksheets

- **Check final stocksheets** are **supported by** count records

- **Ensure** that **continuous stock records** have been **adjusted** to the amounts physically counted or measured, and that differences have been investigated

- **Confirm cut-off** by using details of the last serial number of goods inwards and outwards notes; and of movements during the stocktake (see below)

- **Check replies** from **third parties** about stock held by or for them

- **Confirm** the client's final **valuation** of stock has been calculated correctly

- **Follow up queries** and **notify problems** to management

5 Stock cut-off

Auditors should consider whether management has instituted adequate procedures to ensure that movements into, within and out of stocks are properly identified and reflected in the accounting records in the **correct accounting period**. These are known as 'cut-off' procedures.

Cut-off is most critical to the accurate recording of transactions in a manufacturing enterprise at particular points in the accounting cycle.

- Point of purchase and receipt of goods and services
- Requisitioning of raw materials for production
- Transfer of completed work-in-progress to finished goods stocks
- Sale and despatch of finished goods

Purchase invoices should be recorded as liabilities only if the goods were received prior to the stock count. A schedule of 'goods received not invoiced' should be prepared, and items on the list should be accrued for in the accounts. Sales cut-off is generally more straightforward to achieve correctly than purchases cut-off. Invoices for goods despatched after the stock count should not appear in the profit and loss accounts for the period.

Prior to the stock-take management should make arrangements for cut-off to be properly applied.

(a)   **Appropriate systems of recording** of receipts and despatches of goods should be in place, and also a system for documenting materials requisitions. Goods received notes (GRNs) and goods despatched notes (GDNs) should be sequentially pre-numbered.

(b)   **Final GRN and GDN** and **materials requisition numbers should be noted**. These numbers can then be used to check subsequently that purchases and sales have been recorded in the current period.

(c)   **Arrangements** should be made to ensure that the **cut-off arrangement** for stock held by **third parties** are satisfactory.

There should ideally be no movement of stocks during the stock count. Preferably, receipts and despatches should be suspended for the full period of the count. It may not be practicable to suspend all deliveries, in which case any deliveries which are received during the count should be segregated from other stocks and carefully documented.

Example: Cut off

Zebra Ltd buys its primary raw material from Giraffe Ltd. An order is placed for 20 kilos of the raw material to be delivered on the year end date, 31 March, when a stocktake will be taking place. The delivery (which is one of several to be made by Giraffe's driver in the region where Zebra operates) leaves Giraffe on 30 March. The invoice is put into the post by the accounts department.

At Zebra, the stocktake starts at 6am. The accounts department receives the invoice from Giraffe and processes it. However, the Giraffe driver has had a breakdown and does not make the delivery until 1 April. The invoice total was £50.

The impact of this cut off problem on the accounts of Zebra Ltd can be seen in the following sets of figures:

	Accounts including cut off error		Accounts having been corrected	
	£	£	£	£
Sales		100,000		100,000
Opening stock	1,000		1,000	
Purchases	75,050		75,000	
	76,050		76,000	
Closing stock	1,000		1,000	
Cost of sales		75,050		75,000
Gross profit		24,995		25,000

Profit has been understated because the purchase invoice was processed in March (that is, before the year end date) even though the goods were not received until after the year end. In the second set of figures, the invoice has been **excluded from purchases** because although the invoice had been received, the **goods had not been received**, so the **liability is not recognised**.

You should note that this shows a **lack of control** in the accounts department, who should have matched the invoice to the delivery note before processing it.

5.1 Audit procedures on cut-off

At the stocktake the auditors should carry out the following procedures.

- **Record all movement notes** relating to the period, including:

  - All interdepartmental requisition numbers
  - The last goods received notes(s) and despatch note(s) prior to the count
  - The first goods received notes(s) and despatch note(s) after the count

- **Observe** whether correct cut-off procedures are being followed in the despatch and receiving areas

- **Discuss procedures** with company staff performing the count to ensure they are understood

- **Ensure** that **no goods finished** on the day of the count are **transferred** to the warehouse

During the final audit, the auditors will use the cut-off information from the stocktake to perform the following tests.

- **Match up** the last **goods received notes** with **purchase invoices** and ensure the **liability** has been **recorded** in the **correct period** (Only goods received before the year end should be recorded as purchases)

- **Match up** the last **goods despatched notes** to **sales invoices** and ensure the **income** has been **recorded** in the **correct period** (Only stocks despatched before the year-end should be recorded as sales)

- **Match up** the **requisition notes** to the **work in progress** details for the receiving department to ensure correctly recorded

6 Valuation of stock

Auditors must understand how the company determines the cost of an item for stock valuation purposes. Cost, for this purpose, should include an appropriate proportion of overheads, in accordance with SSAP 9. There are several ways of determining cost. Auditors must ensure that the company is **applying** the method **consistently** and that each year the method used **gives** a **fair approximation** to cost. They may need to support this by additional procedures.

- Reviewing price changes near the year-end
- Ageing the stock held
- Checking gross profit margins to reliable management accounts

The auditors should check that the correct prices have been used to value **raw materials** and **bought in components** valued at actual costs, by **referring** to **suppliers' invoices**. Reference to suppliers' invoices will also provide the auditors with assurance as regards ownership.

If standard costs are used, auditors should **check** the **basis** of the **standards, compare standard costs** with **actual costs** and **confirm** that **variances** are being **accounted for appropriately**.

For work in progress and finished goods, as we saw above, SSAP 9 defines 'cost' as comprising the cost of purchase plus the costs of conversion (production costs). The costs of conversion comprise:

- Costs **specifically attributable** to units of production
- Production overheads
- Other overheads attributable to bringing the product or service to its present location and condition

6.1 Audit procedures

The audit procedures will depend on the methods used by the client to value work in progress and finished goods, and on the adequacy of the system of internal control.

6.1.1 Reasonableness tests

The auditors should consider what tests they can carry out to check the reasonableness of the valuation of finished goods and work in progress. **Analytical procedures** may assist comparisons being made with stock items and stock categories from the previous year's stock summaries. A **reasonableness check** will also provide the auditors with **assurance** regarding **completeness**.

6.1.2 Costs attributable to production

The auditors should carry out the following tests.

- For materials:

  ○ Check costs being used to invoices and price lists

  ○ Confirm appropriate basis of valuation (for example, FIFO) is being used

        ○   Confirm correct quantities are being used when calculating raw material value in work in progress and finished goods

- For labour costs:
  - ○   Check labour costs to wage records
  - ○   Check labour hours to time summaries and production reports
  - ○   Review standard labour costs in the light of actual costs and production

6.1.3 Overhead allocation

The auditors should ensure that the client includes a proportion of overheads **appropriate** to **bringing** the **stock** to its **present location** and **condition**. The basis of overhead allocation should be **consistent** with **prior years** and **calculated** on the **normal level** of **production activity**.

This means that overheads arising from **reduced levels** of **activity, idle time** or **inefficient production should be written off** to the profit and loss account, rather than being included in stock.

In an appendix to SSAP 9 there is general guidance on the allocation of overheads which the auditors should follow. SSAP 9 comments that auditors should note that overheads are **classified by function** when being allocated (for example, whether they are a function of production, marketing, selling or administration).

(a)   All **abnormal conversion** costs (such as idle capacity) must be **excluded**.

(b)   Where **firm sales contracts** have been entered into for the provision of goods or services to customer's specification, **design, marketing and selling costs** incurred before manufacture may be **included**.

(c)   The costs of **general management**, as distinct from functional management, are not directly related to current production and are, therefore, **excluded**.

(d)   The allocation of costs of **central service departments** should depend on the function or functions that the department is serving. **Only** those costs that can reasonably be allocated to the **production function** should be **included**.

(e)   In determining what constitutes **'normal' activity,** a number of factors need to be considered:

- The volume of production which the production facilities are designed to achieve
- The budgeted level of activity for the year under review and for the ensuing year
- The level of activity achieved both in the year under review and in previous years

Although temporary changes in the load of activity may be ignored, persistent variation should lead to revision of the previous norm.

Difficulty may be experienced if the client operates a system of total overhead absorption. It will be necessary for those overheads that are of a general, non-productive nature to be identified and excluded from the stock valuation.

6.1.4 Cost vs Net Realisable Value

Auditors should **compare cost and net realisable value** for each item of stock of all types – raw materials, work in progress and finished goods. Where this is impracticable, the comparison may be done by stock group or category.

Net realisable value is likely to be less than cost when there has been:

- An **increase in costs** or a fall in selling price
- Physical deterioration of stocks
- Obsolescence of products due for example to changes in technology
- A decision as part of a company's marketing strategy to sell products at a loss
- Errors in production or purchasing

The following audit tests are important.

- Review and test the client's system for identifying slow-moving, obsolete or damaged stock

- Follow up any such items that were identified at the stocktaking, ensuring that the client has made adequate provision to write down the items to net realisable value

- Examine stock records to identify slow-moving items; it may be possible to incorporate into a computer audit program certain tests and checks such as listing items whose value or quantity has not moved over the previous year

- Examine the prices at which finished goods have been sold after the year-end and ascertain whether any finished goods items need to be reduced below cost

- Review quantities of goods sold after the year end to determine that year end stock has been, or will be, realised

- If significant quantities of finished goods stock remain unsold for an unusual time after the year-end, consider the need to make appropriate provision

For work in progress, the **ultimate selling price** should be **compared** with the **carrying value** at the year end plus **costs to be incurred** after the year end to bring work in progress to a finished state.

Example: stock valuation

Sunflower Ltd has made the following purchases of the component X.

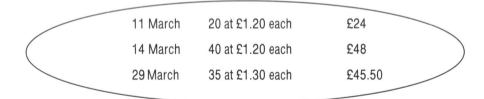

11 March	20 at £1.20 each	£24
14 March	40 at £1.20 each	£48
29 March	35 at £1.30 each	£45.50

Prior to these purchases, Sunflower had not had any X in stock.

During March, 55 Xs were used in production. Of that production, 5 Ys containing ½ an X each are left in stock at the year end date, 31 March. Sunflower values its stock using FIFO, having been told by its auditors in a previous audit that LIFO was an unacceptable basis under SSAP 9.

Value of Xs in raw materials at 31 March

The goods remaining in stock at 31 March are:

95 units purchased less 55 units used = 40 units

  35 at £1.30 (being the last in)
  5 at £1.20 (being the next most recent in)

  40 units = £51.50

The auditors would then vouch this stock valuation by obtaining a copy of the stock history (circled above) and then tracing the last two entries to the purchase invoices to confirm the cost value. They would then ensure that the cost price was attributed to this element of finished goods:

Value of Xs in finished goods at 31 March

5 Ys (which use Xs in production) are in stock. They contain ½ an X each. As the final 40 units have been designated raw materials, the Xs used in this finished goods must (by applying the same rule of FIFO) be valued at £1.20 each, or £0.60 per Y.

The auditors would vouch this by obtaining a breakdown of the stock cost of a Y and ensuring that the cost attributed to a X was 60p. They would not need to trace this to a purchase invoice, as this has been done above. They would also verify any other costs allocated to a Y, for example, labour costs or overheads.

Lastly, they would ensure that if the stock is valued at cost, the NRV of a Y is higher than that cost. This would be done by checking to any after year end date sales of Ys (sales invoice) or a price list or catalogue, if no sales had been made. If no sales had been made, the auditors should check that there were fair reasons for no sales having been made, or whether the stock is obsolete and should be written down in the accounts.

Goods valued at LIFO

SSAP 9 does not permit goods to be valued using LIFO. In a skills based assessment you could be given a stock history, the value attributed to a stock line in the financial statements and some purchase invoices and asked to audit stock. If the goods were valued using LIFO, you would have to observe that this valuation was incorrect, and might have to quantify the error.

In this example, if the goods had been valued at LIFO, the figures would have been:

40 units in stock at 31 March:

  20 at £1.20 (11 March delivery)
  20 at £1.20 (14 March delivery)

  40 units = £48

Raw material stock would have been understated by £3.50.

The 2½ Xs valued as part of Ys in finished goods would be at the correct value by chance, because the five next units would still have come out of the 14 March delivery. If the stock movements were more complex, this valuation might also have been wrong.

Activity 12.1

Chantal has never attended a stocktake before and is uncertain about what to do.

For Chantal's benefit list what she should do before attending the stocktake and during the stocktake, and summarise the problems she might face.

Anton has provided you with a summary of the stock-taking instructions for the year-end, which is given below. Discuss the strengths and weaknesses of these instructions and indicate the improvements that could be made.

STOCK-TAKING INSTRUCTIONS

(a) Arun Khanna, chief accountant, has overall responsibility for the stock count but he is to be assisted by Mr Wells, the storeman, to whom the stocktaking teams are to report, and who will be responsible for the detailed organisation on the count.

(b) Five stock count teams are to carry out the actual count, each team to be responsible for a predetermined section of the warehouse. Each team comprises 2 persons, one from the accounting department and the other from the warehouse.

(c) Each stock count team is to meet Mr Wells at 07.30 hours on 29 December 2002 and will be provided with pre-numbered and pre-printed stock sheets for the section of the warehouse.

(d) During the count both members of the stock count team are to count the stock independently of each other. In the event of differences arising between stock counted and the quantity shown on the stock sheets, the quantity counted is to be entered alongside the original quantity and must be initialled by the senior member of the count team.

(e) Each stock count sheet is to be signed by the senior member of the count team and the bin or rack cards held in the warehouse are to be adjusted, if necessary, to actual quantities counted. All cards are to be initialled to show that the count has been made.

(f) Any goods that appear to be in poor condition are to be deducted from the quantity appearing on the stock sheets, such action again to be supported by initials of the senior member of the count team.

(g) Any queries during the count are to be referred to Mr Wells to whom stock sheets are to be returned at the conclusion of the count. Mr Wells is responsible for ensuring that all stock count sheets have been returned and for forwarding them to Mr Khanna for valuation.

Key learning points

☑ The audit of stocks and work in progress is difficult and time consuming, because of problems of control over stock (affecting existence and cut-off) and problems over valuation.

☑ The valuation and disclosure rules for stock are laid down in SSAP 9 and CA 1985.

☑ Stocktake procedures are vital as they provide evidence which cannot be obtained elsewhere or at any other time about the quantities and conditions of stocks and work in progress.

    – Before the stocktake auditors should ensure audit **coverage** of **stock-taking** is **appropriate**, and that the client's **stock-taking instructions** have been reviewed.

    – During the stocktake the auditors should check the stock count is being carried out according to instructions, carry out test counts, and watch for third party, slow moving stock, cut-off problems.

    – After the stocktake the auditors should check that final stock sheets have been properly compiled from stock count records and that book stock records have been appropriately adjusted.

☑ Auditors should check cut-off by noting the serial numbers of items received and despatched just before and after the year-end, and subsequently checking that they have been included in the correct period.

☑ Auditing the valuation of stock includes:

    – Checking the allocation of overheads is appropriate
    – Confirming stock is carried at the lower of cost and net realisable value

Quick quiz

1   Under what headings does the Companies Act 1985 require stock to be classified?

2   What methods of identifying cost of stock does the Companies Act allow to be used? Which method is not allowed by SSAP 9?

3   Complete the definition, using the words given below.

.... is defined by SSAP ...... as that expenditure which has been incurred in the ....
.... in bringing the product or service to its present location and condition. This includes the .... plus .... (costs of conversion) appropriate to bringing the .... to its present location and condition.

normal course of business, purchase price, production cost, cost, 9, stock

4   Name three methods of stocktaking

     1   ....

     2   ....

     3   ....

5   When should the following stocktaking tests take place?

     (a)   Check client staff are following instructions
     (b)   Review previous year's stocktaking arrangements
     (c)   Assess method of accounting for stocks
     (d)   Trace counted items to final stock sheets
     (e)   Check replies from third parties about stock held for them
     (f)   Conclude as to whether stocktake has been properly carried out
     (g)   Gain an overall impression of levels and values of stocks
     (h)   Consider the need for expert help

BEFORE	DURING	AFTER

6   Name four points in the accounting cycle when cut off is critical.

     1   ....

     2   ....

     3   ....

     4   ....

7   Give four occasions when the net realisable value of stock is likely to fall below cost.

     1   ....

     2   ....

     3   ....

     4   ....

Answers to quick quiz

1   Companies Act 1985 prescribes the following headings.

    •   Raw materials and consumables
    •   Work in progress
    •   Finished goods and goods for resale
    •   Payments on account

2   Companies Act 1985 allows the following methods of stock valuation to be used.

    •   First in first out (FIFO)
    •   Last in first out (LIFO) (not allowed by SSAP 9)
    •   Weighted average cost
    •   Other similar methods

3   cost, 9, normal course of business, purchase price, production cost, stock

4   •   Year end
    •   Pre/post year end
    •   Continuous

5   (a)   DURING   (b)   BEFORE   (c)   BEFORE   (d)   AFTER
    (e)   AFTER   (f)   DURING   (g)   DURING   (h)   BEFORE

6   •   The point of purchase and receipt of goods
    •   The requisitioning of raw materials for production
    •   The transfer of WIP to finished goods
    •   The sale and despatch of finished goods

7   Any of:

    •   An increase in costs or a fall in selling price
    •   Physical deterioration of stocks
    •   Obsolescence of products
    •   A decision as part of a marketing strategy to manufacture and sell at a loss
    •   Errors in production or purchasing

Activity checklist

This checklist shows which performance criteria, range statement or knowledge and understanding point is covered by each activity in this chapter. Tick off each activity as you complete it.

Activity

12.1

This activity deals with Performance Criteria 17.1.G Select or devise appropriate tests in accordance with organisation's procedures, 17.2.A: Conduct tests correctly and as specified in the audit plan, record tests properly and draw valid conclusions from them, 17.2.B: Establish the existence, completeness, ownership, valuation and description of assets and liabilities and gather appropriate evidence to support these findings, 17.2.C: Identify all matters of an unusual nature and refer them promptly to the audit supervisor and 17.2.D: Identify and record material and significant errors, deficiencies or other variations from standard and report them to the audit supervisor.

chapter 13

Fixed assets

Contents

1 The problem
2 The solution
3 Tangible fixed assets
4 Intangible fixed assets
5 Investments

Performance criteria

17.1.G Select or devise appropriate tests in accordance with organisation's procedures

17.2.A Conduct tests correctly and as specified in the audit plan, record tests properly and draw valid conclusions from them

17.2.B Establish the existence, completeness, ownership, valuation and description of assets and liabilities and gather appropriate evidence to support these findings

17.2.C Identify all matters of an unusual nature and refer them promptly to the audit supervisor

17.2.D Identify and record material and significant errors, deficiencies or other variations from standard and report them to the audit supervisor

Range statement

17.1 Accounting systems: purchases; sales; stock; expenses; balance sheet items

17.1 Accounting systems that are: manual; computerised

17.1/2 Tests: tests of control; substantive

1 The problem

Chantal has been allocated the audit of fixed assets, as it is generally a low risk audit area. Fixed assets break down into three areas, intangibles, tangibles and investments.

How should all these assets be audited?

2 The solution

Tangible fixed assets, such as land and buildings, plant and machinery and motor vehicles will be the major items that many companies own, and hence the figure for tangible fixed assets is likely to be very material in the accounts. That said, the major tangible fixed assets tend to be few in number, so that not many items have to be tested in order to gain assurance about a large proportion of the amount shown.

Assertions of particular significance for tangible fixed assets are **rights and obligations** (that is, ownership), **existence and valuation**. Different tests will be needed on ownership and existence. Although ownership may be verified by inspecting appropriate documentation (for example land deeds or vehicle registration documents) those documents do not guarantee that the asset still exists. Physical inspection of the asset may be required to prove existence.

Valuation is the other important assertion generally. The auditors will concentrate on **testing** any **valuations** made **during the year**, and also whether asset values appear reasonable given asset usage and condition. A very important aspect of testing valuation is **reviewing depreciation rates**. Auditors should check that the rates used appear reasonable and are consistently applied from year to year.

Fewer companies have **intangible fixed assets**. These include patents, trademarks, goodwill and research and development. Many are capitalised because of **expectations** management has about the **future income** they will yield, so auditors will need to consider whether those **expectations** appear to be **reasonable**. There are specific accounting standards on research and development and goodwill, so auditors will need to confirm that the requirements of these standards have been followed.

Gaining sufficient assurance concerning the client's **ownership** of investments can be a particular problem.

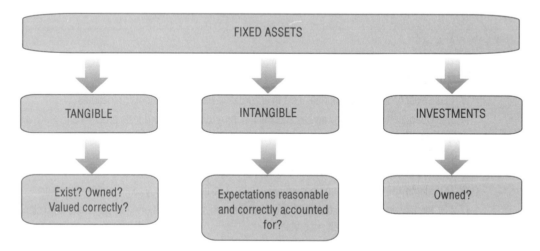

3 Tangible fixed assets

As we have seen, a key element of a good internal control system is a **fixed asset register**, which should help identify assets. In any event auditors should record movements in fixed assets in their working papers. Auditors should also ensure that the company has good controls over substantial asset expenditure and disposals.

3.1 Summary of audit procedures

3.1.1 Completeness

- **Obtain** or **prepare** a **summary** of tangible fixed assets showing:

  - Gross book value
  - Accumulated depreciation
  - Net book value

  and reconcile with the opening position

- Compare fixed assets in the general ledger with the fixed assets register and obtain explanations for differences

- Check whether assets which physically exist are recorded in the fixed asset register

- If a fixed asset register is not kept, obtain a schedule showing the original cost and present depreciated value of major fixed assets

- Reconcile the schedule of fixed assets with the general ledger

3.1.2 Existence

- **Confirm** that the **company physically inspects** all items in the fixed asset register each year

- **Inspect assets,** concentrating on high value items and additions in year. Confirm items inspected:

  - Exist
  - Are in use
  - Are in good condition

- Review records of income yielding assets to see whether all income has been received

- Reconcile opening and closing vehicles by numbers as well as amounts

3.1.3 Valuation

- **Verify valuation** to valuation certificate

- **Consider reasonableness** of **valuation**, reviewing:

  - Experience of valuer
  - Scope of work
  - Methods and assumption used

- Check revaluation surplus has been correctly calculated

- Consider whether permanent diminution in value of assets has occurred

3.1.4 Ownership

- **Verify title** to land and buildings by inspection of:

  ○   Title deeds
  ○   Land registry certificates
  ○   Leases

- Obtain a certificate from solicitors/bankers:

  ○   **Stating purpose** for which the deeds are being held (custody only)
  ○   **Stating deeds** are **free** from **mortgage** or **lien**

- Inspect registration documents for vehicles held

- Confirm all vehicles used for the client's business

- Examine documents of title for other assets (including purchase invoices, architects' certificates, contracts, hire purchase or lease agreements)

3.1.5 Additions (to confirm rights and obligations, valuation and completeness)

- **Verify purchase price of additions** by inspection of architects' certificates, solicitors' completion statements, suppliers' invoices etc.

- **Check capitalisation** of **expenditure** is correct by considering for fixed assets additions and items in relevant expense categories (repairs, motor expenses, sundry expenses) whether:

  ○   Capital/revenue distinction correctly drawn
  ○   Capitalisation in line with consistently applied company policy

- Check **purchases** have been **properly allocated** to correct fixed asset accounts

- Check **purchases** have been **authorised** by directors/senior management

- **Ensure** that appropriate **claims** have been made for **grants**, and grants received and receivable have been received

- **Check additions** have been **recorded** in fixed asset register and general ledger

3.1.6 Self-constructed assets

- **Verify material** and **labour** costs and **overheads** to invoices and wage records.
- **Ensure expenditure** has been **analysed correctly** and **properly charged** to capital
- **Check no profit element** has been included in costs

3.1.7 Disposals (to confirm rights and obligations, valuation and completeness)

- **Verify disposals** with supporting documentation, checking transfer of title, sales price and dates of completion and payment

- **Check calculation** of profit or loss

- **Check** that **disposals** have been **authorised**

- **Consider** whether **proceeds** are **reasonable**

- If the property was **used as security**, ensure **release from security** has been correctly made

- For **significant disposals**, consider impact upon other areas of business and whether disposal should be disclosed under FRS 3

3.1.8 Depreciation

- Review depreciation rates applied in relation to:

  ◦ Asset lives
  ◦ Replacement policy
  ◦ Past experience of gains and losses on disposal
  ◦ Consistency with prior years and accounting policy
  ◦ Possible obsolescence

- Check **depreciation** has been **charged on all assets** with a limited useful life

- For **revalued assets**, ensure that the charge for **depreciation** is **based** on the **revalued amount**

- **Check calculation** of depreciation rates

- **Compare ratios** of depreciation to fixed assets (by category) with:

  ◦ Previous years
  ◦ Depreciation policy rates

- Ensure no further depreciation provided on fully depreciated assets

- Check that depreciation policies and rates are disclosed in the accounts

3.1.9 Charges and commitments

- **Review for evidence** of charges in statutory books and by company search

- **Review leases** of leasehold properties to ensure that company has fulfilled covenants set out in the leases

- **Examine invoices received after year-end, orders and minutes** for evidence of capital commitments

213

3.1.10 Insurance

- **Review insurance policies** in force for all categories of tangible fixed assets and consider the adequacy of their insured values and check expiry dates

Activity 13.1

Chantal will be carrying out the audit of fixed assets, using the schedule of fixed assets additions which the client has provided below.

Describe the audit tests she should carry out:

(a) To confirm existence, ownership and valuation of the printer, the leased van and leased lacing machine.

(b) To confirm whether the cost of the training course should be treated as capital or revenue expenditure. Describe what should happen if you decide that the training course should be treated as revenue expenditure.

(c) To test the depreciation charge of £15,000 on motor vehicles.

SUMMARY OF FIXED ASSET ADDITIONS

	£000	*How acquired*
Printer	17	purchased
Lacing machine	8	leased
Overhaul of stores shelving	12	purchased
New van	12	leased
Signwriting	1	purchased
Training course for workshop technician	2	purchased
New doors for shop	3	purchased

The leasing creditors are included in the trade creditor balances.

Activity 13.2

Chantal has encountered the following problems during the audit of fixed assets.

(a) Anton has stated that the motor vehicles she wished to inspect cannot be inspected, as they are all being driven by salesmen who are not due to return to office until after the accounts are signed.

(b) A large machine, previously written off by the client has been brought back into use at a valuation of £10,000 because of problems with its replacements. The £10,000 has been included as a re-valuation in this year's accounts.

Outline the audit work that should be carried out in the light of the problems found.

4 Intangible fixed assets

The types of asset we are likely to encounter under this heading include patents, licences, trade marks, development costs and goodwill. All intangibles have a finite economic life and should hence be amortised.

4.1 Tests on intangible assets

4.1.1 General

- **Prepare analysis** of movements on cost and amortisation accounts

4.1.2 Ownership

- Obtain confirmation of all patents and trademarks held by a patent agent
- Verify payment of annual renewal fees

4.1.3 Valuation

- **Review specialist valuations** of intangible assets, considering:

    ◦ Qualifications of valuer
    ◦ Scope of work
    ◦ Assumptions and methods used

- **Confirm carried down balances** represent **continuing value**, which are proper charges to future operations.

4.1.4 Additions

- **Inspect purchase agreements**, **assignments** and **supporting documentation** for purchase prices of intangible assets acquired in period
- **Confirm purchases** have been **authorised**
- **Verify amounts capitalised** of patents developed by the company with supporting costing records

4.1.5 Amortisation

- Review amortisation

    ◦ Check computation
    ◦ Confirm that rates used are reasonable

4.1.6 Income from intangibles

- **Review sales returns** and **statistics** to verify the reasonableness of income derived from patents, trademarks and licences.

- **Examine audited accounts** of third party sales covered by a patent, licence or trademark owned by the company

4.2 Goodwill

Key tests are as follows.

- Agree consideration to a sales agreement

- Confirm valuation of assets acquired is reasonable

- Check purchased goodwill is calculated correctly (it should reflect the difference between the fair value of the consideration given and the aggregate of the fair values of the separable net assets acquired)

- Check goodwill does not include non-purchased goodwill

- Review amortisation

  - Test calculation
  - Assess whether amortisation rates are reasonable

- **Ensure valuation** of **goodwill** is **reasonable** by reviewing prior year's accounts and discussion with the directors

4.3 Development costs

The key audit tests largely reflect the criteria laid down in SSAP 13.

- Check accounting records to confirm:

  - **Project** is **clearly defined** (separate cost centre or nominal ledger codes)
  - **Related expenditure** can be **separately identified**, and certified to invoices, timesheets

- Confirm feasibility and viability

  - Examine market research reports, feasibility studies, budgets and forecasts
  - Consult client's technical experts

- **Review budgeted revenues** and **costs** by examining results to date, production forecasts, advance orders and discussion with directors

- **Review calculations** of **future cash flows** to ensure resources exist to complete the project

- **Review previously deferred expenditure** to ensure SSAP 13 criteria are still justified

- **Check amortisation:**
  - ○ Commences with production
  - ○ Charged on a systematic basis

The good news for the auditors in this audit area is that many companies adopt a prudent approach and write off research and development expenditure in the year it is incurred. The auditors' concern in these circumstances is whether the profit and loss account charge for research and development is complete, accurate and valid.

5 Investments

This section applies to companies where dealing in investments is secondary to the main objectives of the company. Under the general heading of 'investments' four distinct items are considered.

- Investment properties (not covered here)
- Investments in companies, whether listed or unlisted, fixed interest or equity
- Income arising from the investments
- Investment in subsidiary and associated companies

(Note. The following comments apply equally to investments treated as fixed or current.)

The key controls over investments are:

(a) **Authorisation** over investment dealing. Authorisation from high level management should be required.

(b) Segregation of duties:

- The recording and custody roles should be kept separate.

- As investments may be misappropriated by being pledged as collateral, those responsible for custody should not have access to cash.

5.1 Existence and rights and obligations

Stockbrokers should not normally be entrusted with the safe custody of share certificates on a continuing basis since they have ready access to the Stock Exchange.

Auditors should not therefore rely on a certificate from a broker stating that he holds the company's securities. If securities are being transferred over the year-end the auditors should nevertheless obtain a broker's certificate but the transaction should be further verified by examining contract notes, and in the case of purchases, examination of the title documents after the year-end.

5.1.1 Substantive tests

- **Examine certificates** of **title** to investments listed in investment records and confirm that they are:
  - ○ Bona fide complete title documents
  - ○ In the client's name
  - ○ Free from any charge

- Examine confirmation from third party investment custodians (such as banks) and check:
  - Investments are in client's name
  - Investments are free from charge or lien
- **Inspect certificates** of **title** which are held by third parties who are not bona fide custodians
- **Inspect blank transfers** and **letters of trust** to confirm client owns shares in name of nominee
- **Review minutes** and **other statutory books** for evidence of charging and pledging

5.2 Additions and disposals

5.2.1 Additions

- **Verify purchase prices** to agreements, contract notes and correspondence
- **Confirm purchases** were **authorised**
- **Check** with Stubbs, Extel or appropriate financial statements that all **reported capital changes** (bonus or rights issues) have been correctly **accounted for** during the period

5.2.2 Disposals of investments

- **Verify disposals** with contract notes, sales agreements or correspondence.
- **Check** whether investment **disposals** have been **authorised**
- **Confirm** that **profit** or **loss** on sale of investments has been **correctly calculated** taking account of:
  - Bonus issue of shares
  - Consistent basis of identifying cost of investment sold
  - Rights issues
  - Accrued interest
  - Taxation

5.3 Valuation

The auditors should establish that the company's policy on valuing investments has been correctly applied and is consistent with previous years, for example cost or market value.

5.3.1 Substantive tests

- **Confirm** the **value** of **listed investments** by reference to the Stock Exchange Daily Lists or the quotations published in the *Financial Times* or *Times*. (The middle market value should be used.)
- Review accounts of unlisted investments and:
  - Check the **basis on** which the **shares** are **valued** (expert help may be required)
  - **Ensure** that the **valuation** of the investment is **reasonable**

- **Check** that **no substantial fall** in the value of the investments has taken place since the balance sheet date

- **Consider** whether there are any **restrictions** on **remittance** of **income** and ensure these are properly disclosed

- **Check** whether **current asset investments** are included at the **lower of cost** or **net realisable value**

5.4 Investment income

The basis of recognising investment income may vary from company to company particularly for dividends, for example:

- Credit taken only when received (cash basis)
- Credit taken when declared
- Credit taken after ratification of the dividend by the shareholders in general meeting

A consistent basis must be applied from year to year.

5.4.1 Substantive tests

- **Check** that all **income** due has been **received**, by reference to Stubbs or Extel cards for listed investments, and financial statements for unlisted investments

- **Review investment income** account for **irregular** or unusual **entries**, or those not apparently pertaining to investments held (particular attention should be paid to investments bought and sold during the year)

- **Ensure** that the **basis** of **recognising** income is **consistent** with previous years

- **Compare investment income** with **prior years** and **explain** any **significant fluctuations**

- **Consider whether** there are likely to be any **restrictions** on **realisation** of the investment or remittance of any income due (especially for investments abroad) and ensure these are properly disclosed in the financial statements

If the client is a charity or pension scheme, auditors should check that tax deducted at source has been reclaimed from the Inland Revenue.

5.5 General tests

Other tests that are likely to be carried out include the following.

- **Obtain** or prepare a **statement** to be placed on the current file **reconciling the book value** of listed and unlisted investments at the last balance sheet date and the current balance sheet date (tests completeness)

- **Ensure** that the **investments** are **properly disclosed and categorised** in the financial statements into listed and unlisted

Key learning points

☑ The disclosure and valuation requirements for all fixed assets under CA 1985 are relevant here.

☑ Key areas when testing tangible fixed assets are:

- Confirmation of ownership
- Inspection of fixed assets to confirm existence
- Valuation by third parties
- Adequacy of depreciation rates

☑ Intangible assets may cause audit problems in the areas of:

- Capitalisation (whether the assets should be capitalised)
- Amortisation

☑ Investments (if quoted) should be valued at mid-market price at the balance sheet date.

☑ Auditors may need to inspect share certificates to confirm ownership.

Quick quiz

1   Complete the control procedures.

    (a)   Acquisitions are properly ....

    (b)   Disposals are .... and proceeds ....

    (c)   Security .... over fixed assets are ....

    (d)   .... is reviewed ....

2   Complete the table, showing which tests are designed to provide evidence about which financial statement assertion.

Completeness	Existence
Valuation	Rights and obligations

(a)	Inspect assets	(e)	Review depreciation rates
(b)	Verify to valuation certificate	(f)	Verify material on self-constructed asset to invoices
(c)	Refer to title deeds	(g)	Examine invoices after the year end
(d)	Compare assets in ledger to fixed asset register	(h)	Review repairs in general ledger

3   Name two tests to confirm rights and obligations concerning charges and commitments.

    1   ....

    2   ....

4   How should auditors test income from intangible assets?

5   In what circumstances can development expenditure be deferred under SSAP 13?

6   How would an auditor test whether the valuation of listed investments is reasonable?

Answers to quick quiz

1   (a)   authorised
    (b)   authorised, accounted for
    (c)   arrangements, sufficient
    (d)   depreciation, every year

2

Completeness		Existence	
(d) Compare assets in ledger to register		(a) Inspect assets	
(h) Review repairs in general ledger			
Valuation		**Rights and obligations**	
(b) Verify to valuation certificate		(c) Refer to title deeds	
(e) Review depreciation rates		(g) Examine invoices after the year end	
(f) Verify material on self-constructed assets to invoice			

3   Two of:

   • Review for evidence of charges in statutory books and by company search
   • Review leases of leasehold properties to ensure the company has fulfilled covenants
   • Examine invoices received after year end, orders and minutes for capital commitments

4   Auditors should test income from intangible fixed assets by reviewing sales returns and statistics to verify the reasonableness of income. They should also examine audited accounts of third party sales, when the third parties are operating under a patent, licence or trademark owned by the company.

5   Development expenditure can be deferred and carried as an intangible fixed asset when:

   (a)   There is a clearly defined project.

   (b)   The expenditure on the project is separately identifiable.

   (c)   The outcome of the project has been assessed with reasonable certainty. Consider:

      • Its technical feasibility
      • Its ultimate commercial viability
      • Its costs being more than covered by future revenues

   (d)   Adequate resources will be available to complete the project.

6   The valuation of listed investments should be confirmed by referring to the Stock Exchange Daily Lists, or the quotations published in the *Financial Times* or *Times*.

Activity checklist

This checklist shows which performance criteria, range statement or knowledge and understanding point is covered by each activity in this chapter. Tick off each activity as you complete it.

Activity

13.1   ☐   This activity deals with performance criteria 17.1.G: Select and devise appropriate tests in accordance with the organisation's procedures.

13.2   ☐   This activity deals with Performance Criteria 17.1.G: Select or devise appropriate tests in accordance with organisation's procedures, 17.2.A: Conduct tests correctly and as specified in the audit plan, record tests properly and draw valid conclusions from them, 17.2.B: Establish the existence, completeness, ownership, valuation and description of assets and liabilities and gather appropriate evidence to support these findings, 17.2.C: Identify all matters of an unusual nature and refer them promptly to the audit supervisor and 17.2.D: Identify and record material and significant errors, deficiencies or other variations from standard and report them to the audit supervisor.

chapter 14

Debtors and cash

Contents

1   The problem
2   The solution
3   Debtors
4   Bad debts
5   Sales
6   Bank
7   Cash

Performance criteria

17.1.G Select or devise appropriate tests in accordance with organisation's procedures

17.2.A Conduct tests correctly and as specified in the audit plan, record tests properly and draw valid conclusions from them

17.2.B Establish the existence, completeness, ownership, valuation and description of assets and liabilities and gather appropriate evidence to support these findings

17.2.C Identify all matters of an unusual nature and refer them promptly to the audit supervisor

17.2.D Identify and record material and significant errors, deficiencies or other variations from standard and report them to the audit supervisor

Range statement

17.1   Accounting systems: purchases; sales; stock; expenses; balance sheet items

17.1   Accounting systems that are: manual; computerised

17.1   Tests: tests of control; substantive

1 The problem

How should the other assets on the balance sheet be audited?

2 The solution

With debtors, auditors are primarily concerned to prove that:

- Debtors represent **amounts** due to the company (the assertions of existence and rights and obligations).
- **Adequate provision** has been made for bad debts, discounts and returns (valuation).
- **Cut-off of goods** despatched and invoiced is satisfactory (measurement, rights and obligations).

The primary procedure for obtaining evidence of the correctness of rights and obligations of debtor balances is the **debtors' circularisation**, asking debtors for confirmation of balances owed. Satisfactory responses to the circularisation are strong audit evidence, as they are **written evidence** from **third parties**. You need to know the specific procedures auditors follow when carrying out a circularisation. Inevitably auditors will not always obtain exact confirmation from all of the debtors circularised, and you should be aware of what auditors do in those circumstances.

Although debtors may agree that they owe the amount stated in the client's books, that does not mean that they will pay that amount. Therefore auditors will also need to carry out tests to confirm the **valuation** of debtors and the **adequacy** of **bad debt provisions**. Provision for bad debts may be made against specific debts. Alternatively there may be a general provision, say X% of trade debtors, or X% of all overdue debts.

Finally **cut-off** will need to be tested. Most often this will be done along with testing of stock and purchases cut-off. The main concern of auditors when testing sales will be that sales have been **completely** recorded.

The other major current asset is **cash at bank** and in hand. Cash at bank will be confirmed by obtaining confirmation in the form of a **bank letter** from the clients' bank(s) of balances held at the year-end. Auditors will then check that the balances shown in the bank letter can be reconciled to the balances shown in the client's records by carrying out a bank reconciliation or checking the reconciliation that the client has prepared.

Cash in hand can be confirmed by a **cash count**. Cash counts are not carried out on many audits since cash balances held as floats are small. However you need to know the procedures involved, because cash counts may be necessary when the amount of cash passing through a business is large (retail operations, for example), or a cash count is performed to test controls over cash as well as to substantiate the balances held.

3 Debtors

Much of the auditors' detailed work will be based on a selection of debtors' balances chosen from a listing of sales ledger balances, prepared by the client or auditors.

Ideally the list should be aged, showing the period or periods of time money has been owed. The following substantive procedures are necessary to check the **completeness** and **accuracy** of a client-prepared list.

- Check the balances from the individual sales ledger accounts to the list of balances and vice versa
- Check the total of the list to the sales ledger control account
- Add up the list of balances and the sales ledger control account
- Confirm whether list of balances reconciles with the sales ledger control account

3.1 The debtors' circularisation

The verification of trade debtors by contacting them directly to confirm balances (direct circularisation) is the normal means of checking whether debtors owe bona fide amounts due to the company. Circularisation should produce a written statement from each debtor contacted that the amount owed at the date of the circularisation is correct. This is, prima facie, reliable audit evidence, being from an independent source and in 'documentary' form.

Ideally the circularisation should take place immediately after the year-end and hence cover the year-end balances to be included in the balance sheet. However, time constraints may make it impossible to achieve this ideal. In these circumstances it may be acceptable to carry out the circularisation **prior to the year-end** provided that circularisation occurs no more than three months before the year-end and internal controls are strong.

Circularisation is essentially an act of the **client**, who alone can authorise third parties to divulge information to the auditors. Should the client refuse to co-operate in the circularisation the auditors will have to consider whether they should **qualify** their **audit report**, as they may not be able to satisfy themselves, by means of other audit procedures, as to the validity and accuracy of the debtor balances.

When circularisation is undertaken the method of requesting information from the debtor may be either 'positive' or 'negative'.

- Under the **positive** method the debtor is requested to confirm the accuracy of the balance shown or state in what respect he is in disagreement.

- Under the **negative** method the debtor is requested to reply **only** if the amount stated is disputed.

The positive method is generally preferable as it is designed to encourage definite replies from those circularised. The negative method may be used if the client has good internal control, with a large number of small accounts. In some circumstances, say where there is a small number of large accounts and a large number of small accounts, a combination of both methods may be appropriate.

The following is a specimen 'positive' confirmation letter.

MANUFACTURING CO LIMITED

15 South Street
London

Date

Messrs   (debtor)

In accordance with the request of our auditors, Messrs Arthur Daley & Co, we ask that you kindly confirm to them directly your indebtedness to us at (insert date) which, according to our records, amounted to £.......... as shown by the enclosed statement.

If the above amount is in agreement with your records, please sign in the space provided below and return this letter direct to our auditors in the enclosed stamped addressed envelope.

If the amount is not in agreement with your records, please notify our auditors directly of the amount shown by your records, and if possible detail on the reverse of this letter full particulars of the difference.

Yours faithfully,

For Manufacturing Co Limited

Reference No: ....

(Tear off slip)

The amount shown above is/is not * in agreement with our records as at

Account No   ....   Signature   ....

Date   ....   Title or position   ....

* The position according to our records is shown overleaf.

Note:

- The letter is on the client's paper, signed by the client.
- A copy of the statement is attached.
- The reply is sent directly to the auditor in a pre-paid envelope.

The statements will normally be prepared by the client's staff, from which point the auditors, as a safeguard against the possibility of fraudulent manipulation, must maintain **strict control** over the **checking** and **despatch** of the statements. Precautions must also be taken to ensure that undelivered items are returned, not to the client, but to the auditors' own office for follow-up by them.

Auditors will normally only circularise a sample of debtors. If this sample is to yield a meaningful result it must be based upon a complete list of all debtor accounts. In addition, when constructing the sample, the following classes of account should receive special attention:

- Old unpaid accounts
- **Accounts written off** during the period under review
- **Accounts** with **credit balances**
- **Accounts** settled by **round sum payments**

Similarly, the following should not be overlooked:

- Accounts with nil balances
- **Accounts** which have been **paid** by the date of the examination

Auditors may apply stratification techniques to ensure that a sufficient proportion of debtors are confirmed.

3.2 Follow-up of debtors' circularisation

Auditors will have to carry out further work in relation to those debtors who:

- **Disagree** with the **balance stated** (positive and negative circularisation)
- **Do not respond** (positive circularisation only)

In the case of disagreements, the debtor response should have identified specific amounts which are disputed. Disagreements can arise for the following reasons.

(a)   There is a **dispute** between the client and the customer. The reasons for the dispute would have to be identified, and provision made if appropriate against the debt.

(b) **Cut-off problems** exist, because the client records the following year's sales in the current year or because goods returned by the customer in the current year are not recorded in the current year. Cut-off testing may have to be extended (see below).

(c) The customer may have sent the **monies before** the year-end, but the monies were **not recorded** by the client as receipts until **after** the year-end. Detailed cut-off work may be required on receipts.

(d) Monies received may have been posted to the **wrong account** or a cash-in-transit account. Auditors should check if there is evidence of other mis-posting. If the monies have been posted to a cash-in-transit account, auditors should ensure this account has been cleared promptly.

(e) Customers who are also suppliers may **net off balances** owed and owing. Auditors should check that this is allowed.

(f) **Teeming and lading, stealing** monies and **incorrectly posting** other receipts so that no particular debtor is seriously in debt is a fraud that can arise in this area. If auditors suspect teeming and lading has occurred, detailed testing will be required on cash receipts, particularly on prompt posting of cash receipts.

When the positive request method is used the auditors must follow up by all practicable means those debtors who **fail to respond**. Second requests should be sent out in the event of no reply being received within two or three weeks and if necessary this may be followed by telephoning the customer, with the client's permission.

After two, or even three, attempts to obtain confirmation, a list of the outstanding items will normally be passed to a responsible company official, preferably independent of the sales accounting department, who will arrange for them to be investigated.

3.2.1 Additional procedures where circularisation is carried out before year-end

The auditors will need to carry out the following procedures where their circularisation is carried out before the year-end.

- Review and reconcile entries on the sales ledger control account for the intervening period

- Verify sales entries from the control account by checking sales day book entries, copy sales invoices and despatch notes

- Check that appropriate credit entries have been made for goods returned notes and other evidence of returns/allowances to the sales ledger control account

- Select a sample from the cash received records and ensure that receipts have been credited to the control account

- Review the list of balances at the circularisation date and year end and investigate any unexpected movements or lack of them (it may be prudent to send further confirmation requests at the year end to material debtors where review results are unsatisfactory)

- **Carry out analytical review** procedures, comparing debtors' ratios at the confirmation date and year-end

- **Carry out** year end **cut-off tests**, in addition to any performed at the date of the confirmation (see below)

3.2.2 Evaluation and conclusions

All circularisations, regardless of timing, must be properly recorded and evaluated. All **balance disagreements** and **non-replies** must be **followed up** and their effect on total debtors evaluated. **Differences** arising that merely represent **invoices** or **cash in transit** (normal timing differences) generally do not require adjustment, but disputed amounts, and errors by the client, might require adjustments.

3.3 Alternative procedures

If it proves impossible to get confirmations from individual debtors, **alternative procedures** include the following.

- Check receipt of cash after date

- Verify valid purchase orders if any

- Examine the account to see if the balance outstanding represents specific invoices and confirm their validity

- Obtain explanations for invoices remaining unpaid after subsequent ones have been paid

- Check if the balance on the account is growing, and if so, why

- Test company's control over the issue of credit notes and the write-off of bad debts

Activity 14.1

(a)   For the benefit of Chantal, describe the audit procedures that should be followed when planning and performing a circularisation to be carried out at the client's year end. (You are not required to consider follow-up procedures.)

(b)   You have undertaken a debtors' circularisation. Explain what you will do in response to the following replies:

(i)   Balance agreed by debtor
(ii)   Balance not agreed by debtor
(iii)   Debtor is unable to confirm the balance because of the form of records kept by the debtor
(iv)   Debtor does not reply to the circularisation

4 Bad debts

The extent of testing is likely to depend on the strength of controls over credit terms and slow payers, the client's previous record of bad debts, and the proportion of debts that are overdue.

4.1 Procedures

- **Confirm necessity/adequacy** of provision against **write-off** of debts by review of correspondence, solicitors' debt collection, agencies' letters, liquidation statements

- Examine customer files on overdue debts, and **assess** whether **provision** is required in the circumstances

- **Consider** whether **amounts owed** may be **not recovered** where there have been:
    - Round sum payments on account
    - Invoices unpaid after subsequent invoices paid

- **Review customer files/correspondence** from solicitors for evidence of potential bad debts

- **Confirm general provisions** for bad debts
    - Calculation correct
    - Formula used reasonable and consistent with previous years

- **Examine credit notes** issued after the year-end for **provisions** that should be made against current period balances.

- **Check accuracy** of **aged debtor analysis** by comparing analysis with dates on invoices

- **Investigate unusual features** on aged debtors analysis, such as:
    - Unapplied credits
    - Unallocated cash

- **Investigate unusual items** in the sales ledger, such as:
    - Journal entries transferring balances from one account to another
    - Journal entries that clear post year-end debtor balances
    - Balances not made up of specific invoices
    - Sales ledger accounts with significant adjustments or credit notes

Auditors should also consider the collectability of material debtor balances other than those contained in the sales ledger. Auditors should request certificates of loan balances from employees and others, and inspect the authority if necessary.

4.1.1 Inter-company indebtedness

Where significant trading occurs between group companies the auditors should have ascertained as a result of their tests of controls whether trading has been at arm's length. As regards the balances at the year end, the following substantive procedures are suggested.

- **Confirm balances** owing from group and associated companies (current and loan accounts) with the other companies' records (directly, or by contacting other group members' auditors)

- **Ensure** that **cut-off procedures** have operated properly regarding inter company transfers

- **Assess reliability** of amounts owing

- **Ascertain** the **nature** of the entries comprised in the balances at the year end.

- **Ensure** that any **management charges** contained therein have been **calculated** on a **reasonable** and **consistent basis** and have been acknowledged by the debtor companies

4.1.2 Prepayments

The extent of audit testing will depend on the materiality of the amounts.

- **Verify prepayments** by reference to the cash book, expense invoices, correspondence and so on

- **Check calculations** of prepayments

- **Review** the **detailed profit and loss account** to ensure that all likely prepayments have been provided for

- **Review** the **prepayments** for **reasonableness** by comparing with prior years and using analytical procedures where applicable

5 Sales

Debtors will often be tested in conjunction with sales. Auditors are seeking to obtain evidence that sales are **completely** and **accurately recorded**. This will involve carrying out certain procedures to test for **completeness** of sales and also testing **cut-off**.

5.1 Completeness and occurrence of sales

Analytical review is likely to be important when testing completeness. Auditors should consider the following.

- The **level of sales** over the year, compared on a month-by-month basis with the previous year
- The effect on sales value of **changes in quantities** sold
- The effect on sales value of changes in **products** or **prices**
- The level of **goods returned, sales allowances** and **discounts**
- The **efficiency of labour** as expressed in sales or pre-tax profit per employee

In addition auditors must record reasons for changes in the **gross profit margin** ($\frac{\text{Gross profit}}{\text{Turnover}} \times 100\%$).

Analysis of the gross profit margin should be as detailed as possible, ideally broken down by **product area** and **month or quarter**.

As well as analytical review, auditors may feel that they need to test completeness of recording of individual sales in the accounting records. To do this, auditors should start with the documents that first record sales (**goods despatched notes** or **till rolls** for example). They should trace details of sales recorded in these through intermediate documents such as the sales **day book invoices** and **summaries through** to the **sales ledger**.

Auditors must **ensure** that the **population of documents** from which the sample is originally taken is itself complete, by checking for example the completeness of the sequence of goods despatched notes. Auditors should also **review reconciliations** of the sales ledger control account and other relevant reconciliations, and **investigate unusual items**.

If on the other hand, the auditors suspect that sales may have been **invalidly** recorded (may **not** have **occurred)**, then the sample will be taken from the sales ledger and confirmed to supporting documentation (orders, despatch notes and such like).

5.2 Measurement of sales

Other tests that may be carried out on sales include:

- Check the pricing calculations and additions on invoices
- Check whether discounts have been properly calculated
- Check whether VAT has been added appropriately
- Check casting of the sales ledger accounts and sales ledger control account

Auditors should also check the **measurement** and **validity** of **credit notes** by tracing debits in the sales account to credit notes, and **checking credit notes** to **supporting documentation** for **authorisation**, and evidence that the sales did take place.

5.3 Sales cut-off

During the stocktake the auditors will have obtained details of the last serial numbers of goods outward notes issued before the commencement of the stocktaking.

The following substantive procedures are designed to test that goods taken into stock are not also treated as sales in the year under review and, conversely, goods despatched are treated as sales in the year under review and not also treated as stock.

- Check goods despatched and returns inwards notes around year-end to ensure:

    ◦ Invoices and credit notes are dated in the correct period
    ◦ Invoices and credit notes are posted to the sales ledger and general ledger in the correct period

- **Reconcile entries** in the **sales ledger control account** around the **year-end** to daily batch invoice totals ensuring batches are posted in correct year

- **Review sales ledger control account** around year-end for **unusual items**

- **Review material after-date invoices, credit notes** and **adjustments** and ensure that they are properly treated as following year sales

5.3.1 Goods on sale or return

Care should be exercised to ensure that goods on sale or return are properly treated in the accounts. Except where the client has been notified of the sale of the goods they should be reflected in the accounts as **stock** at cost and not as debtors, otherwise profits may be incorrectly anticipated.

Activity 14.2

AJ (Paper) Ltd do not normally provide against specific bad debts, but instead make a general bad debt provision. This year the general provision is 5% of debtors.

Task

State the audit work Chantal should perform on the company's bad debt provision.

6 Bank

The audit of bank balances will need to cover **completeness**, **existence**, **rights and obligations** and **valuation**. All of these elements can be audited directly through the device of obtaining third party confirmations from the client's banks and reconciling these with the accounting records, having regard to cut-off. As preparation, the auditors should update details of bank accounts held, ensuring the client holds accounts with bona fide banks.

6.1 Bank reports

The standard request to the bank includes information about account and balance details, facilities, securities, and additional banking relationships. Supplementary information is concerned with requests for trade finance information, and derivatives and commodity trading information.

The procedure for requesting information from the bank is simple but important.

(a) The banks will require **explicit written authority** from their client to disclose the information requested.

(b) The **auditors' request** must **refer** to the **client's letter** of authority and the date thereof. Alternatively it may be countersigned by the client or it may be accompanied by a specific letter of authority.

(c) In the case of joint accounts, **letters of authority** signed by all **parties** will be necessary.

(d) Such **letters** of **authority** may either **give permission** to the bank to disclose information for a specific request or grant permission for an indeterminate length of time.

(e) The request should **reach** the **branch manager** at least **two weeks in advance** of the client's **year-end** and should state both that year-end date and the previous year-end date.

(f) The **auditors** should themselves **check** that the bank response covers all the information in the standard and other responses.

6.1.1 Bank confirmation request letter – illustration

[XXXXXX Bank plc
25 XXX Street
Warrington
Cheshire
WA1 1XQ]

Dear Sirs,

In accordance with the agreed practice for provision of information to auditors, please forward information on our mutual client(s) as detailed below on behalf of the bank, its branches and subsidiaries. This request and your response will not create any contractual or other duty with us.

COMPANIES OR OTHER BUSINESS ENTITIES
(attach a separate listing if necessary)

[Parent Company Ltd
Subsidiary 1 Ltd
Subsidiary 2 Ltd]

AUDIT CONFIRMATION DATE (30 APRIL 2000)

Information required	Tick
Standard	
Trade finance	
Derivative and commodity trading	
Custodian arrangements	
Other information (see attached)	

The authority to disclose information signed by your customer is attached / already held by you (delete as appropriate). Please advise us if this authority is insufficient for you to provide full disclosure of the information requested.

The contract name is [John Caller]   Telephone [01 234 5678]

Yours faithfully,
[XXX Accountants]

6.1.2 Standard request for information

The following information should always be disclosed by banks upon receipt of a request for information for audit purposes. Responses should be given in the order below and if no information is available then this must be stated as 'None' in the response.

1   **Account and balance details**

Give full titles of all bank accounts including loans, (whether in sterling or another currency) together with their account numbers and balances. For accounts closed during the 12 months up to the audit confirmation date give the account details and date of closure.

Note. Also give details where your customer's name is joined with that of other parties and where the account is in a trade name.

State if any account or balances are subject to any restriction(s) whatsoever. Indicate the nature and extent of the restriction, eg garnishee order.

2   **Facilities**

Give the following details of all loans, overdrafts and associated guarantees and indemnities:

- Term
- Repayment frequency and/or review date
- Details of period of availability of agreed finance, ie finance remaining undrawn
- Detail the facility limit

3   **Securities**

With reference to the facilities detailed in (2) above give the following details:

- Any security formally charged (date, ownership and type of charge). State whether the security supports facilities granted by the bank to the customer or to another party.

   Note. Give details if a security is limited in amount or to a specific borrowing or if to your knowledge there is a prior, equal or subordinate charge.

- Where there are any arrangements for set-off of balances or compensating balances eg back to back loans, give particulars (ie date, type of document and accounts covered) of any acknowledgement of set-off, whether given by specific letter of set-off or incorporated in some other document.

4   **Additional banking relationships**

State if you are aware of the customer(s) having any additional relationships with branches or subsidiaries of the Bank not covered by the response. Supply a list of branches etc.

6.2 Cut-off

Care must be taken to ensure that there is no **window dressing**, by checking cut-off carefully. Window dressing in this context is usually manifested as an attempt to overstate the liquidity of the company by:

(a)   Keeping the cash book open to take credit in the year for **remittances actually received after** the year end, thus enhancing the balance at bank and reducing debtors

(b)   **Recording cheques** as **paid** in the period under review which are not actually despatched until after the year end, thus decreasing the balance at bank and reducing creditors

A combination of (a) and (b) can contrive to present an artificially healthy looking current ratio.

With the possibility of (a) above in mind, where lodgements have not been cleared by the bank until the new period the auditors should **examine** the **paying-in slip** to ensure that the amounts were actually paid into the bank on or before the balance sheet date.

As regards (b) above, where there appears to be a particularly **large number** of **outstanding cheques** at the year-end, the auditors should check whether these were **cleared within** a **reasonable time** in the new period. If not, this may indicate that despatch occurred after the year-end.

6.3 Summary of bank balance procedures

The following suggested substantive balance sheet tests summarise the principal audit procedures discussed above relevant to bank balances. The procedures apply to all bank accounts.

- **Obtain standard bank confirmations** from each bank with which the client conducted business during the audit period

- **Check arithmetic** of bank reconciliation

- **Trace cheques shown as outstanding** from the bank reconciliation to the cash book prior to the year-end and to the **after date bank statements** and **obtain explanations** for any large or unusual **items not cleared** at the time of the audit

- **Verify** by checking pay-in slips that **uncleared bankings** are **paid in** prior to the year end, and check uncleared bankings are cleared quickly after the year-end

- **Verify** balances per cash book according to the reconciliation with **cash book** and **general ledger**

- **Verify** the **bank balances** with reply to **standard bank letter** and with the bank statements

- **Scrutinise** the cash book and bank statements before and after the balance sheet date for **exceptional entries** or **transfers** which have a material effect on the balance shown to be in hand

- **Identify** whether any **accounts** are **secured** on the **assets** of the company

- **Consider** whether there is a **legal right** of **set-off** of overdrafts against positive bank balances

- **Determine** whether the **bank accounts** are **subject** to any **restrictions**

- Obtain explanations for all items in the cash book for which there are no corresponding entries in the bank statement and vice versa

7 Cash

Cash balances/floats are often individually immaterial. They may require some audit emphasis because of the opportunities for fraud that could exist where internal control is weak due for example to lack of segregation of duties, failure to bank receipts promptly or inadequate custody arrangements.

However, in enterprises such as hotels, the amount of cash in hand at the balance sheet date could be considerable; the same goes for retail organisations.

Where the auditors determine that cash balances are potentially material they may conduct a cash count, ideally at the balance sheet date. Rather like attendance at stocktaking, the conduct of the count falls into three phases: planning, the count itself and follow up procedures.

7.1 Planning

Planning is an essential element, for it is an important principle that all cash balances are counted at the same time as far as possible. Cash in this context may include unbanked cheques received, IOUs and credit card slips, in addition to notes and coins.

As part of their planning procedures the auditors will hence need to determine the **locations** where cash is held and which of these locations warrant a count. Planning decisions will need to be recorded on the current audit file including:

- **Precise** time of the count(s) and location(s)
- **Names** of the **audit staff** conducting the counts
- **Names** of the **client staff** intending to be present at each location

Where a location is not visited it may be expedient to obtain a letter from the client confirming the balance.

7.2 Cash count

(a) All cash/petty **cash books** should be **written up** to date in ink (or other permanent form) at the time of the count.

(b) All **balances** must be **counted** at the **same time**.

(c) All **negotiable securities** must be **available** and **counted** at the time the cash balances are counted.

(d) At **no time** should the **auditors** be left **alone** with the cash and negotiable securities.

(e) **All cash** and securities **counted** must be **recorded** on working papers subsequently filed on the current audit file, reconciliations should be prepared where applicable (for example imprest petty cash float).

7.3 Follow-up procedures

These should ensure that:

- Certificates of cash-in-hand are obtained as appropriate.
- Unbanked cheques/cash receipts have subsequently been paid in and agree to the bank reconciliation.
- IOUs and cheques cashed for employees have been reimbursed.
- IOUs or cashed cheques outstanding for unreasonable periods of time have been provided for.
- The balances as counted are reflected in the accounts (subject to any agreed amendments because of shortages and so on).

Activity 14.3

For Chantal's benefit:

(a)   List the contents of a standard bank letter for audit purposes.
(b)   Explain what tests auditors should normally carry out on the bank reconciliation.

Activity 14.4

A member of the company's staff has recently been dismissed for embezzling petty cash. Anton is concerned with the procedures operating over petty cash, and he has asked you to carry out a surprise cash count. Although petty cash is not material for audit purposes, you agree to his request, and you ask Chantal to assist you.

Set out for Chantal the main procedures that she should carry out when performing a cash count.

Key learning points

☑   Circularisation of debtors is a major procedure. Generally circularisation will be positive (debtors confirm client's figures are correct).

☑   Auditors must follow up:

    –   Debtor disagreements
    –   Failure by debtors to respond

☑   Testing of the bad debt provision and sales cut-off is also important.

☑   Bank balances are usually confirmed directly with the bank by a bank letter. Balances confirmed by the bank must be reconciled to the balances shown in the client cash book.

☑   Cash balances should be checked if irregularities are suspected.

Quick quiz

1   The negative method of debtors' circularisation should only be used if the client has a good internal control and a small number of large debtors accounts.

True

False

2   Name four types of account which should receive special attention when picking a sample for a debtors' circularisation.

1   ....

2   ....

3   ....

4   ....

3   Complete the following tests which aim to confirm the valuation of bad debts.

(a)   Confirm adequacy of provision by reviewing correspondence with

(i)   ....

(ii)   ....

(b)   Examine .... issued after the year end for provisions that should be made against current period balances.

4   Name three things that can be considered when undertaking analytical review on sales.

1   ....

2   ....

3   ....

5   Summarise the procedure for obtaining confirmation from a client's bank.

1   ....

2   ....

3   ....

4   ....

5   ... .

6   ....

6   Complete these two of the audit tests performed to verify the bank reconciliation.

(a)   Trace cheques shown as outstanding on the .... to the ....
prior to the year end and ....
....

(b)   Obtain satisfactory explanations for all items in the ………………….. …………………… for which there is no corresponding entry in the …………………….. ………………….. and ………….. …………………… .

7   Give two examples of business where cash floats could be considerable.

1   ……………………………………………

2   ……………………………………………

8   What planning matters relating to a cash count should be recorded in the current audit file?

1   ……………………………………………

2   ……………………………………………

3   ……………………………………………

Answers to quick quiz

1   False

2   The following accounts require special attention in a debtors' circularisation.

- Old unpaid accounts
- Accounts written off during the period under review
- Accounts with credit balances
- Accounts settled by round-sum payments

3   (a)   debtors, solicitors
     (b)   credit notes

4   1   Level of sales, month by month
     2   Price
     3   Goods returned

5   (1)   The banks will require **explicit written authority** from their client to disclose the information requested.

     (2)   The **auditors' request** must **refer** to the **client's letter** of authority and the date thereof. Alternatively it may be countersigned by the client or it may be accompanied by a specific letter of authority.

     (3)   In the case of joint accounts, **letters of authority** signed by all **parties** will be necessary.

     (4)   Such **letters** of **authority** may either **give permission** to the bank to disclose information for a specific request or grant permission for an indeterminate length of time.

     (5)   The request should **reach** the **branch manager** at least **two weeks in advance** of the client's **year-end** and should state both that year-end date and the previous year-end date.

     (6)   The **auditors** should themselves **check** that the bank response covers all the information in the standard and other responses.

6   (a)   bank reconciliation, cash book, after date bank statements
     (b)   cash book bank statements, bank letter

7   Hotels
        Retail operations

8   Time of count
        Names of client staff attending
        Names of audit staff attending

Activity checklist

This checklist shows which performance criteria, range statement or knowledge and understanding point is covered by each activity in this chapter. Tick off each activity as you complete it.

Activity

14.1		This activity deals with Performance Criteria 17.1.G: Select or devise appropriate tests in accordance with organisation's procedures and 17.2.A: Conduct tests correctly and as specified in the audit plan, record tests properly and draw valid conclusions from them and 17.2.B: Establish the existence, completeness, ownership, valuation and description of assets and liabilities and gather appropriate evidence to support these findings and 17.2.G: Identify all matters of an unusual nature and refer them promptly to the audit supervisor and 17.2.D: Identify and record material and significant errors, deficiencies or other variations from standard and report them to the audit supervisor
14.2		This activity deals with Performance Criteria 17.1.G: Select or devise appropriate tests in accordance with organisation's procedures
14.3		This activity deals with Performance Criteria 17.1.G: Select or devise appropriate tests in accordance with organisation's procedures
14.4		This activity deals with Performance Criteria 17.1.G: Select or devise appropriate tests in accordance with organisation's procedures

chapter 15

Liabilities, share capital, reserves & statutory books

Contents

1   The problem
2   The solution
3   Current liabilities
4   Purchases and expenses
5   Long-term liabilities
6   Share capital, reserves and statutory books

Performance criteria

17.1.G   Select or devise appropriate tests in accordance with organisation's procedures

17.2.A   Conduct tests correctly and as specified in the audit plan, record tests properly and draw valid conclusions from them

17.2.B   Establish the existence, completeness, ownership, valuation and description of assets and liabilities and gather appropriate evidence to support these findings

17.2.C   Identify all matters of an unusual nature and refer them promptly to the audit supervisor

17.2.D   Identify and record material and significant errors, deficiencies or other variations from standard and report them to the audit supervisor

Range statement

17.1   Accounting systems: purchases; sales; stock; expenses; balance sheet items; payroll

17.1   Accounting systems that are: manual; computerised

17.1   Tests: tests of contol; substantive

1 The problem

Creditors is often one of the most sensitive areas of a company's accounts. It significantly affects the company's liquidity, and may be closely related to limits on bank borrowing or loan agreements. There may thus be significant incentives for a company to carry creditors at less than their true value. How should creditors be audited to ensure they are not understated?

The Companies Act has detailed provisions governing share capital, reserves and statutory books. How can auditors obtain evidence that the statutory requirements have been met?

2 The solution

Much of testing creditors is focused on the **completeness** of recording and liability recognition. Supplier statements provide good third party evidence of this. Analytical procedures can also help to indicate whether purchases have been recorded completely.

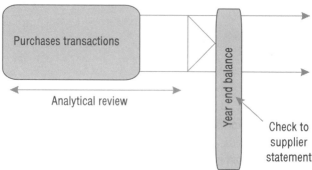

The company is required to keep statutory records of share capital and other matters, and to make returns to the Registrar of Companies. The auditors will refer to these to gain evidence about disclosures in the financial statements.

3 Current liabilities

The purchases cycle tests of controls will have provided the auditors with some assurance as to the completeness of liabilities. Auditors should however be particularly aware, when conducting their balance sheet work, of the possibility of understatement of liabilities. As regards **trade creditors**, auditors should particularly consider the following.

- Is there a **satisfactory cut-off** between goods received and invoices received, so that purchases and trade creditors are recognised in the correct year?

- Do trade creditors represent **all the bona fide amounts due** by the company?

The list of creditors' balances will be one of the principal sources from which the auditors will select their samples for testing. The listing should be extracted from the purchase ledger by the client. The auditors will carry out the following substantive tests to verify that the extraction has been properly performed and is **complete**.

- Check from the purchase ledger accounts to the list of balances and vice versa
- Reconcile the total of the list with the purchase ledger control account
- Cast the list of balances and the purchase ledger control account

The client should also prepare a detailed schedule of trade and sundry accrued expenses.

3.1 Completeness and accuracy of trade creditors

The most important test when considering **trade creditors** is comparison of suppliers' statements with purchase ledger balances. This provides evidence of **existence, rights and obligations** and **completeness.**

When selecting a sample of creditors to test, auditors must be careful not just to select creditors with large year-end balances. Remember, it is errors of **understatement** that auditors are primarily interested in when reviewing creditors, and errors of understatement could occur equally in creditors with low or nil balances as with high balances.

Therefore, when comparing supplier statements with year-end purchase ledger balances, auditors should include within their sample creditors with nil or negative purchase ledger balances. Auditors should be particularly wary of low balances with major suppliers.

You may be wondering as we normally carry out a debtors' circularisation whether we would also circularise creditors. The answer is generally no. The principal reason for this lies in the nature of the purchases cycle: third party evidence in the form of suppliers' invoices and even more significantly, suppliers' statements, is available as part of the standard documentation of the cycle.

In the following circumstances the auditors may, however, determine that a circularisation is necessary.

    (a)   Where suppliers' statements are, for whatever reason, unavailable or incomplete

    (b)   Where weaknesses in internal control or the nature of the client's business make possible a material misstatement of liabilities that would not otherwise be picked up

    (c)   Where it is thought that the client is deliberately trying to understate creditors

    (d)   Where the accounts appear to be irregular or if the nature or size of balances or transactions is abnormal

In these cases confirmation requests should be sent out and processed in a similar way to debtors' confirmation requests. 'Positive' requests will be required.

4 Purchases and expenses

When testing purchases, auditors are testing whether they have **occurred**, are **measured correctly** and have been made for **valid reasons**, (that goods and services purchased have provided benefits to the company). They are also checking for **accuracy of recording** of purchases so again cut-off procedures will be important.

4.1 Validity of purchases

As with sales, **analytical procedures** will be important. Auditors should consider:

- The **level of purchases** over the year, compared on a month-by-month basis with the previous year
- The effect on value of purchases of **changes in quantities purchased**

- The effect on value of purchases of changes in **products** purchased (for example a change in ingredients), or **prices of products**

- How the **ratio of trade creditors to purchases** compares with previous years

- How the **ratio of trade creditors to stock** compares with previous years

- How **major expenses** other than purchases compare with previous years

In addition auditors may carry out the following additional substantive tests on individual purchases or expenses.

- **Check purchases and expenses recorded** in the **general or purchase ledger** or **cash book** to supporting documentation (books of prime entry, invoices, delivery notes, purchase orders) considering:

  ○ Whether **purchases** and **expenses** are **valid** (invoices addressed to the client, for goods and services ordered by the client, for the purposes of the business)

  ○ Whether **purchases** and **expenses** have been allocated to the correct **purchase** or **general ledger** account

  ○ Whether amounts have been **calculated correctly**

- Consider **reasonableness of deductions** from purchases or expenses by reference to subsequent events

- Consider whether **valid debts** are **recorded** in **purchase ledger** by **checking credit notes**

If auditors are concerned about the completeness of recording of purchases, the following tests may be necessary.

- Check a sample of purchase orders/goods received notes to purchase invoices
- Review the file of unprocessed invoices and obtain explanations
- Check the total of the purchase day book to the general ledger
- Analytically review the gross profit percentage and obtain explanations for fluctuations

4.2 Purchases cut-off

The procedures applied by the auditors will be designed to ascertain whether:

- Goods received for which no invoice has been received are accrued.
- Goods received which have been invoiced but not yet posted are accrued.
- Goods returned prior to the year-end are excluded from stock and trade creditors.

At the year-end stocktaking the auditors will have made a note of the last serial numbers of goods received notes. Suggested substantive procedures are as follows.

- **Check from goods received notes** with serial numbers before the year-end to ensure that invoices are either:

  ○ Posted to purchase ledger prior to the year-end, or
  ○ Included on the schedule of accruals

- **Review the schedule of accruals** to ensure that goods received after the year-end are not accrued

- **Check from goods returned notes prior to year-end** to ensure that **credit notes** have been **posted** to the purchase ledger prior to the year-end or accrued

- **Review large invoices** and **credit notes** included after the year-end to ensure that they refer to the following year

- **Reconcile daily batch invoice totals** around the year-end to purchase ledger control ensuring batches are posted in the correct year

- **Review** the **control account** around the year-end for **any unusual items**

4.3 Verification of accruals

Checking the **completeness** and **valuation** of accruals is an area that lends itself to analytical procedures and reconciliation techniques. Care must be taken with statutory liabilities such as PAYE and VAT where there is, arguably, an expectation that the auditors verify these liabilities regardless of materiality.

You should note in particular with accruals the variety of sources which may indicate possible accruals. These include **last year's accruals**, **expense items** where an accrual would be expected, and **invoices received** and **cash paid** after the year-end.

Auditors should also use their **knowledge** of the **business** to consider whether there are accruals which they would expect to be there, but which may not be invoiced or paid until long after the year-end.

The following substantive procedures are suggested.

- Check that accruals are fairly calculated and verify by reference to subsequent payments and supporting documentation

- Review the profit and loss account and prior years' figures and consider liabilities inherent in the trade to ensure that all likely accruals have been provided

- Scrutinise payments and invoices received made after year-end to ascertain whether they should be accrued

- Consider basis for round sum accruals and ensure it is consistent with prior years

- Ascertain why any payments on account are being made and ensure that the full liability is provided

- For provisions (other than provisions for depreciation, tax and bad debts):

  ○ **Prepare a schedule** of any **provisions** indicating their purpose and basis, showing details of movement during the period

  ○ **Decide** whether any of the **provisions** are **sufficiently material** to be separately disclosed in the accounts; in particular consider whether any provisions need to be disclosed in accordance with FRS 3

For PAYE and VAT the following approach should be adopted.

- **PAYE**. Normally this should represent one month's deductions. **Check amount paid to Inland Revenue** by inspecting receipted annual declaration of tax paid over, or returned cheque

- **VAT**. **Check reasonableness** to **next VAT return** (either the year-end will coincide with a VAT period-end, in which case the accounts should agree with the VAT return, or the liability should be an appropriate part of the liability for the first period ending after the year-end). **Verify last amount paid** in year per cash book to VAT return

4.4 Wages and salaries

Although auditors may test other expenses solely by analytical review, they may carry out more detailed testing on wages and salaries, partly because of the consequences of failure to deduct PAYE and NIC correctly.

Analytical procedures will nonetheless be used to give some assurance on wages and salaries. Auditors should consider:

- Wages and salaries levels month-by-month with previous years
- Effect on wages and salaries of salary changes during the year
- Average wage per month over the year
- Sales/profits per employee

In addition auditors may carry out the following substantive tests.

4.4.1 Occurrence

- Check individual remuneration per payroll to personnel records, records of hours worked or salary agreements and such like.

- Confirm existence of employees on payroll by meeting them or attending wages payout.

- Check benefits (pensions) on payroll to supporting documentation.

4.4.2 Measurement

- **Check accuracy of calculation** of **benefits**

- **Check whether calculation of statutory deductions** (PAYE, NIC) is **correct**

- **Check validity of other deductions** (for example, pension contributions or share save) by agreement to supporting documentation (personnel files, conditions of pension scheme) and **check accuracy of calculation** of other deductions

4.4.3 Completeness

- **Check** a sample of employees from **personnel records** and ensure **included** in **payroll records**
- **Check details** of **joiners** and ensure **recorded** in **correct month**
- **Check casts of payroll records**
- **Confirm payment of net pay** per payroll records to **cheque or bank transfer** summary
- **Agree net pay** per cash book to **payroll**
- **Scrutinise payroll** and **investigate** unusual items

Activity 15.1

You are carrying out the audit of creditors and accruals.

The AJ (Paper) Ltd operates a central warehouse to which all raw materials are delivered. Stores reception checks all deliveries for quantity and quality to the delivery note, and the stores receptionist completes a goods received note, keeping one copy and sending one copy to the purchase ledger department.

The purchase ledger department receives invoices, and when details have been checked as correct, invoices are posted to the purchase ledger. Accounts with suppliers are settled monthly.

Tasks

Describe the audit work you will carry out:

(a)   To confirm purchase cut-off is correct
(b)   To confirm balances on the purchase ledger
(c)   To confirm accruals (you can assume the only accruals are VAT, PAYE and time-apportioned expenses)

Activity 15.2

You are finishing off the detailed audit work on creditors of AJ (Paper) Ltd.

Select a sample of trade creditors at 31 December 2002 (with turnover of > £700,000 in 2002), and reconcile the supplier's statement to the year-end purchase ledger balance. Vouch any reconciling item to source documentation.

The information you require is given on the following pages.

Your working papers should give the test objective and the work done, summarise the results and state the conclusion drawn. You should also show for each creditor chosen how the balance per the supplier's statement reconciles to the balance per the purchase ledger.

Note: In relation to your test, you may assume that all late invoices have been included in the late invoices account, but late credit notes have not been accounted for.

AJ (PAPER) LTD
24/26 Arthur Road
Newcastle upon Tyne
NT1 4LJ

Invoice

I 882469

To:Gray Ltd
   Unit 7
   Netherhall Site
   Middleham MR22 3TL

	Date/Tax point
	29.12.02

| Your reference | Our Order No. | DESPATCHED | | Account |
		Date	Per	
3428	P 661319	–	–	108735

	VAT Rate	£	p
Carriage re: Inv. I 881329	17.5%	45	75
TOTAL GOODS		45	75
VAT		8	00
		53	75

AJ (PAPER) LTD

24/26 Arthur Road
Newcastle upon Tyne
NT1 4LJ

Credit
Note

C 17832

To: Blacknote
    32 Brixton Road
    London SW9 6BR

	Date/Tax point
	28.03.02

Your reference	Our Order No.	DESPATCHED		Account
		Date	Per	
PO 4289	P 661342	–	–	108442

	VAT Rate	£	p
20 Damaged boxes	17.5%	237	36
TOTAL GOODS		237	36
VAT		41	53
		278	89

AJ (PAPER) LTD

24/26 Arthur Road
Newcastle upon Tyne
NT1 4LJ

Despatch
Note

DN 482761

To: Rossney & Co
327 Scelwith Road
Aberdeen AB11 4PR

				Date/Tax point
				29.12.02

| Your reference | Our Order No. | DESPATCHED | | Account |
		Date	Per	
M 1176299	P 661307	29.12.02	–	107507

	VAT Rate	£	p
Special order boxes	17.5%	10,000	00
Carriage	17.5%	599	43
TOTAL GOODS		10,599	43
VAT		1,854	90
		12,454	33

CREDITOR DETAILS

A special interrogation of the client's computer system has revealed that three suppliers had turnover of over £700,000 during the year and these are shown below.

Extracts from purchase ledger

A/c no	Supplier	Code	No	Date	Value	Balance
117342	Forestguard	Inv	7119	31.09.02	12,496.62	
	Paper	Inv	0741	30.10.02	16,865.86	
		Inv	2306	27.11.02	15,477.48	
		Csh	1200	26.12.02	(12,496.62)	32,343.34
234911	Terry's	Inv	5611	20.10.02	19,654.62	
	Paper	Inv	6720	10.11.02	22,856.26	
		Csh	1200	26.11.02	(19,654.62)	22,856.26
235601	Woodcutter	Inv	6504	05.09.02	36,145.27	
		Inv	6788	27.10.02	87.08	
		Inv	6942	16.11.02	568.72	
		Inv	7119	27.11.02	61,035.17	
		Inv	7342	29.12.02	36,145.27	
		CNT	1226	17.11.02	(2,549.30)	
		CSH	1200	26.12.02	(36,801.07)	94,631.14
Total balance 31/12/02						608,315.68

VAT No. 3 719 846 6

FORESTGUARD PAPER

Accounts receivable
48, Dunstable Rd
Newmarket
0312 489 273

A/C AJ (Paper) Ltd
W007
24-26 Arthur Road
Newcastle-upon-Tyne
NT1 4LJ

STATEMENT

at 31 December 2002

Date	Reference	Debit	Credit	Balance
31.9.02	124577119	12,496.62		12,496.62
25.10.02	126200741	16,885.86		29,382.48
25.11.02	127942306	15,477.48		44,859.96
27.12.02	128604003	6,952.48		51,812.44
29.12.02	Cash 001		12,496.62	39,315.82

Inclusive of VAT
Reg office 48, Dunstable Rd, Newmarket Reg No 113459118

STATEMENT

Unit 6
Greycoat Estate
Gloucester
0429 91738

AJ (PAPER) LTD
24-26 ARTHUR ROAD
NEWCASTLE-UPON-TYNE
NT1 4LJ

DATE: 16.12.02

ACCOUNT: 107W004

DATE	DETAILS	DEBIT	CREDIT
18.09.02	Invoice 47342880	10,417.42	
20.09.02	Invoice 47342939	2,926.84	
21.09.02	Invoice 47343007	5,028.38	
04.10.02	CASH		18,372.64
17.10.02	Invoice 47345611	19,654.62	
08.11.02	Invoice 47346720	22,856.26	
	Total	60,883.52	18,372.64
	Balance	42,510.88	

REG NO 1173458

VAT NO 84891173

STATEMENT

WOODCUTTER LTD

Acton Grange, Gloucestershire, GU11 4PS, 0693 71592

To:

AJ (PAPER) LTD
24/26 ARTHUR ROAD
NEWCASTLE-UPON-TYNE
NT1 4LJ

Date: 31.12.02

DATE	REF		DEBIT	CREDIT	BAL
	NOVEMBER 2002 ACCOUNT				95,286.94
23.12.02	55117342	Inv	36,145.27		131,432.21
30.12.02		Csh		36,801.07	94,631.14
30.12.02	00071483	CNo		4,975.46	89,655.68
	AMOUNT DUE				89,655.68

REG NO   7499188   VAT NO   0119 469823

VAT No. 3 719 846 6

FORESTGUARD PAPER

Accounts receivable
48, Dunstable Rd
Newmarket
0312 489 273

AJ (Paper) Ltd
24-26 Arthur Road
Newcastle-upon-Tyne
NT1 4LJ

INVOICE NUMBER

126200741

Date	Account no.	Transport	Terms
25.10.02	W007		30 DAYS NET

Description	Amount
1,400kg at agreed price	14,353.93
Vat @17.5%	2,511.93
Amount due	16,865.86

RECEIVED

Inv No.	109527
Date	30|10|02
Calcs (sign)	RS
Auth (sign)	AS
NL Code	170 £14,353.93
	900 £8,511.93

Reg office 48, Dunstable Rd, Newmarket Reg No 113459118

5 Long-term liabilities

We are concerned here with long-term liabilities comprising debentures, loan stock and other loans repayable at a date more than one year after the year-end.

Auditors will primarily try and determine:

- **Completeness:** whether all long-term liabilities have been disclosed

- **Measurement:** whether interest payable has been calculated correctly and included in the correct accounting period

- **Disclosure:** whether long-term loans and interest have been correctly disclosed in the financial statements

5.1 Substantive procedures applicable to all audits

The following suggested substantive procedures are relevant.

- **Obtain/prepare schedule of loans** outstanding at the balance sheet date showing, for each loan: name of lender, date of loan, maturity date, interest date, interest rate, balance at the end of the period and security

- **Compare opening balances** to previous year's working papers

- **Test the clerical accuracy** of the analysis

- **Compare balances** to the **general ledger**

- **Check name** of **lender** to **register** of **debenture holders** or equivalent (if kept)

- **Trace new borrowings** and **repayments** to **entries** in the **cash book**

- **Confirm repayments** are in accordance with **loan agreement**

- **Examine cancelled cheques** and **memoranda of satisfaction** for **loans repaid**

- **Verify** that **borrowing limits** imposed either by articles or by other agreements are **not exceeded**

- **Examine signed Board minutes** relating to **new borrowings/repayments**

- **Obtain direct confirmation** from **lenders** of the amounts outstanding, accrued interest and what security they hold

- **Verify interest charged** for the period and the adequacy of accrued interest

- **Confirm assets charged** have been **entered** in the **register of charges** and **notified** to the **Registrar**

- **Review restrictive covenants** and provisions relating to default:
  - **Review** any **correspondence** relating to the loan
  - **Review confirmation** replies for non-compliance
  - If a **default appears** to exist, **determine** its **effect**, and **schedule findings**

- Review minutes, cash book to check if all loans have been recorded

6 Share capital, reserves and statutory books

This section discusses three areas which, although only tenuously related, are often bracketed together for audit purposes. The audit objectives are to ascertain that:

- Share capital has been properly classified and disclosed in the financial statements and changes properly authorised.

- Movements on reserves have been properly authorised and, in the case of statutory reserves, only used for permitted purposes.

- Statutory records have been properly maintained and returns properly and expeditiously dealt with.

6.1 Share capital, reserves and distributions

The issued share capital as stated in the accounts must be **agreed** in total with the **share register**. An examination of transfers on a test basis should be made in those cases where a company handles its own registration work.

Where the registration work is dealt with by independent registrars, auditors will normally examine the reports submitted by them to the company, and obtain from the registrars at the year-end a certificate of the share capital in issue.

Company law prescribes that:

(a) The directors must have the **general powers of management** to be able to allot shares.

(b) The directors must not exercise that power without **authority** from the **members**. That authority may either be given by the company's **articles** or by **resolution** passed in **general meeting** (s 80 of the Companies Act).

(c) The directors must respect the **pre-emption rights** of **existing members**. Under s 89 of the Companies Act directors must first offer shares to holders of similar shares in proportion to their holdings. A private company can permanently exclude these rules in its memorandum and articles. Any company can decide by special resolution that the rules should not apply on a specific occasion.

Auditors should take particular care if there are any movements in reserves that cannot be distributed, and should **confirm** that these movements are **valid**.

The following suggested substantive procedures are relevant.

6.1.1 Share capital

- Agree the authorised share capital with the memorandum and articles of association
- Agree changes to authorised share capital with properly authorised resolutions

6.1.2 Issue of shares

- **Verify any issue** of share capital or other changes during the year with general and board **minutes**

- **Ensure issue or change** is within the **terms** of the **memorandum** and **articles** of association, and directors possess appropriate authority to issue shares

- Confirm that **cash** or **other consideration** has been **received** or **debtor(s) is included** as called up share capital not paid

- **Confirm** that any **premium** on issue of shares has been **credited** to the **share premium** account

- Where a public company has issued shares for **non-cash consideration,** check fair **value** has been **received for** the shares, and that valuation reports have been obtained

- For **redeemable shares** issued, check their **terms provide** for payment on **redemption**

6.1.3 Transfers of shares

- **Verify transfers of shares** shown in the register of members by reference to:
  - Correspondence
  - Completed and stamped transfer forms
  - Cancelled share certificates
  - Minutes of directors' meeting if director approval is required for transfers

- **Check the balances** on **shareholders' accounts** in the register of members and the total list with the amount of issued share capital in the general ledger

6.1.4 Dividends

- **Agree dividends** paid and proposed to **authority** in minute books and **check calculation** with **total share capital** issued to ascertain whether there are any outstanding or unclaimed dividends

- **Check dividend payments** with **documentary evidence** (say, the returned dividend warrants)

- **Check** that **dividends do not contravene** the distribution provisions of the **Companies Act 1985**

6.1.5 Reserves

- **Check movements on reserves** to supporting **authority**

- **Ensure that movements on reserves do not contravene the Companies Act 1985** and the memorandum and articles of association

- **Confirm** that the company can **distinguish** those reserves at the balance sheet date that are **distributable** from those that are **non-distributable**

- **Ensure appropriate disclosures** are made in the company's accounts. (These include the requirement to show movements on reserves during the year, and the FRS 3 requirement to include a statement of total gains and losses, and a statement of shareholders' funds)

6.2 Statutory books

Suggested substantive procedures are as follows.

6.2.1 Register of directors and secretaries

- **Update permanent file** giving details of directors and secretary
- **Verify** any **changes** with the **minutes** and ensure that the necessary details have been filed at Companies House
- **Verify** that the **number of directors complies** with the **articles**

6.2.2 Register of directors' interests in shares and debentures

- **Ensure** that **directors' interests** are **noted** on the permanent file for cross-referencing to directors' reports
- Ensure that directors' shareholdings comply with the articles

6.2.3 Minute books of directors' and general meetings

- **Obtain photocopies** or **prepare extracts** from the **minute books** of meetings concerning financial matters, cross-referencing them to appropriate working papers
- **Ensure** that **extracts** of **agreements** referred to in the minutes are **prepared** for the permanent file
- **Check agreements** with the company's seal book where one is kept
- **Note the date** of the last **minute reviewed**
- **Check** that **meetings** have been **properly convened** and that quorums attended them

6.2.4 Register of interests in shares (if applicable)

- **Scrutinise register** and verify that it appears to be in order
- Ensure that significant interests are noted on the permanent file

6.2.5 Register of charges

- Update permanent file schedule from the register
- Ensure that any assets which are charged as security for loans from third parties are disclosed in the accounts
- Obtain confirmation that there are no charges to be recorded if no entries are recorded in the register
- Consider carrying out company search at Companies House to verify the accuracy of the register

6.2.6 Accounting records

- Consider whether the accounting records are adequate to:
  - Show and explain the company's transactions
  - Disclose with reasonable accuracy, at any time, the financial position of the company
  - Comply with the Companies Act by recording money received and expended, assets and liabilities, year-end stock and stock-taking, sales and purchases
  - Enable the directors to ensure that the accounts give a true and fair view

6.2.7 General ledger and journals

- Check opening balances in general ledger to previous year's audited accounts
- Check additions of general ledger accounts
- Review general ledger accounts and ensure significant transfers and unusual items are *bona fide*
- Review the journal and ensure that significant entries are authorised and properly recorded
- Check extraction and addition of trial balance (if prepared by the clients)

6.2.8 Returns

- Check that the following returns have been filed properly:
  - Annual return and previous year's accounts
  - Notices of change in directors or secretary
  - Memoranda of charges or mortgages created during the period
  - VAT returns
  - Other tax returns

6.2.9 Directors' service contracts

- **Inspect copies** of directors' service contracts or memoranda
- **Ensure** that they are **kept** at either:
  - The registered office
  - The principal place of business
  - The place where the register of members is kept, if not the registered office
- Verify that long-term service contracts (lasting more than five years) have been approved in general meeting

6.3 Directors' emoluments

The auditors have a duty to include in their report the required disclosure particulars of directors' emoluments and transactions with directors, if these requirements have not been complied with in the accounts (s 237).

The auditors will have carried out an evaluation of salaries payroll procedures, including the system in operation for directors' salaries, earlier in the audit. At the year end, they can probably concentrate on limited substantive work designed to ensure that **the final figures in** the **accounting records** are **complete** and the **disclosure requirements** in respect of directors have been **complied with**.

Auditors may have particular problems here in relation to **non-recurring payments** and **benefits in kind**, as, if the auditors have no previous knowledge of the existence of such items, they are often difficult to detect. Consideration should always be given as to whether some of the more common types of benefit exist (for example a company car or cheap loans).

The auditors should carry out the following general procedures.

- **Ascertain** whether **monies payable or benefits** in kind provided have been **properly approved** in accordance with the company's memorandum and articles of association and that they are not prohibited by the Act

- **Confirm** that all **monies payable** and **benefits receivable** in relation to the current accounting period have been **properly accounted for**, unless the right to any of these has been waived by inspecting:

  - Salary records
  - Service contracts
  - Board minutes
  - Other relevant records

- Review **directors' service contracts**

- **Review** the company's **procedures** to ensure that all directors **advise** the board of all disclosable emoluments

- **Review the procedures** for ensuring that any **payments made to former directors** of the company are identified and properly disclosed

- **Consider** the **need** for any **amounts** included in directors' remuneration to be **further disclosed** in accordance with the Companies Act 1985 (for example property rented by directors from a company at below market rental)

In accordance with the Companies Act 1985 the amount to be disclosed for a benefit in kind is its **estimated money value**. Where the value used is based upon estimates the auditors must ensure that such estimates are made at an appropriate level (for example by the board of directors). On occasions it may be almost impossible to place a meaningful value on the benefit. In such cases it might be advisable for the directors to provide an explanatory note at the foot of the directors' emoluments note.

Under the Companies Act 1985 rules emoluments in respect of a person's accepting office as director shall be treated as emoluments in respect of his services as director.

Key learning points

☑   The largest figure in current liabilities will normally be trade creditors generally checked by comparison of suppliers' statements with purchase ledger accounts.

☑   A creditors' circularisation might be appropriate, although they are relatively rare in practice compared to the frequency of debtors' circularisations.

☑   Accruals can be significant in total. Expense accruals will tend to repeat from one year to the next. Auditors should review after-date invoices and payments, and consider whether anything else that would have been expected has not been accrued.

☑   Long-term liabilities are usually authorised by the board and should be well documented.

☑   Share capital, reserves and statutory books will usually be examined together in an audit.

☑   The main concern with share capital and reserves (including distributions) will be that all transactions comply with the Companies Act.

☑   When auditing statutory books auditors should consider whether:

–   The company has complied with the Companies Act
–   The records contain information that affects other areas of the audit

☑   Auditors should ensure that directors' emoluments have been completely recorded in the accounts.

Quick quiz

1   What are the two primary objectives of balance sheet work on liabilities?

    1   ....

    2   ....

2   Nil balances should not be included in a supplier statement test.

    True   ☐

    False ☐

3   Give two instances where creditors' circularisation is required.

    1   ....

    2   ....

4   Give four things auditors should consider when carrying out analytical review on wages and salaries.

    1   ....

    2   ....

    3   ....

    4   ....

5   Complete the definition

    Long term liabilities comprise ...., ...-........................... and other loans .... at a date .... a year .... the year end.

6   What are the audit objectives relating to share capital?

    1   ....

    2   ....

    3   ....

7   Name three audit procedures in relation to minutes of director's meetings

    1   ....

    2   ....

    3   ....

8   Name three sources of information on director's emoluments.

    1   ....

    2   ....

    3   ....

Answers to quick quiz

1 To ensure (1) completely and (2) accurately recorded

2 False

3 1 Supplier statements are unavailable
   2 Weak internal controls

4 1 Salary rate changes
   2 Average wage by month over the year
   3 Sale/employee
   4 Payroll proof in total

5 debentures, loan-stock, repayable, more than, after.

6 Share capital has been (1) properly classified and (2) disclosed in the financial statements and changes are (3) properly authorised

7 1 Cross reference extracts from minutes regarding financial matters to working papers
   2 Include extracts of agreements referred to in the minutes for the permanent file
   3 Note the date of the last meeting reviewed

8 1 Salary records
   2 Service contracts
   3 Board minutes

Activity checklist

This checklist shows which performance criteria, range statement or knowledge and understanding point is covered by each activity in this chapter. Tick off each activity as you complete it.

Activity

15.1 ☐ This activity deals with Performance Criteria 17.1.G: Select or devise appropriate tasks in accordance with the organisation's procedures.

15.2 ☐ This activity deals with Performance Criteria 17.1.G: Select or devise appropriate tests in accordance with organisation's procedures, 17.2.A: Conduct tests correctly and as specified in the audit plan, record tests properly and draw valid conclusions from them, 17.2.B: Establish the existence, completeness, ownership, valuation and description of assets and liabilities and gather appropriate evidence to support these findings, 17.2.C: Identify all matters of an unusual nature and refer them promptly to the audit supervisor and 17.2.D: Identify and record material and significant errors, deficiencies or other variations from standard and report them to the audit supervisor.

chapter 16

Audit completion

Contents

1 The problem
2 The solution
3 Overall review of financial statements
4 Going concern
5 Management representations
6 Subsequent events
7 Contingencies
8 Communication
9 Completion

Performance criteria

17.2.C Identify all matters of an unusual nature and refer them promptly to the audit supervisor

17.2.D Identify and record material and significant errors, deficiencies or other variations from standard and refer them to the audit supervisor

17.3.D Discuss and agree your preliminary calculations and recommendations with the audit supervisor

Range statement

17.1/2 Tests: tests of control; substantive

Knowledge and understanding

1 A general understanding of the legal duties of auditors: the content of reports; the definition of proper records

1 The problem

Andrew and Chantal have completed much of their detailed audit work on the Balance Sheet. However, Tariq is still not in a position to be able to give an opinion on the financial statements. How should the audit be completed to enable the audit partner to come to his audit opinion?

2 The solution

There are various reviews that auditors carry out to complete an audit. They must also complete a report to the partner, appraising the partner of all the key issues that have arisen during the audit and how they have been dealt with, together with any implications for the audit report.

A key matter to deal with is the matter of management representations. The auditors will have asked management many questions during the course of the audit. In some cases, management's answers may provide the only evidence auditors have on a particular subject. Auditors need to handle such evidence very carefully.

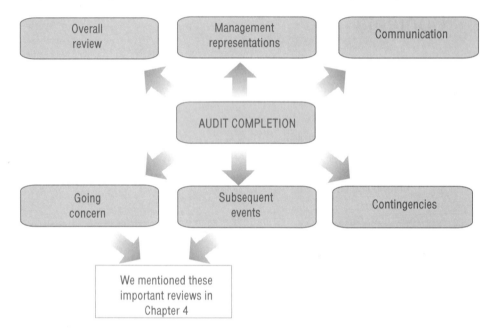

3 Overall review of financial statements

Once the bulk of the substantive procedures have been carried out, the auditors will have a draft set of financial statements which should be supported by appropriate and sufficient audit evidence. SAS 470 *Overall review of financial statements* states that:

> 'Auditors should carry out such a review of the financial statements as is sufficient, in conjunction with the conclusions drawn from the other audit evidence obtained, to give them a reasonable basis for their opinion on the financial statements.'

This review requires appropriate skill and experience on the part of the auditors.

3.1 Compliance with accounting regulations

'Auditors should consider whether the information presented in the financial statements is in accordance with statutory requirements and that the accounting policies employed are in accordance with accounting standards, properly disclosed, consistently applied and appropriate to the entity.'

The SAS suggests that, when compliance with statutory requirements and accounting standards is considered, the auditors may find it useful to use a **checklist**. In fact, it is quite common, particularly in large firms which audit plcs and other complex businesses, to have a variety of pre-printed checklists for different types of client.

Auditors should also consider whether the financial statements as a whole and the assertions contained therein are consistent with their knowledge of the entity's business and with the results of other audit procedures, and the manner of disclosure is fair.

3.2 Analytical procedures

In Chapter 11 we discussed how analytical review procedures are used as part of the overall review procedures at the end of an audit. Analytical review at the final stage must cover:

- Important accounting ratios
- Related items
- Changes in products or customers
- Price and mix changes
- Wages changes
- Variances
- Trends in production and sales
- Changes in material and labour content of production
- Other profit and loss account expenditure
- Variations caused by industry or economy factors

As at other stages, significant fluctuations and unexpected relationships must be investigated and documented.

4 Going concern

In Chapter 4 we talked about the responsibility of the auditors for checking that the directors' assessment of going concern is reasonable. SAS 130 *Going concern basis in financial statements* gives guidance about the procedures auditors should undertake.

The SAS gives guidance to auditors in the context of the going concern basis in financial statements which are required to be properly prepared under the Companies Act and to show a true and fair view.

4.1 Audit procedures

'When forming an opinion as to whether financial statements give a true a fair view, the auditors should consider the entity's ability to continue as a going concern, and any relevant disclosures in the financial statements.'

The audit procedures will be based on the directors' deliberations and the information they used. The auditors must assess whether the audit evidence is sufficient and whether they agree with the directors' judgement.

4.2 Audit evidence

'The auditors should assess the adequacy of the means by which the directors have satisfied themselves that:

(a)   it is appropriate for them to adopt the going concern basis in preparing the financial statements; and

(b)   the financial statements include such disclosures, if any, relating to going concern as are necessary for them to give a true and fair view.

For this purpose:

(a)   the auditors should make enquiries of the directors and examine appropriate available financial information; and

(b)   having regard to the future period to which the directors have paid particular attention in assessing going concern, the auditors should plan and perform procedures specifically designed to identify any material matters which could indicate concern about the entity's ability to continue as a going concern.'

4.2.1 Preliminary assessment

The auditors' approach includes a preliminary assessment, when the overall audit plan is being developed, of the risk that the entity may be unable to continue as a going concern. The auditors should consider:

(a)   **Whether the period** to which the directors have paid particular attention in assessing going concern is **reasonable** in the client's circumstances

(b)   The **systems**, or other means (formal or informal), **for timely identification of warnings of future risks** and uncertainties the entity might face

(c)   **Budget and/or forecast information** (cash flow information in particular) produced by the client, and the quality of the systems (or other means, formal or informal) in place for producing this information and keeping it up to date

(d)   Whether the **key assumptions** underlying the budgets and/or forecasts appear appropriate in the circumstances, including consideration of:

- Projected profit
- Forecast levels of working capital
- The completeness of forecast expenditure
- Whether the client will have sufficient cash at periods of maximum need
- The financing of capital expenditure and long-term plans

(e) The **sensitivity of budgets and/or forecasts** to variable factors both within the control of the directors and outside their control

(f) Any **obligations, undertakings or guarantees** arranged with other entities (in particular, lenders, suppliers and group companies)

(g) The **existence, adequacy and terms of borrowing facilities**, and supplier credit

(h) The **directors' plans** for resolving any matters giving rise to the concern (if any) about the appropriateness of the going concern basis. In particular, the auditors may need to consider whether:

- The plans are realistic
- The plans are likely to resolve any problems foreseen
- The directors are likely to put the plans into practice effectively

The auditors' and directors' procedures can be very simple in some cases, particularly in the case of smaller companies, where budgets and forecasts are not normally prepared and no specific systems are in place to monitor going concern matters.

4.2.2 The auditors' examination of borrowing facilities

The auditors will usually:

- **Obtain confirmations** of the existence and terms of bank facilities
- **Make** their own **assessment** of the intentions of the bankers relating thereto

These procedures will become more important if for example, the client is **dependent** on **borrowing facilities** shortly due for renewal, correspondence between the bankers and the entity reveals that the **last renewal** of facilities was **agreed with difficulty**, or a **significant deterioration in cash flow** is predicted.

If the auditors cannot satisfy themselves then, in accordance with the audit reporting standard (SAS 600), they should consider whether the relevant matters need to be:

- **Disclosed in the financial statements** in order that they give a true and fair view, and/or
- **Referred to in the auditors' report** (by an explanatory paragraph or a qualified opinion)

4.2.3 Determining and documenting the auditors' concerns

The following are given as examples of indicators of an entity's inability to continue as a going concern.

GOING CONCERN	
Financial	An excess of liabilities over assets
	Net current liabilities
	Necessary borrowing facilities have not been agreed
	Default on terms of loan agreements, and potential breaches of covenant
	Significant liquidity or cash flow problems
	Major losses or cash flow problems which have arisen since the balance sheet date and which threaten the entity's continued existence

GOING CONCERN	
	Substantial sales of fixed assets not intended to be replaced
	Major restructuring of debts
	Denial of (or reduction in) normal terms of trade credit by suppliers
	Major debt repayment falling due where refinancing is necessary to the entity's continued existence
	Inability to pay debts as they fall due
Operational	Fundamental changes to the market or technology to which the entity is unable to adapt adequately
	Externally forced reductions in operations (for example, as a result of legislation or regulatory action)
	Loss of key management or staff, labour difficulties or excessive dependence on a few product lines where the market is depressed
	Loss of key suppliers or customers or technical developments which render a key product obsolete
Other	Major litigation in which an adverse judgement would imperil the entity's continued existence
	Issues which involve a range of possible outcomes so wide that an unfavourable result could affect the appropriateness of the going concern basis

Auditors may still obtain sufficient appropriate audit evidence in such situations to conclude that the going concern basis is still appropriate. Further procedures such as discussions with the directors and further work on forecasts may be required. Where auditors consider that there is a significant level of concern about the going concern basis, they might write to the directors suggesting the need to take suitable advice.

4.3 Assessing disclosures in the financial statements

The main concern here is **sufficiency** of disclosure:

- Where there are going concern worries
- Where the future period the directors have considered is less than one year

The auditors must assess whether the statements show a true and fair view and whether their opinion should be qualified, as well as whether all matters have been satisfactorily disclosed.

4.4 Reporting on the financial statements

The SAS summarises, in flowchart form, how auditors formulate their opinion as to whether the financial statements give a true and fair view and this is shown on the next page.

Going concern and reporting on the financial statements

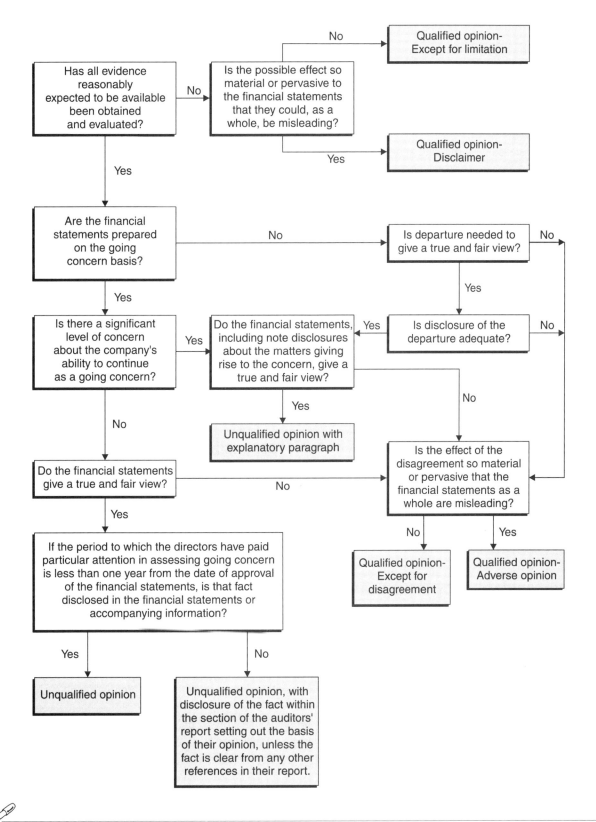

The following matters must be included in the financial statements for disclosure to be regarded as adequate.

- A statement that the financial statements have been prepared on the **going concern basis**
- A statement of the **pertinent facts**
- The **nature** of the concern
- A statement of the **assumptions** adopted by the directors, which should be clearly distinguishable from the pertinent facts
- (Where appropriate and practicable) a statement regarding the directors' **plans for resolving the matters** giving rise to the concern
- Details of any **relevant actions** by the directors

5 Management representations

The auditors receive many representations during the audit and some may be critical to obtaining sufficient appropriate audit evidence. Representations may also be required for general matters, for example, full availability of accounting records. Written confirmation of oral representations avoids confusion and disagreement. The written confirmation may take the form of:

(a) A **representation letter** from **management** (see example below)

(b) A **letter from the auditors** outlining their understanding of management's representations, duly acknowledged and confirmed in writing by management

(c) **Minutes of meetings of the board** or directors, or similar body, at which such representations are approved

5.1 Acknowledgement by directors of their responsibility for the financial statements

The auditors should obtain evidence that the directors acknowledge their collective responsibility for the preparation of the financial statements and have approved the financial statements. Auditors normally do this when they receive a signed copy of the financial statements which incorporate a relevant statement of the directors' responsibilities.

5.2 Representations by management as audit evidence

In addition to representations relating to responsibility for the financial statements, the auditors may wish to rely on management representations as audit evidence. SAS 440 *Management representations* says:

> 'Auditors should obtain written confirmation of representations from management on matters material to the financial statements when those representations are critical to obtaining sufficient appropriate audit evidence.'

Such matters should be discussed with those responsible for giving the written confirmation, to ensure that they understand what they are confirming. Written confirmations are normally required of appropriately senior management. Only matters which are material to the financial statements should be included in a letter of representation. When the auditors receive such representations they should:

(a)   Seek corroborative audit evidence

(b)   Evaluate whether the representations made by management appear reasonable and are consistent with other audit evidence obtained, including other representations

(c)   Consider whether the individuals making the representations can be expected to be well-informed on the particular matters

The SAS then makes a very important point.

'Representations by management cannot be a substitute for other (expected) audit evidence. If auditors are unable to obtain sufficient appropriate audit evidence regarding a matter which may have a material effect on the financial statements and such audit evidence is expected to be available, this constitutes a limitation in the scope of the audit, even if a representation from management has been received on the matter.'

There are two instances given in the SAS where management representations may be the only audit evidence available.

- **Knowledge of the facts is confined to management**, for example, the facts are a matter of management intention.

- **The matter is principally one of judgement or opinion**, for example, the trading position of a particular customer.

There may be occasions when the representations received do not agree with other audit evidence obtained.

Auditors should seek written representation from directors about their conclusion that the company is a **going concern**. If the directors are unhappy to give such representation, the auditors should consider the implication of this for the validity of the assumption.

'If a representation appears to be contradicted by other audit evidence, the auditors should investigate the circumstances to resolve the matter and consider whether it casts doubt on the reliability of other representations.'

Investigations of such situations will normally begin with further enquiries of management. The representations may have been misunderstood or, alternatively, the other evidence misinterpreted. If explanations are insufficient or unforthcoming, then further audit procedures may be required.

5.3 Basic elements of a management representation letter

A management representation letter should:

- Be addressed to the auditors
- Contain the specified information
- Be appropriately dated
- Be approved by those with specific knowledge of the relevant matters

The auditors will normally request that the letter is:

- Discussed and agreed by the board of directors (or equivalent)
- Signed on its behalf by the chairman and secretary before the auditors approve the financial statements

The letter will usually be **dated on** the day the financial statements are **approved**, but if there is any significant delay between the representation letter and the date of the auditors' report, then the auditors should consider the need to obtain further representations.

5.4 Action if management refuses to provide written confirmation of representations

'If management refuses to provide written confirmation of a representation that the auditors consider necessary, the auditors should consider the implications of this scope limitation for their report.'

In these circumstances, the auditors should consider whether it is appropriate to rely on other representations made by management during the audit.

5.5 Example of a management representation letter

An **example** of a management representation letter is provided in an appendix to the SAS. It is **not** a standard letter, and representations do not have to be confirmed in letter form.

(Company letterhead)

(To the auditors)   (Date)

We confirm to the best of our knowledge and belief, and having made appropriate enquiries of other directors and officials of the company, the following representations given to you in connection with your audit of the financial statements for the period ended 31 December 20...

(1)   We acknowledge as directors our responsibilities under the Companies Act 1985 for preparing financial statements which give a true and fair view and for making accurate representations to you. All the accounting records have been made available to you for the purpose of your audit and all the transactions undertaken by the company have been properly reflected and recorded in the accounting records. All other records and related information, including minutes of all management and shareholders' meetings, have been made available to you.

(2)   The legal claim by ABC Limited has been settled out of court by a payment of £258,000. No further amounts are expected to be paid, and no similar claims have been received.

(3)   In connection with deferred tax not provided, the following assumptions reflect the intentions and expectations of the company:

    (a)   capital investment of £450,000 is planned over the next three years;

    (b)   there are no plans to sell revalued properties; and

    (c)   we are not aware of any indications that the situation is likely to change so as to necessitate the inclusion of a provision for tax payable in the financial statements.

(4)   The company has not had, or entered into, at any time during the period any arrangement, transaction or agreement to provide credit facilities (including loans, quasi-loans or credit transactions) for directors or to guarantee or provide security for such matters.

(5) There have been no events since the balance sheet date which necessitate revision of the figures included in the financial statements or inclusion of a note thereto.

As minuted by the board of directors at its meeting on .... (date)

....

Chairman   Secretary

Examples of other issues which may be the subject of representations from management include:

- The extent of the purchase of goods on terms which include reservation of title by suppliers

- The absence of knowledge of circumstances which could result in losses on long-term contracts

- The reasons for concluding that an overdue debt from a related party is fully recoverable

- Confirmation of the extent of guarantees, warranties or other financial commitments relating to subsidiary undertakings or related parties

Activity 16.1

(a) For Chantal's benefit explain what the main purposes of a letter of representation are and how far auditors can rely on the audit evidence it provides.

(b) Draft appropriate representations to cover the following circumstance.

A long-term material balance of £200,000 owed by Y Limited, has been outstanding for nine months at the year-end. The reason for the delay in repayment has been cash flow problems, but the associate's cash flow has improved since the year-end and the directors are confident the debt can be recovered. The company has made a number of small, regular progress payments.

6 Subsequent events

Post balance sheet events are those events, both favourable and unfavourable, which occur between the balance sheet date and the date on which the financial statements are approved by the board of directors.

Adjusting events are post balance sheet events which provide additional evidence of conditions existing at the balance sheet date. They include events which because of statutory conventional requirements are reflected in financial statements. **Non-adjusting events** are post balance sheet events which concern conditions which did not exist at the balance sheet date. You should know how these items are accounted for from your other AAT studies.

In respect of each disclosable post balance sheet event, the notes to the financial statements should state:

- The **nature** of the event
- An **estimate** of the financial effect, or a statement that it is not practicable to make such an estimate

6.1 SAS 150 *Subsequent events*

Subsequent events are those relevant events (favourable or unfavourable) which occur and those facts which are discovered between the period end and the laying of the financial statements before the members or equivalent.

Relevant events are those which:

- Provide additional evidence relating to conditions existing at the balance sheet date or

- Concern conditions which did not exist at the balance sheet date, but which may be of such materiality that their disclosure is required to ensure the financial statements are not misleading.

SAS 150 states that auditors should consider the effect of subsequent events on the financial statements and on their report and should perform procedures designed to obtain sufficient appropriate audit evidence that all material subsequent events up to the date of their report which require adjustment of, or disclosure in, the financial statements have been identified and properly reflected therein.

6.2 Audit procedures

These procedures should be applied to any matters examined during the audit which may be susceptible to change after the year end. They are in addition to tests on specific transactions after the period end, for example cut-off tests.

PROCEDURES TESTING SUBSEQUENT EVENTS	
Enquiries of management	Status of items involving **subjective judgement**/ accounted for using preliminary data
	New **commitments**, borrowings or guarantees
	Sales or destruction of **assets**
	Issues of **shares/debentures** or changes in business structure
	Developments involving **risk areas, provisions** and **contingencies**
	Unusual accounting adjustments
	Major events (eg going concern problems) affecting appropriateness of accounting policies for estimates
Other procedures	**Consider procedures** of management for identifying subsequent events
	Read minutes of general board/committee meetings
	Review latest accounting records and financial information

These procedures should be performed as near as possible to the date of the auditors' report. Reviews and updates of these procedures may be required, depending on the length of the time between the procedures and the signing of the auditors' report and the susceptibility of the items to change over time.

As you know, the financial statements are the directors' responsibility. The directors should therefore inform the auditors of any material subsequent events between the date of the auditors' report and the date the financial statements are issued. The auditors do not have any obligation to perform procedures, or make enquires regarding the financial statements after the date of their report.

If the financial statements are amended, the auditors should extend the subsequent events procedures to the date of their new report, carry out any other appropriate procedures and issue a new audit report dated the day it is signed.

The SAS gives the appropriate procedures which the auditors should undertake when the directors revise the financial statements.

- **Carry out the audit procedures** necessary in the circumstances

- **Consider**, where appropriate, whether Stock Exchange or financial services regulations require the **revision to be publicised** or a regulator to be informed

- **Review the steps taken by the directors** to ensure that anyone in receipt of the previously issued financial statements together with the auditors' report thereon is informed of the situation

- **Issue a new report** on the revised financial statements

When the auditors issue a **new report** they:

- **Refer in their report to the note to the financial statements** which more extensively discusses the reason for the revision of the previous accounts

- **Refer to the earlier report** issued by them on the financial statements

- **Date** their new report **not earlier** than the date the revised financial statements are approved

- **Have regard** to the **guidance** relating to reports on revised annual financial statements and directors' reports as set out in APB's Practice Note 8 *Reports by auditors under company legislation in the United Kingdom*

Where the directors do not revise the financial statements but the auditors feel they should be revised, and where the statements have been issued but not yet laid before the members, or if the directors do not intend to make an appropriate statement at the AGM, then the auditors should consider steps to take, on a timely basis, to prevent reliance on their report. For example, they could make a statement at the AGM. The auditors have no right to communicate to the members directly in writing.

7 Contingencies

You should know the accounting requirements relating to provisions and contingencies. The key distinction is between provisions which are accrued in the accounts, and contingent assets and liabilities, which are not accrued but which may be disclosed.

7.1 Procedures

The audit tests that should be carried out on provisions and contingent assets and liabilities are as follows.

- **Obtain details** of all **provisions** which have been included in the **accounts** and all **contingencies** that have been disclosed

- **Obtain** a **detailed analysis** of all **provisions** showing opening balances, movements and closing balances

- **Determine** for each material provision **whether** the **company** has a **present obligation** as a result of past events by:

    ◦ **Review** of **correspondence** relating to the item

    ◦ **Discussion** with the **directors**. Have they created a valid expectation in other parties that they will discharge the obligation?

- **Determine** for each material provision **whether** it is **probable** that a **transfer of economic benefits** will be required to settle the obligation by the following tests:

    ◦ **Check** whether any **payments** have been **made** in the post balance sheet period in respect of the item

    ◦ **Review of correspondence** with solicitors, banks, customers, insurance company and suppliers both pre and post year end

    ◦ **Send** a **letter** to the **solicitor** to obtain their views (where relevant)

    ◦ **Discuss** the **position** of similar **past provisions** with the directors, were these provisions eventually settled?

    ◦ **Consider** the **likelihood** of **reimbursement**

- **Recalculate** all **provisions** made

- **Compare** the **amount provided** with any post year end payments and with any amount paid in the past for similar items

- In the event that it is not possible to estimate the amount of the **provision, check** that this **contingent liability** is **disclosed** in the accounts

- **Consider** the **nature** of the **client's business**; would you expect to see any other provisions eg warranties?

Activity 16.2

For Chantal's benefit:

(a) Explain what general procedures auditors should carry out when reviewing post balance sheet events.

(b) What information relating to after the balance sheet date, might be relevant, and why, in the following audit areas?

   (i)   Stock
   (ii)   Trade creditors and accruals

(c) Outline how auditors should obtain evidence about legal claims in which clients are involved.

8 Communication

It is vital that the audit senior keeps in contact with the more senior members of the audit team and appraises them of key issues arising.

This will enable the senior members of the team to react to matters they need to react to in the audit, for example, adjustments to risk assessments and materiality levels and also help the audit partner to come to his audit conclusion.

The audit senior will keep in regular contact with the supervisor about how the audit is going. The supervisor may well attend site for part of the audit as well. He will certainly visit at least once to conduct a **review** of the audit work carried out.

8.1 Review

As we discussed in Chapter 7, each member of the audit team will be involved in reviewing the work of junior members of the team. The supervisor and probably the audit manager will attend site to review work carried out.

The engagement partner is unlikely to review the audit file until the audit has been completed and the audit team have left site, so the audit manager must ensure that the audit has been completed satisfactorily.

8.2 Report to partner

The audit team will compile a report for the benefit of the partner to be maintained in the audit file which will summarise the key findings during the audit.

As the audit manager will have reviewed the audit file, the engagement partner will not necessarily review the entire file. The report to partner will point the partner in the direction of key issues arising, should he want to review the audit work carried out in more detail.

9 Completion

9.1 Summarising errors

In evaluating whether the financial statements give a true a fair view, auditors should assess the materiality of the aggregate of uncorrected misstatements. The aggregate of uncorrected misstatements comprises:

(a) **Specific misstatements** identified by the auditors, including uncorrected misstatements identified during the audit of the previous period if they affect the current period's financial statements

(b) Their **best estimate** of **other misstatements** which cannot be quantified specifically

If the auditors consider that the aggregate of misstatements may be material, they must consider reducing audit risk by extending audit procedures or requesting the directors to adjust the financial statements (which the directors may wish to do anyway). The auditors should consider the implications for their audit report if:

- The directors refuse to adjust.

- The extended audit procedures do not enable the auditors to conclude that the aggregate of uncorrected misstatements is not material.

The summary of errors will not only list errors from the current year, but also those in the previous year(s). This will allow errors to be highlighted which are reversals of errors in the previous year, such as in the valuation of closing/opening stock. Cumulative errors may also be shown, which have increased from year to year.

SCHEDULE OF UNADJUSTED ERRORS

| | 20X2 | | | | 20X1 | | | |
| | P & L account | | Balance sheet | | P & L account | | Balance sheet | |
	Dr	Cr	Dr	Cr	Dr	Cr	Dr	Cr
	£	£	£	£	£	£	£	£
(a) ABC Ltd debt unprovided	10,470			10,470	4,523			4,523
(b) Opening/ closing stock under-valued*	21,540			21,540		21,540	21,540	
(c) Closing stock undervalued		34,105	34,105					
(d) Opening unaccrued expenses								
Telephone*		453	453		453			453
Electricity*		905	905		905			905
(e) Closing unaccrued expenses								
Telephone	427			427				
Electricity	1,128			1,128				
(f) Obsolete stock write off	2,528			2,528	3,211			3,211
Total	36,093	35,463	35,463	36,093	9,092	21,540	21,540	9,092
*Cancelling items	21,540			21,540				
		453	453					
		905	905					
	14,553	34,105	34,105	14,553				

The schedule will be used by the audit manager and partner to decide whether the client should be requested to make adjustments to the financial statements.

9.2 Completion checklists

Audit firms frequently use checklists which must be signed off to ensure that all final procedures have been carried out, all material amounts are supported by sufficient appropriate evidence, etc. An example follows.

Audit completion checklist

Client:

Period ended:

Instructions:

1   All questions must be answered by ticking one of the columns as appropriate.

2   Any 'No' answer must be reference to the 'points for partner' schedule.

Section I – To be completed by manager	Yes	No	N/A	*Reference to point for partner schedule*

Permanent audit file
1   Have the following been updated in the course of the audit:
(a) Flowcharts and related documentation for:
    (i) computer systems?
    (ii) non-computer systems?
(b) Internal/key control evaluation questionnaire conclusions?
(c) Details of the client organisation?
(d) Financial history?				

2 Is a current letter of engagement in force?				
Transaction (interim) audit file 3 Were walk-through tests performed to confirm our record of the accounting systems?				
4 Was the audit programme tailored?				
5 Was adequate audit attention given to internal control weaknesses				
6 Were levels of audit testing (compliance and substantive) appropriate?				
7 Have audit programmes been signed off as complete?				
8 Are there adequate explanations of work done and are conclusions drawn?				
9 Is there evidenced of the review of work?				
10 Have weaknesses arising on the interim audit been reported to management in a formal letter?				
11 Has the client replied to the weaknesses already notified in respect of matters arising from the previous year's audit?				
12 Have major internal control weaknesses previously notified been rectified?				

	Yes	No	N/A	Reference to point for partner schedule
Final (balance sheet) audit file				
13 Have lead schedules been prepared for each audit area and cross-referenced and agreed with the financial statements?				
14 Have all the working papers been installed and dated by the members of staff who prepared them?				
15 Have all the working papers been cross-references				
16 Do the working papers show comparative figures where appropriate?				
17 Have audit conclusions been drawn for each balance sheet audit areas as appropriate				
18 Has the balance sheet audit programme been completed, initialled and cross-referenced to the working papers?				
19 Have the necessary profit and loss account schedules been prepared and do they agree with the detailed accounts?				
20 Current asset: (a) Were debtors circularised and were the results satisfactory? (b) Was the client's stocktaking attended and were the results satisfactory? (c) Is the basis of stock and work in progress valuation satisfactory and correctly disclosed in the account?				
21 Liabilities: (a) Were creditors circularised and were the results satisfactory? (b) Have all liabilities, contingent liabilities, and capital commitments been fully accounted for or noted in the accounts?				
Audit completion 22 Have formal representations been obtained or has a draft letter been set up (including representations in respect of each director regarding transactions involving himself and his connected persons required to be disclosed by the Companies Act 1985)				
23 Have all audit queries been satisfactorily answered?				

	Yes	No	N/A	Reference to point for partner schedule
24 Post balance sheet event review: (a) Has a comprehensive review been performed and evidenced? (b) Has the review been carried out at the most recent date possible with regard to the anticipated date of the audit report?				
25 Have all audit queries been satisfactorily answered?				
26 Have all closing adjustments been agreed with the client?				
27 Are you satisfied that all material instances where we have not received the information and explanations we require have been referred to in the points for partner schedule?				
28 Review of working papers? (a) Have you reviewed all the working papers? (If not, briefly describe review procedure adopted) (b) Have arrangements been made for the financial statements to be reviewed by: (i) a second partner (a brief review or special review)? and/or (ii) the audit review panel? (c) Has the planning memorandum and, where applicable, client risk evaluation questionnaire been completed?				
Subsidiary and associated companies 29 Where secondary auditors have been involved in the audit of subsidiary and associated companies, have we: (a) Sent our group accounts audit questionnaire? (b) Received satisfactory answers? or (c) Reviewed and approved the working papers of secondary auditors?				
30 Have all accounts of subsidiary and associated companies been approved by the directors and audited?				
31 If any of the audit reports have been qualified has the fact and nature of the qualification been referred to in the points for partner schedule?				
Financial statements and directors' report 32 Is the financial statements layout in accordance with the firm's standard accounts pack?				
33 Has the analytical review memorandum been properly completed and are the review conclusions consistent with the conclusions drawn in respect of our other audit work?				

		Yes	No	N/A	Reference to point for partner schedule
34	Is the reliance placed on analytical review reasonable in the circumstances?				
35	Is any proposed dividend covered by the distributable profits as disclosed in the financial statements?				
36	Has the firm's accounting disclosure checklist been completed to ensure that the financial statements and directors' report comply with: (a) the Companies Act 1985? (b) Statements of Standard Accounting Practice and Financial Reporting Standards? (c) Stock Exchange requirements? (d) Other reporting requirements?				
37	Has the directors' report been reviewed for consistency with the financial statements?				
38	Has other financial information to be issued with the audited financial statements (eg contained in the Chairman's Statement or Employee Accounts) been reviewed for consistency with the financial statements?				

Audit Manager ....   Date...

Section II – To be completed by the reporting partner	Yes	No	Comments
1 Has Section I of the checklist been satisfactorily completed?			
2 Have all the points on the 'points for partner' schedule been satisfactorily resolved or are there any material matters outstanding which should be referred to the audit panel?			
3 Has your review of the current and permanent file indicated that the working paper evidence is sufficient to enable you to form an opinion on the financial statements, having regard to the firm's audit manual procedures?			
4 Are the conclusions you have drawn from your overall review of the financial statements based on your knowledge of the client, consideration of the analytical review memorandum, review of post balance sheet events and where appropriate, client risk evaluation questionnaire, consistent with those contained in the detailed working papers?			
5 Have all improvements which you consider could be made in the conduct of future audits been noted on 'points forward' (for consideration at the audit debriefing)?			
6 (a) Are there any specialist areas in which the client could benefit from our expertise, for example tax planning? (b) Has the provision of such services been drawn to his attention?			

I confirm that the report of the auditors will be unqualified*/unqualified with an explanatory paragraph*/qualified* as set out in the attached draft financial statements.

Reporting Partner ....   Date ....

* Delete as appropriate

Activity 16.3

Draft any sections of the Report to Partner you feel are relevant from the audit work you and Chantal have done at AJ (Paper) Ltd for the year ended 31 December 2002.

Key learning points

☑ The auditors must perform and document an overall review of the financial statements before they can reach an opinion, covering:

 – Compliance with statute and accounting standards
 – Consistency with audit evidence
 – Overall reasonableness

☑ Analytical procedures should be used at the final stage of audit. The review should cover:

 – Key business ratios
 – Related items in accounts
 – The effect of known changes on the accounts

☑ Evaluation of going concern is most important. Auditors should consider the future plans of directors and any signs of going concern problems which may be noted throughout the audit. Bank facilities may have to be confirmed.

☑ When reporting on the accounts, auditors should consider whether the going concern basis is appropriate, and whether disclosure of going concern problems is sufficient.

☑ Representations from management should generally be restricted to matters that cannot be verified by other audit procedures.

☑ Any representations should be compared with other evidence and their sufficiency assessed.

☑ Auditors should consider the effect of subsequent events (after the balance sheet date) on the accounts.

☑ Auditors have a responsibility to review subsequent events before they sign their audit report, and may have to take action if they become aware of subsequent events between the date they sign their audit report and the date the financial statements are laid before members.

☑ The audit of contingencies involves reviewing the company's dealing with solicitors, and is generally connected to the subsequent events review.

☑ As part of their completion procedures, auditors should consider whether the aggregate of uncorrected misstatements is material.

Quick quiz

1   What are the five principal considerations in a review of the financial statements for consistency and reasonableness?

    1   ....

    2   ....

    3   ....

    4   ....

    5   ....

2   Complete the table putting the indicators of an entity's inability to continue as a going concern under the correct headings.

Financial	Operational	Other

(a) Litigation   (c) Fundamental changes to market   (e) Denial of trade credit by suppliers

(b) Inability to pay due debts   (d) Loss of key customers   (f) Loss of key management

3   The directors must satisfy themselves that the going concern basis in the financial statements is appropriate.

True   ☐

False   ☐

4   Name two instances given in SAS 440 of when management representation may be the only audit evidence available.

    1   ....

    2   ....

5   What types of misstatement might be included in the aggregate of uncorrected misstatements?

6 In evaluating whether the financial statement give a true and fair view, auditors should assess the materiality of the aggregate of uncorrected misstatements.

True ☐

False ☐

7 Complete the definition, using the words given in the box below.

…………………… …………………. are those which provide …………………. evidence relating to the conditions ……………………….. and the balance sheet date, or concern …………….. which …………… ……………. ……………… at the balance sheet date, but which may be of such …………………. that their ………………….. is required to ensure the financial statements are not misleading.

> events, existing, relevant, not, conditions, exist, additional, did, disclosure, materiality

Answers to quick quiz

1 When reviewing accounts for consistency and reasonableness auditors should consider:

1 Whether the accounts reflect the information and explanations and the conclusions reached during the audit

2 Whether the review reveals any new factors which may affect the presentation and disclosure of the accounts

3 The results of analytical procedures at the end of the audit

4 Whether the presentation of the accounts may have been unduly influenced by the directors

5 The effect of the aggregate of uncorrected misstatements

2

Financial	Operational	Other
(b)	(c)	(a)
(e)	(d)	
	(f)	

3 True

4 • When facts are confined to management
• When the matter is one of management judgement

5 Misstatements that may be included in the statement are specific misstatements identified by the auditors, and the auditors' best estimate of other misstatements.

6 True

7 Relevant events, additional, existing, conditions, did not exist, materiality, disclosure

Activity checklist

This checklist shows which performance criteria, range statement or knowledge and understanding point is covered by each activity in this chapter. Tick off each activity as you complete it.

Activity

16.1 ☐ This activity deals with Performance Criteria 17.2.C: Identify all matters of an unusual nature and refer them promptly to the audit supervisor and 17.2.D: Identify and record material and significant errors, deficiencies or other variations from standard and report them to the audit supervisor.

16.2 ☐ This activity deals with Performance Criteria 17.2.C: Identify all matters of an unusual nature and refer them promptly to the audit supervisor and 17.2.D: Identify and record material and significant errors, deficiencies or other variations from standard and report them to the audit supervisor and 17.3.D: Discuss and agree your preliminary conclusions and recommendations with the audit supervisor.

16.3 ☐ This activity deals with Performance Criteria 17.2.C: Identify all matters of an unusual nature and refer them promptly to the audit supervisor and 17.2.D: Identify and record material and significant errors, deficiencies or other variations from standard and report them to the audit supervisor and 17.3.D: Discuss and agree your preliminary conclusions and recommendations with the audit supervisor.

chapter 17

Group audits

Contents

1   The problem
2   The solution
3   Principal auditors and other auditors
4   Procedures
5   Reporting considerations

Performance criteria

All the performance criteria and range statements apply to group audits.

Range statement

All the performance criteria and range statements apply to group audits.

1 The problem

Chantal has been booked on another audit. It is a large audit of a group of companies. Khan Associates is auditing the parent company and two of the subsidiaries, but another firm will be auditing another subsidiary and other associated companies.

Chantal has been asking Andrew how group audits work. How can two firms of auditors be involved in one audit?

2 The solution

First, Chantal is under a misapprehension about the audit of a group. It is not merely **one** audit.

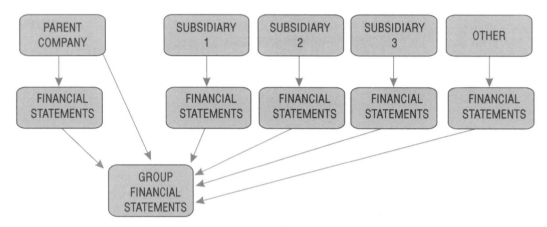

Each set of financial statements will be audited. Connection between the firms of auditors is only relevant for the group financial statements.

Note that the majority of the contents of the group financial statements have already been audited. Khan Associates will audit the intra-company aspects and the additional group disclosures. They can rely on their own audit of the parent and subsidiaries 1 and 2, and may seek to rely on the other auditors' work for the rest of the group, in a similar way to them relying on the work of the expert.

Auditing standards give guidance on how this works, in SAS 510 *The relationship between principal auditors and other auditors,* which we will look at here.

3 Principal auditors and other auditors

Principal auditors are the auditors with responsibility for reporting on the financial statements of an entity when those financial statements include financial information of one or more components audited by other auditors.

Other auditors are auditors, other than the principal auditors, with responsibility for reporting on the financial information of a component which is included in the financial statements audited by the principal auditors. Other auditors include affiliated firms, whether using the same name or not, and correspondent firms, as well as unrelated auditors.

Component is a division, branch, subsidiary, joint venture, associated undertaking or other entity whose financial information is included in financial statements audited by the principal auditors.

The duty of the principal auditors is to report on the group accounts, including therefore all entities included in the group accounts. The principal auditors have **sole responsibility** for this opinion even where the group financial statements include amounts derived from accounts which have not been audited by them. As a result, they cannot discharge their responsibility to report on the group financial statements by an unquestioning acceptance of component companies' financial statements, whether audited or not.

3.1 Rights of principal auditors

The principal auditors have the following rights:

(a) The **right to require from the other auditors** of a UK-incorporated company such **information and explanations** as they may reasonably require (s 389A(3) CA 1985)

(b) The right to **require the parent company** to take all reasonable steps to **obtain reasonable information** and explanations from the subsidiary and this will include foreign subsidiaries (s 389A(4) CA 1985)

Even where their responsibilities in this regard are not set down by statute (for example where the component company is an associated company not a subsidiary), the other auditors should appreciate that the component company's financial statements will ultimately form a part of the group financial statements.

In principle, the other auditors should therefore be prepared to co-operate with the principal auditors and make available such information as the principal auditors may require in order to discharge their duties as auditors of the group financial statements.

The principal auditors must decide how to take account of the work carried out by the other auditors. The extent of the procedures adopted by the principal auditors will be determined by the **materiality** of the amounts derived from the financial statements of components of the group, and the **level of risk** that the auditors are willing to accept that such statements contain material errors.

SAS 510 sets out that auditors have sufficient involvement to give an opinion on group accounts. The principal auditors should not be so far removed from large parts of the group audit that they are unable to form an opinion. The SAS suggests that, in this context, the principal auditors should consider the following.

- The **materiality** of the portion of the financial statements which they do not audit

- The **degree of their knowledge** regarding the business of the components

- The **nature of their relationship** with the firms acting as other auditors

- Their **ability** where necessary to **perform additional procedures** to enable them to act as principal auditors

- The **risk of material misstatements** in the financial statements of the components audited by other auditors

4 Procedures

SAS 510 says:

> 'When planning to use the work of other auditors, principal auditors should consider the professional qualifications, experience and resources of the other auditors in the context of the specific assignment.'

The initial enquires of this nature will be concerned with:

- The other auditors' membership of a professional body
- The **reputation** of any firm to which the other auditors are affiliated

> 'Principal auditors should obtain sufficient appropriate audit evidence that the work of the other auditors is adequate for the principal auditors' purposes.'

In order to obtain such evidence at the planning stage, the principal auditors should advise the other auditors of the use they intend to make of their work and make arrangement for the co-ordination of their audit efforts. The principal auditors will inform the other auditors about the following matters.

- **Areas** requiring **special consideration** (key risks, control environment)
- Procedures for the identification of disclosable inter-group transactions
- Procedures for notifying principal auditors of unusual circumstances
- The timetable for completion of the audit
- The independence requirements
- The relevant accounting, auditing and reporting requirements

The other auditors should give representations on independence and accounting, auditing and reporting requirements.

The nature, timing and extent of the principal auditors' procedures will depend on the individual circumstances of the engagement (for example, risk and materiality) and their assessment of the other auditors. Procedures that the principal auditors may use include the following.

- **Discussions** with the other auditors about their audit procedures
- **Review** of a **written summary** of those procedures (perhaps using a questionnaire or checklist)
- **Review** of the other auditors' **working papers**

These procedures may be unnecessary if evidence has already been obtained of adequate quality control over the other auditors' work, for example, through inter-firm reviews within affiliated firms.

Having received the agreed work, documentation etc from the other auditors the principal auditors need to consider the significant findings of the other auditors. This consideration may involve the following.

- **Discussions** with the other auditors and with the directors or management of the component

- **Review** of copies of **reports to directors** or **management** issued by the other auditors

- **Supplementary tests**, performed by the principal auditors or by the other auditors, on the financial statements of the component

The other auditors should co-operate with the principal auditors and assist them by drawing to their attention any matters they discover in their audit which they feel is likely to be relevant to the principal auditors' work. They may do so:

- By **direct communication** (with permission from the component or where there is a statutory obligation)
- By reference in their audit report

If the other auditors are unable to perform any aspect of their work as requested, they should inform the principal auditors.

4.1 Information supplied by principal auditors

The other auditors have **sole responsibility** for their audit opinion on the financial statements of the component they audit. They should **not** rely on the principal auditors informing them of matters which might have an impact on the financial statements of the component. If they wish to do so, they should seek representations directly from the directors or management of the entity audited by the principal auditors.

The principal auditors have no obligation, statutory or otherwise, to provide information to other auditors. Where during the course of their audit, they discover matters which they consider may be relevant to the other auditors' work, they should discuss and agree an appropriate course of action with the directors of the entity which they audit. This may involve the principal auditors communicating directly with the other auditors, or the directors informing the component or the other auditors.

If the circumstances are such that the information cannot be passed to the other auditors, for example due to sensitive commercial considerations, the principal auditors should take **no further action**. To divulge such information in these situations would be a breach of client confidentiality.

5 Reporting considerations

The SAS makes the following important points about the principal auditors' report.

> 'When the principal auditors are satisfied that the work of the other auditors is adequate for the purposes of their audit, *no reference* to the other auditors is made in the principal auditors' report.
>
> The principal auditors have sole responsibility for their audit opinion and a reference to the other auditors in the principal auditors' report may be misunderstood and interpreted as a qualification of their opinion or a division of responsibility, neither of which is appropriate.'

The principal auditors must consider the implications for their report when they **cannot** obtain sufficient evidence about the work of the other auditors, and it has not been possible to perform additional procedures in respect of the component's financial statements.

The reports of other auditors on the component's financial statements may contain a qualified opinion or an explanatory paragraph referring to an uncertainty.

In such cases the principal auditors should consider whether the subject of the qualification or fundamental uncertainty is of **such nature and significance**, in relation to the financial statements of the entity on which they are reporting, that it should be reflected in their audit report.

Key learning points

☑ Principal auditors (group auditors) have sole responsibility for the opinion on the group accounts. They should consider whether their participation is sufficient to allow them to act as principal auditors.

☑ When dealing with other auditors, principal auditors should:

– Identify during planning key audit issues and requirements

– Gain sufficient assurance about other auditors' work (by discussions, checklists, review of working papers)

– Consider the significant findings of other auditors

☑ Other auditors should co-operate with the principal auditors.

Quick quiz

1   Match the auditors with the correct definition.

     (a)   Principal auditors

     (b)   Other auditors

         (i)   The auditors with responsibility for reporting on the financial statements of an entity when those financial statements include financial information of one or more components by others.

         (ii)   Auditors with responsibility for reporting on the financial information of a component which is included in the financial statements audited by another firm. This includes affiliated firms, whether using the same name or not, and correspondent firms, as well as unrelated auditors.

2   List three rights of principal auditors

     1   ....

     2   ....

     3   ....

3   Complete the matters which the principal auditors must consider in relation to a group audit.

     •   The ....of the portion of the financial statements which they do not audit.

     •   The .... regarding the business of the component.

     •   The .... of their .... with the other auditors.

     •   Their ability, where necessary, to ....
....

     •   The risk of .... in the financial statements not audited by them.

4   Name four factors the principal auditors should take into account when planning the nature, timing and extent of their procedures.

     1   ....

     2   ....

     3   ....

     4   ....

Answers to quick quiz

1   (a)(i), (b)(ii)

2   1   Statutory rights and duties in relation to audit of holding company

   2   Right to require information and explanations of auditors of a UK incorporated company included in the consolidation

   3   Right to require the parent company to take all reasonable steps to obtain information and explanations from the subsidiary.

3   Materiality, degree of their knowledge, nature, relationship, perform additional procedures, material misstatements.

4   1   Assessment of other auditors
   2   Risks
   3   Materiality of components
   4   Relationship with clients

P A R T D

Preparing draft reports

chapter 18

Reports to
management

Contents

1   The problem
2   The solution
3   Reports to those charged with governance
4   Reports to management

Performance criteria

17.1.D Record significant weaknesses in control correctly

17.3.A Prepare clear and concise draft reports relating to the audit assignment and submit them for review
         and approval in line with organisational procedures

17.3.B Draw valid conclusions and provide evidence to support them

17.3.C Make constructive and practicable recommendations

Range statement

17.3   Draft reports relating to a manual system

Knowledge and understanding

11   Management letters which include systems weaknesses, clerical/accounting mistakes, disagreement re
         accounting policies or treatment

1 The problem

Anton has asked Tariq if the audit team can appraise him of relevant audit matters and of any weaknesses they observe in the systems and financial statements.

How should they do that?

2 The solution

Reporting to management and 'those charged with governance', ie directors, is governed by auditing standards. In fact, SAS 610 *Communication of audit matters to those charged with governance* sets out that auditors must communicate certain matters with directors. One such matter is major control weaknesses. Auditors would traditionally report control weakness to management, for example the accountant, as well.

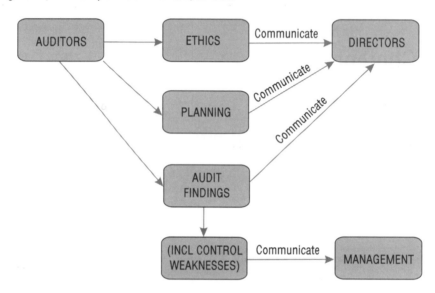

3 Reports to those charged with governance

Those charged with governance are those persons entrusted with the supervision, control and direction of an entity. Those charged with governance include the directors of a company or other body, the partners, proprietors, committee of management or trustees or other forms of entity, or equivalent persons responsible for directing the entity's affairs and preparing its financial statements.

Management is those persons who have executive responsibility for the conduct of the entity's operations and the preparation of its financial statements.

SAS 610 requires that auditors should communicate relevant matters relating to the audit of the financial statements to those charged with governance of the entity. Such communications should be on a sufficiently prompt basis to enable those charged with governance to take appropriate action.

It is also important to the audit process that the two parties **share available information**, and that the auditors can make **constructive observations** to the entity.

3.1 The communication process

Many of the factors in the communication process, such as, 'to whom?' 'when?' 'how often?' will depend on the size of the entity and the environment in which it operates. The SAS suggests that form and timing must be planned and determined according to the recipients, who might be the **board of directors**, or the **audit committee**. The SAS states that, **ordinarily**, before discussing matters with those charged with governance, the auditors are likely to **discuss them with management**. Sometimes, particularly in smaller entities, management and directors will be the same people.

Similarly, the **form** of the communication will depend upon circumstances. It may be **written** or **oral**. Matters to consider are:

- The size, structure, and communication process of the entity
- The nature, sensitivity and significance of the matters arising
- Statutory or regulatory requirements
- Arrangements made by the parties, as outlined above

3.2 Relevant matters

3.2.1 Matters of independence and objectivity

It is particularly important to discuss matters of independence with clients who are listed on a stock exchange.

3.2.2 Planning matters

Planning matters to communicate might include materiality, material misstatements, approach to internal controls, extent to which external auditors intend to rely on internal auditors and any work to be undertaken by other auditors.

3.2.3 Audit findings

These will include:

- Expected modifications to the auditors' report

- Unadjusted misstatements

- Material weaknesses in the accounting and internal control systems identified during the audit

- Their views about the qualitative aspects of the entity's accounting practices and financial reporting

- Matters specifically required by other Auditing Standards to be communicated to those charged with governance and

- Any other relevant matters relating to the audit.

The auditors should discuss significant misstatements with those charged with governance. It might be that the auditors want the financial statements amended, while the directors do not want to make amendments. If this is the case, the SAS advises that the auditors seek confirmation of their reasons by written representation.

3.3 Third parties

There may be occasion when third parties are interested in the report to those charged with governance. The auditor should ensure that the recipients of the letter understand that it is not intended for third parties.

It might be appropriate to include a **disclaimer** in the letter, stating that it is for the sole use of the addressee and must not be quoted or referred to without the written consent of the auditor.

4 Reports to management

The main purposes of reports to management are for auditors to communicate various points that have come to their attention during the audit.

- The **design** and **operation** of the **accounting and internal control systems,** including suggestions for their improvement

- **Other constructive advice**, for example comments on potential economies or improvements in efficiency

- **Other matters**, for example comments on adjusted and unadjusted errors in the financial statements or on particular accounting policies and practices

4.1 Material weaknesses in the accounting and internal control systems

A **material weakness** is one which may result in a **material misstatement** in the financial statements. If it is corrected by management, it need not be reported, but the discovery and correction should be documented.

To be effective, the report should be made **as soon as possible** after **completion** of the **audit procedures**. A written report is usual, but some matters may be raised orally with a file note to record the auditors' observation and the directors' response. Where no report is felt to be necessary, the auditors should inform management that no material weaknesses have been found. They would still be required to report to those charged with governance.

Where the audit work is performed on more than one visit, the auditors will normally report to management after the interim audit work has been completed as well as after the final visit.

The final report to management can cover the following issues.

(a)   **Additional matters** under the same headings as the interim letter, if sent

(b)   Details of **inefficiencies** or **delays** in the agreed timetable for preparation of the accounts or of workings schedules which delayed the completion of the audit and may have resulted in increased costs

(c)   Any **significant differences** between the **accounts** and any **management accounts** or budgets which not only caused audit problems but also detract from the value of management information

(d)   Any results of the auditors' **analytical procedures** of which management may not be aware and may be of benefit to them

If the auditors choose not to send a formal letter or report but consider it preferable to discuss any weaknesses with management, the discussion should be **minuted** or otherwise recorded in writing. Management should be provided with a copy of the note.

The auditors should explain in their report to management that it **only** includes those matters which came to their attention as a result of the audit procedures, and that it should not be regarded as a comprehensive statement of all weaknesses that exist or all improvements that might be made.

The auditors should request a **reply** to all the points raised, indicating what action management intends to take as a result of the comments made in the report. If **previous points** have **not** been **dealt with effectively** and they are still considered significant, the auditors should enquire why action has not been taken.

The report may contain matters of varying levels of significance and thus make it difficult for senior management to identify points of significance. The auditors can deal with this by giving the report a **'tiered' structure** so that major points are dealt with by the directors or the audit committee and minor points are considered by less senior personnel.

Other points to note about the management letter are as follows.

- The recommendations should take the form of **suggestions** backed up by **reason and logic**.

- The letter should be in **formal terms** unless the client requests otherwise.

- **Weaknesses** that **management** are aware of but **choose not to do anything about** should be **mentioned** to protect the auditors.

- If management or staff have **agreed to changes**, this should be mentioned in a letter.

4.2 Third parties interested in reports to directors or management

Any report made to directors or management should be regarded as a confidential communication. The auditors should therefore not normally reveal the contents of the report to any third party without the prior written consent of the directors or management of the company.

In practice, the auditors have little control over what happens to the report once it has been despatched. Occasionally management may provide third parties with copies of the report, for example their bankers or certain regulatory authorities.

Thus care should be taken to protect the auditors' position from exposure to liability in negligence to any third parties who may seek to rely on the report. Accordingly, the auditors should state clearly in their report that it has been prepared for the private use of the client.

4.3 Specimen management letter

A specimen letter is provided below which demonstrates how the principles described in the previous paragraphs are put into practice.

SPECIMEN MANAGEMENT LETTER

ABC & Co
Certified Accountants
29 High Street
London, N10 4KB

The Board of Directors,

Manufacturing Co Limited,

15 South Street

London, S20 1CX

1 April 20X8

Members of the board,

Financial statements for the year ended 31 May 20X8

In accordance with our normal practice we set out in this letter certain matters which arose as a result of our review of the accounting systems and procedures operated by your company during our recent interim audit.

We would point out that the matters dealt with in this letter came to our notice during the conduct of our normal audit procedures which are designed primarily for the purpose of expressing our opinion on the financial statements of your company. In consequence our work did not encompass a detailed review of all aspects of the system and cannot be relied on necessarily to disclose defalcations or other irregularities or to include all possible improvements in internal control.

1   *Purchases: ordering procedures*

Present system

During the course of our work we discovered that it was the practice of the stores to order certain goods from X Ltd orally without preparing either a purchase requisition or purchase order.

Implications

There is therefore the possibility of liabilities being set up for unauthorised items and at a non-competitive price.

Recommendations

We recommend that the buying department should be responsible for such orders and, if they are placed orally, an official order should be raised as confirmation.

2   *Purchase ledger reconciliation*

Present system

Although your procedures require that the purchase ledger is reconciled against the control account on the nominal ledger at the end of every month, this was not done in December or January.

Implications

The balance on the purchase ledger was short by some £2,120 of the nominal ledger control account at 31 January 20X8 for which no explanation could be offered. This implies a serious breakdown in the purchase invoice and/or cash payment batching and posting procedures.

Recommendations

It is important in future that this reconciliation is performed regularly by a responsible official independent of the day to day purchase ledger, cashier and nominal ledger functions.

3 *Sales ledger: credit control*

Present system

As at 28 February 20X8 debtors account for approximately 12 weeks' sales, although your standard credit terms are cash within 30 days of statement, equivalent to an average of about 40 days (6 weeks) of sales.

Implications

This has resulted in increased overdraft usage and difficulty in settling some key suppliers accounts on time.

Recommendations

We recommend that a more structured system of debt collection be considered using standard letters and that statements should be sent out a week earlier if possible.

4 *Preparation of payroll and maintenance of personnel records*

Present system

Under your present system, just two members of staff are entirely and equally responsible for the maintenance of personnel records and preparation of the payroll. Furthermore, the only independent check of any nature on the payroll is that the chief accountant confirms that the amount of the wages cheque presented to him for signature agrees with the total of the net wages column in the payroll. This latter check does not involve any consideration of the reasonableness of the amount of the total net wages cheque or the monies being shown as due to individual employees.

Implications

It is a serious weakness of your present system, that so much responsibility is vested in the hands of just two people. This situation is made worse by the fact that there is no clearly defined division of duties as between the two of them. In our opinion, it would be far too easy for fraud to take place in this area (eg by inserting the names of 'dummy workmen' into the personnel records and hence on to the payroll) and/or for clerical errors to go undetected.

Recommendations

(i)   Some person other than the two wages clerks be made responsible for maintaining the personnel records and for periodically (but on a surprise basis) checking them against the details on the payroll;

(ii) The two wages clerks be allocated specific duties in relation to the preparation of the payroll, with each clerk independently reviewing the work of the other;

(iii) When the payroll is presented in support of the cheque for signature to the chief accountant, that he should be responsible for assessing the reasonableness of the overall charge for wages that week.

> Our comments have been discussed with your finance director and the chief accountant and these matters will be considered by us again during future audits. We look forward to receiving your comments on the points made. Should you require any further information or explanations do not hesitate to contact us.
>
> This letter has been produced for the sole use of your company. It must not be disclosed to a third party, or quoted or referred to, without our written consent. No responsibility is assumed by us to any other person.
>
> We should like to take this opportunity of thanking your staff for their co-operation and assistance during the course of our audit.
>
> Yours faithfully
>
> ABC & Co

Activity 18.1

During the audit of AJ (Paper) Ltd you have ascertained the following weaknesses within the systems of internal control.

(a) The ordering, recording and payment for purchases of materials are made by the administration department manager.

(b) When goods have been completed they are transferred to the finished goods area to await loading for delivery: these goods are not checked to ensure they agree with the customer order.

(c) All production department workers are paid on an hourly basis as per the hours on their time records. These records are completed by each worker on a weekly basis and are not checked by the supervisor prior to being submitted to the payroll department.

(d) The office workers are paid monthly by direct transfer to their bank accounts: any changes to the salaries are notified verbally to the payroll department by the personnel manager.

Required

Based on the above information, draft the management letter giving:

(i)   A description of the weakness
(ii)   Implications of the weakness
(iii) Recommendations to address the weakness

BPP
PROFESSIONAL EDUCATION

Key learning points

☑ Auditing standards require auditors to communicate audit matters with those charged with governance.

☑ Audit matters include:
- Ethical matters (independence and objectivity)
- Planning
- Audit findings (including major control weaknesses)

☑ Auditors will often also report control weaknesses to management.

☑ If the report is made verbally, the auditors should minute the conversation.

☑ Weakness reporting usually takes the format:
- Weakness
- Consequence
- Recommendation

Quick quiz

1   Auditors can never be liable to third parties on the information contained within the report communicating audit matters to those charged with governance.

True   [   ]

False [   ]

2   What matters should the report to those charged with governance cover?

3   What format will the report to management take?

1   ....

2   ....

3   ....

4   Auditors should always communicate with management in writing:

True   [   ]

False [   ]

Answers to quick quiz

1   False

2   Relevant audit matters:

- Re independence/objectivity

- Planning matters

- Audit findings, for example,

   ○   Central weaknesses
   ○   Unadjusted errors
   ○   Expected modifications to the audit report

3   (1)   Weakness
    (2)   Consequence
    (3)   Recommendation

4   False

Activity checklist

This checklist shows which performance criteria, range statement or knowledge and understanding point is covered by each activity in this chapter. Tick off each activity as you complete it.

Activity

18.1 ☐ This activity details with Performance Criteria 17.1.D: Record significant weaknesses in control correctly and 17.3.A: Prepare clear and concise draft reports relating to the audit assignment and submit them for review and approval in line with organisational procedures and 17.3.B: Draw valid conclusions and provide evidence to support them and 17.3.C: Make constructive and practicable recommendations.

chapter 19

The external audit opinion

Contents

1   The problem
2   The solution
3   Statutory requirements
4   Unqualified report
5   Qualified audit reports
6   Reporting inherent uncertainty

Performance criteria

17.3.A Prepare clear and concise draft reports relating to the audit assignment and submit them for review and approval in line with organisational procedures

17.3.B Draw valid conclusions and provide evidence to support them

17.3.C Make constructive and practicable recommendations

Range statement

17.3   Draft reports relating to a manual system

1 The problem

Auditors have to report on truth and fairness to shareholders. How can they do that in a way that 'non-accounting' shareholders will understand? And how can they ensure that the public do not misunderstand the nature of their professional duties and what the audit report means?

2 The solution

SAS 600 *Auditors' report on financial statements* sets out a **standard** audit report that should be used for all audits. It contains key elements designed to help users understand what an audit is and the opinion that is given. Auditors either give an unqualified or qualified audit opinion.

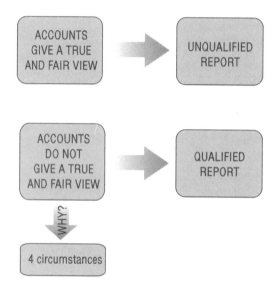

It may also be necessary to include an explanatory paragraph in an unqualified report to give more emphasis to a significant matter or to provide additional disclosure.

3 Statutory requirements

An **unqualified** audit report communicates an assurance to the user, that an independent examination of the accounts has discovered no material problems and that the accounts show a **true and fair view**. We will discuss truth and fairness in the next section of this chapter.

An unqualified report also conveys certain implications. These are unstated because the auditors only report **by exception**. In other words, these assumptions will only be mentioned (by a **qualified** audit report) if they do not hold true. An unqualified report implies that (under s 237 Companies Act 1985):

(a) **Proper accounting records** have been kept and proper returns adequate for the audit received from branches not visited.

(b) The **accounts** agree with the **accounting records** and **returns.**

(c)   **All information and explanations** have been **received** as the auditors think necessary and they have had access at all times to the company's books, accounts and vouchers.

(d)   **Details** of **directors' emoluments** and **other benefits** have been correctly **disclosed** in the financial statements.

(e)   Particulars of **loans** and **other transactions** in favour of **directors** and others have been correctly disclosed in the financial statements.

(f)   The **information** given in the **directors' report** is **consistent** with the **accounts**.

The auditors' report should be placed before the financial statements. The directors' responsibilities statement should be placed before the auditors' report, or, as discussed in Chapter 4, the auditors should include it in their report.

4 Unqualified reports

The following is given as an example of an unqualified audit report, as updated by a bulletin in 2001.

UNLISTED ENTITY INCORPORATED IN GREAT BRITAIN OR
NORTHERN IRELAND

Independent auditors' report [1]to the shareholders of XYZ Limited

We have audited the financial statements of (name of entity) for the year ended ... which comprise [2] (state the primary financial statements such as the profit and loss account, the balance sheet, the cash flow statement, the statements of total recognised gains and losses) and the related notes. These financial statements have been prepared under the historical cost convention* (as modified by the revaluation of certain fixed assets) and the accounting policies set out therein.

[3]Respective responsibilities of directors and auditors

The director's responsibilities for preparing the annual report and the financial statements in accordance with applicable law and United Kingdom Accounting Standards are set out in the statement of director's responsibilities.

Our responsibility is to audit the financial statements in accordance with relevant legal and regulatory requirements and United Kingdom Auditing Standards.

We report to you our opinion as to whether the financial statements give a true and fair view and are properly prepared in accordance with the (Companies Act 1985) (Companies (Northern Ireland) Order 1986). We also report to you if, in our opinion, the director's report is not consistent with the financial statements, if the company has not kept proper accounting records, it we have not received all the information and explanations we required for our audit, or if information specified by law or the Listing Rules regarding directors remuneration and transactions with the company is not disclosed.

We read other information contained in the annual report and consider whether it is consistent with the audited financial statements. This other information comprises only (the Director's Report, the Chairman's Statement, the Operating and Financial Review). We consider the implications for our report if we become aware of any apparent misstatements or material inconsistencies with the financial statements. Our responsibilities do not extend to any other information.

---

³**Basis of audit opinion**

We conducted our audit in accordance with United Kingdom Auditing Standards issued by the Auditing Practices Board. An audit includes examination, on a test basis, of evidence relevant to the amounts and disclosures in the financial statements. It also includes an assessment of the significant estimates and judgements made by the directors in the preparation of the financial statements, and of whether the accounting polices are appropriate to the company's circumstances, consistently applied and adequately disclosed.

We planned and performed our audit so as to obtain all the information and explanations which we considered necessary in order to provide us with sufficient evidence to give reasonable assurance that the financial statements are free from material misstatement, whether caused by fraud or other irregularity or error. In forming our opinion we also evaluated the overall adequacy of the presentation of information in the financial statements.

³**Opinion**

In our opinion the financial statements give a true and fair view of the state of the company's affairs as at … and of its profit (loss) for the year then ended and have been properly prepared in accordance with the (Companies Act 1985) (Companies (Northern Ireland) Order 1986).

Registered auditors   ⁴   *Address*

⁵*Date*

Key

The report shows the mandatory requirements of SAS 600:

1   Title identifying to whom the report is addressed

2   Introductory paragraph detailing the financial statements the report refers to

3   Three paragraphs explaining:

   ◦   Respective responsibilities of directors and auditors
   ◦   Basis of opinion
   ◦   Opinion

4   Signature of the auditor (or, by the auditor on behalf of the firm)

5   The date of the report

The report recommends the use of standard format as an aid to the reader, including headings for each section, for example 'Qualified opinion'. The title and addressee and the introductory paragraph are fairly self explanatory. The standard report for a **listed** company contains references to the Stock Exchange rules.

4.1 Statements of responsibility and basic opinion

'(a)   Auditors should distinguish between their responsibilities and those of the directors by including in their report:

   (i)   a statement that the financial statements are the responsibility of the reporting entity's directors;

(ii) a reference to a description of those responsibilities when set out elsewhere in the financial statements or accompanying information; and

(iii) a statement that the auditors' responsibility is to express an opinion on the financial statements.

(b) Where the financial statements or accompanying information (for example the directors' report) do not include an adequate description of directors' relevant responsibilities the auditors' report should include a description of those responsibilities.'

4.2 Explanation of auditors' opinion

'Auditors should explain the basis of their opinion by including in their report:

(a) a statement as to their compliance or otherwise with Auditing Standards, together with the reasons for any departure therefrom;

(b) a statement that the audit process includes:

(i) examining, on a test basis, evidence relevant to the amounts and disclosures in the financial statements;

(ii) assessing the significant estimates and judgements made by the reporting entity's directors in preparing the financial statements;

(iii) considering whether the accounting policies are appropriate to the reporting entity's circumstances, consistently applied and adequately disclosed;

(c) a statement that they planned and performed the audit so as to obtain reasonable assurance that the financial statements are free from material misstatement, whether caused by fraud or other irregularity or error, and that they have evaluated the overall presentation of the financial statements.'

Other than in exceptional circumstances, a departure from an auditing standard is a limitation on the scope of work undertaken by the auditors.

4.3 Expression of opinion

'An auditors' report should contain a clear expression of opinion on the financial statements and on any further matters required by statute or other requirements applicable to the particular engagement.'

An unqualified opinion on financial statements is expressed when in the auditors' judgement they give a true and fair view (where relevant) and have been prepared in accordance with relevant accounting or other requirements. This judgement entails concluding whether inter alia:

(a) The financial statements have been prepared using **appropriate, consistently applied accounting policies**.

(b)   The financial statements have been **prepared** in accordance with **relevant legislation, regulations** or **applicable accounting standards** (and that any departures are justified and adequately explained in the financial statements).

(c)   There is **adequate disclosure** of all information relevant to the proper understanding of the financial statements.

4.4 Date and signature of the auditors' report

'(a)   Auditors should not express an opinion on financial statement until those statements and all other financial information contained in a report of which the audited financial statements form a part have been approved by the directors, and the auditors have considered all necessary available evidence.

(b)   The date of an auditors' report on a reporting entity's financial statements is the date on which the auditors sign their report expressing an opinion on those statements.'

If the date on which the auditors sign the report is later than that on which the directors approve the financial statements, then the auditors must check that the post balance sheet event review has been carried out up to the date they sign their report and that the directors would also have approved the financial statements on that date.

4.5 Forming an opinion on financial statements

Appendix 1 of the SAS considers the process of forming an audit opinion using the flowchart shown on the next page. The flowchart is drawn up on the basis that the directors make no further amendments to the financial statements following the audit.

The principal matters which auditors consider in forming an opinion may be expressed in three questions.

- Have they **completed all procedures necessary** to meet auditing standards and to obtain all the information and explanations necessary for their audit?

- Have the financial statements been **prepared in accordance** with the **applicable accounting requirements**?

- Do the financial statements, as prepared by the directors, give **a true and fair view**?

Note. Requirements are referred to in terms of generally accepted accounting principles.

FORMING AN OPINION ON FINANCIAL STATEMENTS

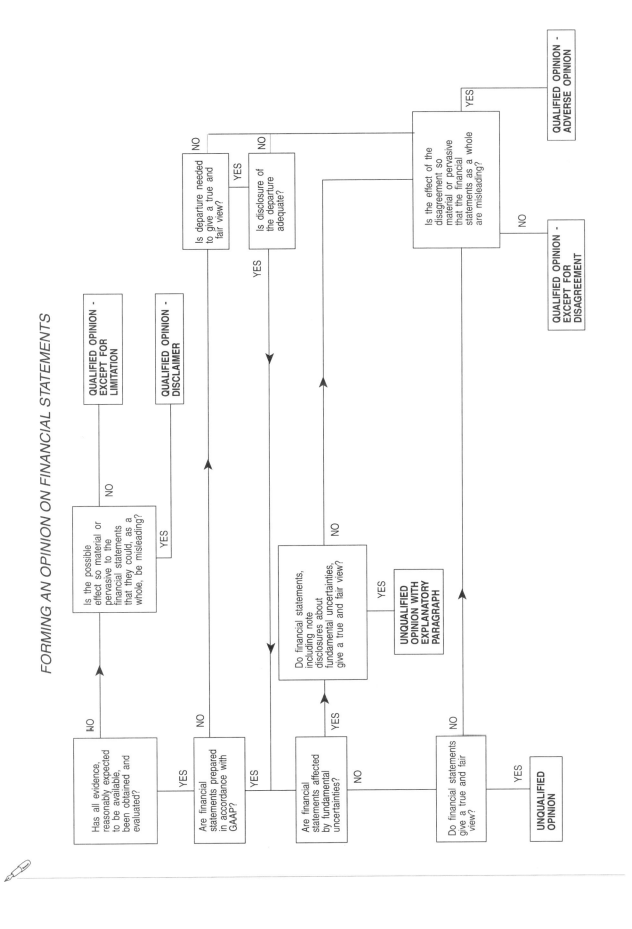

Activity 19.1

The following is a series of extracts from an unqualified audit report.

AUDITORS' REPORT TO THE SHAREHOLDERS OF AJ (PAPER) LIMITED

We have audited *the financial statements on pages .... to ....* which have been prepared under the historical cost convention.

We have conducted our audit *in accordance with Auditing Standards* issued by the Auditing Practices Board. An audit includes examination on a test basis of evidence relevant to the amounts and disclosures in the financial statements.

In our opinion the financial statements give a true and fair view of the state of the company's affairs as at 31 December 2002 and of its profit for the year then ended and have been properly prepared in accordance with the Companies Act 1985.

Tasks

For Chantal's benefit explain the purpose and meaning of the following phrases taken from the above extracts of an unqualified audit report.

(a)   '... the financial statements on pages .... to ....'
(b)   '... in accordance with Auditing Standards.'
(c)   'In our opinion ...'

5 Qualified audit reports

Qualified audit reports arise when auditors do not believe they can state without reservation that the accounts give a true and fair view.

5.1 The qualification 'matrix'

The circumstances giving rise to a qualification of the auditors' opinion will generally fall into one of two categories:

(a)   Where there is a **limitation in the scope of work** which prevents the auditors from forming an opinion on a matter (uncertainty – see SAS 600.7)

(b)   Where the auditors are able to form an opinion on a matter but this **conflicts** with the view given by the financial statements (disagreement – see SAS 600.8)

Either case, uncertainty or disagreement, may give rise to alternative forms of qualification. This is because the uncertainty or disagreement can be:

- Material but not pervasive
- Pervasive to the overall true and fair view

The standard requires that the following forms of qualification should be used in the different circumstances outlined below.

QUALIFICATION MATRIX

Nature of circumstances	Material but not pervasive	Pervasive
Limitation in scope	Except for .. might	Disclaimer of opinion
Disagreement	Except for ...	Adverse opinion

Except for . . . might	Auditors disclaim an opinion on a particular aspect of the accounts which is not considered pervasive.
Disclaimer of opinion	Auditors state they are unable to form an opinion on truth and fairness.
Except for	Auditors express an adverse opinion on a particular aspect of the accounts which is not considered pervasive.
Adverse opinion	Auditors state the accounts do not give a true and fair view.

5.2 Limitations in the scope of the audit

Scope limitations will arise where auditors are unable for any reason to obtain all the information and explanations which they consider necessary for the purpose of their audit, arising from:

(a) Absence of proper accounting records

(b) An inability to carry out audit procedures considered necessary as, for example, where the auditors are unable to obtain satisfactory evidence of the existence or ownership of material assets

The auditors' report should include a description of the factors leading to the limitation in the opinion section of their report. They should issue a disclaimer of opinion when the possible effect of a limitation on scope is so material or pervasive that they are unable to express an opinion on the financial statements.

A qualified opinion should be issued when the effect of the limitation is not as material or pervasive as to require a disclaimer, and the wording of the opinion should indicate that it is qualified as to the possible adjustments to the financial statements that might have been determined to be necessary had the limitation not existed.

When giving this type of qualified opinion, auditors should assess:

(a) The **quantity and type of evidence** which may reasonably be expected to be available to support the figure or disclosure in the financial statements

(b) The **possible effect** on the financial statements of the matter for which insufficient evidence is available

SAS 600 gives the following examples.

Example 8. Qualified opinion: limitation on the auditors' work

(Independent Auditors' report to the shareholders.... as on page 321)

(Respective responsibilities of directors and auditors... as on page 321)

(Basis of opinion: excerpt)

.... or error. However, the evidence available to us was limited because £... of the company's recorded turnover comprises cash sales, over which there was no system of control on which we could rely for the purposes of our audit. There were no other satisfactory audit procedures that we could adopt to confirm that cash sales were properly recorded.

In forming our opinion we also evaluated the overall adequacy of the presentation of information in the financial statements.

Qualified opinion arising from limitation in audit scope

Except for any adjustments that might have been found to be necessary had we been able to obtain sufficient evidence concerning cash sales, in our opinion the financial statements give a true and fair view of the state of the company's affairs as at 31 December 20.. and of its profit (loss) for the year then ended and have been properly prepared in accordance with the Companies Act 1985.

In respect alone of the limitation on our work relating to cash sales:

(a)   we have not obtained all the information and explanations that we considered necessary for the purpose of our audit; and

(b)   we were unable to determine whether proper accounting records had been maintained.

Example 9. Disclaimer of opinion

(Independent Auditors' report to the shareholders.... as on page 321)

(Respective responsibilities of directors and auditors... as on page 321)

(Basis of opinion: excerpt)

.... or error. However, the evidence available to us was limited because we were appointed auditors on (date) and in consequence we were unable to carry out auditing procedures necessary to obtain adequate assurance regarding the quantities and condition of stock and work in progress, appearing in the balance sheet at £.... . Any adjustment to this figure would have a consequential significant effect on the profit for the year.

In forming our opinion we also evaluated the overall adequacy of the presentation of information in the financial statements.

Opinion: disclaimer on view given by financial statements

Because of the possible effect of the limitation in evidence available to us, we are unable to form an opinion as to whether the financial statements give a true and fair view of the state of the company's affairs as at 31 December 20.. or of its profit (loss) for the year then ended. In all other respects, in our opinion the financial statements have been properly prepared in accordance with the Companies Act 1985.

In respect of the limitation on our work relating to stock and work-in-progress:

(a)   we have not obtained all the information and explanations that we considered necessary for the purpose of our audit; and

(b)   we were unable to determine whether proper accounting records had been maintained.

Note. Because of the length of the audit report, we have only shown those parts of each qualified report which differ from the unqualified report shown in Section 4.

5.3 Circumstances giving rise to disagreements

The explanatory notes to SAS 600 suggest that circumstances giving rise to disagreement include the following.

- Inappropriate accounting policies
- **Disagreement** as to the **facts or amounts** included in the financial statements
- **Disagreement** as to the **manner or extent of disclosure** of facts or amounts in the financial statements
- **Failure to comply** with **relevant legislation** or **other requirements**

'Where the auditors disagree with the accounting treatment or disclosure of a matter in the financial statements, and in the auditors' opinion the effect of that disagreement is material to the financial statements:

(a)   the auditors should include in the opinion section of their report:

   (i)   a description of all substantive factors giving rise to the disagreement;
   (ii)   their implications for the financial statements;
   (iii) whenever practicable, a quantification of the effect on the financial statements;

(b)   when the auditors conclude that the effect of the matter giving rise to disagreement is so material or pervasive that the financial statements are seriously misleading, they should issue an adverse opinion;

(c)   in the case of other material disagreements, the auditors should issue a qualified opinion indicating that it is expressed except for the effects of the matter giving rise to the disagreement.'

Example 7. Qualified opinion: disagreement

Previous paragraphs as on page 321

Qualified opinion arising from disagreement about accounting treatment

Included in the debtors shown on the balance sheet is an amount of £Y due from a company which has ceased trading. XYZ plc has no security for this debt. In our opinion the company is unlikely to receive any payment and full provision of £Y should have been made, reducing profit before tax and net assets by that amount.

Except for the absence of this provision, in our opinion the financial statements give a true and fair view of the state of the company's affairs as at 31 December 20.. and of its profit (loss) for the year then ended and have been properly prepared in accordance with the Companies Act 1985.

Example 10. Adverse opinion

Previous paragraphs as on page 321

Adverse opinion

As more fully explained in note ... no provision has been made for losses expected to arise on certain long-term contracts currently in progress, as the directors consider that such losses should be off-set against amounts recoverable on other long-term contracts. In our opinion, provision should be made for foreseeable losses on individual contracts as required by Statement of Standard Accounting Practice 9. If losses had been so recognised the effect would have been to reduce the profit before and after tax for the year and the contract work in progress at 31 December 20.. by £.. .

In view of the effect of the failure to provide for the losses referred to above, in our opinion the financial statements do not give a true and fair view of the state of the company's affairs as at 31 December 19.. and of its profit (loss) for the year then ended. In all other respects, in our opinion the financial statements have been properly prepared in accordance with the Companies Act 1985.

5.3.1 Going concern example

The auditors will qualify their opinion if the directors have paid attention to less than one year as the 'foreseeable future' and have not disclosed that fact, and they consider that the directors have not taken adequate steps to satisfy themselves that it is appropriate for them to adopt the going concern basis. This will be a limitation in the scope of the auditors' work.

The audit report will contain the following paragraph if disclosure is considered adequate.

Basis of opinion: excerpt

Going concern

In forming our opinion, we have considered the adequacy of the disclosures made in note 1 of the financial statements concerning the uncertainty as to the continuation and renewal of the company's bank overdraft facility. In view of the significance of this uncertainty we consider that it should be drawn to your attention but our opinion is not qualified in this respect.

Where the going concern presumption is **inappropriate**:

- Even disclosure in the financial statements of the matters giving rise to this conclusion is not sufficient for them to give a true and fair view.

- The effect on financial statements prepared on that basis is so material or pervasive that the financial statements are seriously misleading.

Accordingly, an **adverse opinion** (that the accounts do not give a true and fair view) is appropriate in such cases.

The directors may prepare financial statements on a basis other than that of a going concern. If the auditors consider this other basis to be appropriate in the specific circumstances, and if the financial statements contain the necessary disclosures, the auditors should not qualify their opinion in this respect.

6 Reporting inherent uncertainty

An **inherent uncertainty** is an uncertainty whose resolution is dependent upon uncertain future events outside the control of the reporting entity's directors at the date the financial statements are approved. A **fundamental uncertainty** is an inherent uncertainty where the magnitude of its potential impact is so great that, without clear disclosure of the nature and implications of the uncertainty, the view given by the financial statements would be seriously misleading.

Inherent uncertainties about the outcome of future events frequently affect a wide range of components of the financial statements. These uncertainties are uncertainties which remain even though auditors have obtained all the evidence they can expect to obtain about the components. SAS 600 gives details of how auditors should approach inherent uncertainties.

> '(a)   In forming their opinion on financial statements, auditors should consider whether the view given by the financial statements could be affected by inherent uncertainties which, in their opinion, are fundamental.
>
> (b)   When an inherent uncertainty exists which:
>
> (i)   in the auditors' opinion is fundamental; and
> (ii)   is adequately accounted for and disclosed in the financial statements;
>
> the auditors should include an explanatory paragraph referring to the fundamental uncertainty in the section of their report setting out the basis of their opinion.
>
> (c)   When adding an explanatory paragraph, auditors should use words which clearly indicate that their opinion on the financial statements is not qualified in respect of its concepts.'

In forming an opinion, auditors take into account:

- The appropriateness of the accounting policies

- The adequacy of the accounting treatment

- Estimates and disclosures of inherent uncertainties in the light of evidence available at the date they express their opinion

Inherent uncertainties are regarded as **fundamental** when they involve a **significant level** of concern about the validity of the **going concern basis** or other matters whose potential effect on the fundamental statements is unusually great. A common example of a fundamental uncertainty is the outcome of major litigation.

The auditor will need to consider:

- The possibility that the estimate included in the accounts may be **subject to change**
- The possible range of values it may take
- The consequences of that range of potential values on the view shown in the financial statements

Example 4. Unqualified opinion with explanatory paragraph describing a fundamental uncertainty.

Fundamental uncertainty (insert just before opinion paragraph)

In forming our opinion, we have considered the adequacy of the disclosures made in the financial statements concerning the possible outcome to litigation against B Limited, a subsidiary undertaking of the company, for an alleged breach of environmental regulations. The future settlement of this litigation could result in additional liabilities and the closure of B Limited's business, whose net assets included in the consolidated balance sheet total £... and whose profit before tax for the year is £... . Details of the circumstances relating to this fundamental uncertainty are described in note .... . Our opinion is not qualified in this respect.

Activity 19.2

What impact would each of the following matters have on the audit report of these clients?

(a)   The audit team were not informed about the year-end stocktake until after it had taken place. Stock is material in the financial statements.

(b)   No provision has been made against a material amount owed by a debtor who is now in liquidation.

(c)   A substantial claim has been lodged against the company by a major customer. The matter is fully explained in the notes to the accounts, but no provision has been made for legal costs or for compensation payable as it is not possible to determine with reasonable accuracy the amounts, if any, which may become payable.

The directors have received legal advice which appears to be reliable that the claim can be successfully defended.

Activity 19.3

Anton mentions that one of the major customers of the company is in serious financial difficulties and looks likely to go into liquidation in the next few months. The relationship with a further major customer is currently in serious difficulties. The directors are however confident about a number of opportunities for business with new customers. The finance director states that appropriate disclosures will be made in the accounts, but wants to know what impact the uncertainties may have on the audit report. You state that you believe that the company is likely to be able to continue as a going concern, but the audit report may need to include an explanatory paragraph because there is a significant inherent uncertainty about the company's status as a going concern.

Draft the explanatory paragraph which may be included within the audit report.

Key learning points

☑ The Companies Act requires specific reference in the audit report to:

- The truth and fairness of the state of the company's affairs at the period-end
- The truth and fairness of the profit or loss
- Whether the accounts have been properly prepared in accordance with the Companies Act

☑ The Companies Act requires certain matters to be reported on by exception:

- Proper accounting records kept and proper returns received
- Accounts in agreement with the accounting records and returns
- All information and explanations received
- Details of directors' emoluments correctly disclosed
- Details of loans and other transactions in favour of directors and related parties correctly disclosed
- Information given in the directors' report consistent with the accounts

☑ SAS 600 Auditors' report on financial statements radically altered the form of both unqualified and qualified audit reports.

☑ The main elements of an unqualified audit report are:

- A title identifying the addressee

- An introductory paragraph identifying the financial statements audited

- Sections dealing with:

  ◦ Responsibilities of directors and auditors
  ◦ Basis of the auditors' opinion
  ◦ A clear statement of opinion

☑ Auditors may qualify their audit opinion on the grounds of uncertainty or limitation of scope; these may be material or fundamental.

☑ Auditors are principally concerned with the correct treatment and disclosure of inherent and fundamental uncertainties, which relate to uncertain future events.

☑ Auditors should include an explanatory paragraph in their audit report if fundamental uncertainties exist.

Quick quiz

1   What should auditors do if the accounts do not contain the details required by the Companies Act concerning directors' emoluments?

2   How according to SAS 600.3 should auditors distinguish between their responsibilities and those of the directors?

3   According to the example given in SAS 600, what must the directors do when preparing financial statements?

4   What are the two explicit opinions and the six implied opinions of the audit report?

     1   ....   1...

     2   ....   2...

                                              3...

                                            4...

                                            5...

                                            6...

5   Complete the standard opinion paragraph.

In our opinion the .... give a .... of the state of the company's affairs as at 31.XX.XX and of its .... (............) for .... and have been .... in accordance with the Companies Act 1985.

6   Complete the diagram by filling in the type of report that would be issued in each situation.

FORMING AN OPINION ON FINANCIAL STATEMENTS

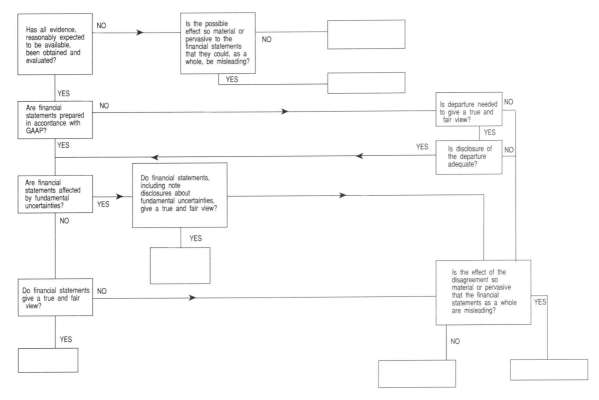

7   Draw the qualification matrix

8   Complete the definition

An .... uncertainty is an uncertainty whose resolution is dependent upon ....
.... outside the control of the reporting entity's directors at ....
.... the financial statements are ....

Answers to quick quiz

1   If the accounts do not contain the disclosures of directors' emoluments required by statute, auditors should qualify their audit report and give the required disclosures in their report.

2   According to SAS 600.3, auditors should state that the financial statements are the responsibility of the directors, make reference to the description of directors' responsibilities if set out elsewhere in the accounts, and state the auditors' responsibility is to express an opinion on the financial statements.

3   When preparing financial statements, directors should:

- Select suitable accounting policies and apply them consistently.
- Make judgements and estimates that are reasonable and prudent.

- State whether applicable accounting standards have been followed, with material departures disclosed and explained (large companies only).

- Prepare the financial statements on the going concern basis unless inappropriate.

4	1	Truth and fairness	1	Proper accounting records kept
	2	Properly prepared	2	Accounts agree with records and returns
			3	All information and explanations received
			4	Details of directors' emoluments correctly disclosed
			5	Particulars of directors' loans disclosed
			6	Information in directors' report consistent with accounts

5   Financial statements, true and fair view, profit (loss) the year then ended, properly prepared

6

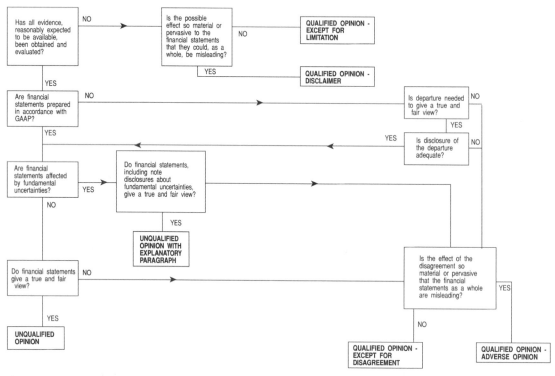

FORMING AN OPINION ON FINANCIAL STATEMENTS

7   QUALIFICATION MATRIX

Nature of circumstances	Material but not pervasive	Pervasive
Disagreement	Except for .. might	Disclaimer of opinion
Limitation in scope	Except for ...	Adverse opinion

Except for . . . might	Auditors disclaim an opinion on a particular aspect of the accounts which is not considered pervasive.
Disclaimer of opinion	Auditors state they are unable to form an opinion on truth and fairness.
Except for	Auditors express an adverse opinion on a particular aspect of the accounts which is not considered pervasive.
Adverse opinion	Auditors state the accounts do not give a true and fair view.

8   inherent, uncertain future events, the date, approved

Activity checklist

This checklist shows which performance criteria, range statement or knowledge and understanding point is covered by each activity in this chapter. Tick off each activity as you complete it.

Activity

19.1 ☐   This activity deals with Performance Criteria 17.3.A: Prepare clear and concise draft reports relating to the audit assignment and submit them for review and approval in line with organisational procedures.

19.2 ☐   This activity deals with Performance Criteria 17.3.A: Prepare clear and concise draft reports relating to the audit assignment and submit them for review and approval in line with organisational procedures and 17.3.B: Draw valid conclusions and provide evidence to support them and 17.3.C: Make constructive and practicable recommendations.

19.3 ☐   This activity deals with Performance Criteria 17.3.A: Prepare clear and concise draft reports relating to the audit assignment and submit them for review and approval in line with organisational procedures and 17.3.B: Draw valid conclusions and provide evidence to support them and 17.3.C: Make constructive and practicable recommendations.

Answers to Activities

Answers to activities

Chapter 1

Answer 1.1

An audit is an exercise designed to provide evidence as to whether the financial statements produced by the directors give a true and fair view of the state of affairs of the company and of the profit or loss for the year, and whether they have been properly prepared in accordance with the Companies Act 1985 and other relevant standards.

The primary duty of the auditors is to report on the truth and fairness of the financial statements. They also have duties to ensure that the company has met other legal requirements, such as maintaining suitable accounting records as required by law.

The auditors have some rights which are enshrined in statute. They have a right of access to company records, as well as rights to information and explanations from company employees and directors. They have the right to attend general meetings of the company and to be heard on any matter that concerns them as auditors. They have the right to receive a copy of any written resolution proposed and to require a general meeting to be held so that the financial statements can be laid before members.

Answer 1.2

Anton must ensure that the company keeps the following records:

- Cash books covering receipts and payments

- Records of all the assets and liabilities of the business, probably incorporating a fixed asset register, debtors and creditors listings and bank statements and reconciliations.

- Statements of stock held at the year end, and

- All stock sheets used in stock counting to come to the statement of stock held

Answer 1.3

Most companies are required by law to have an annual audit, unless they are a qualifying small company or a dormant company. Such an audit must be carried out by a qualified audit practitioner who can give an impartial opinion.

Some companies will also employ staff to carry out work known as internal audit. A large part of internal audit's work is to monitor the effectiveness of internal controls which directors have set up to ensure the smooth running of the company and the safeguarding of company assets.

The work that internal and external auditors do can be similar, particularly in terms of the techniques used. However, a company will not be able to use their internal auditors to carry out the audit required by law, as employees of the company are prohibited from being the external auditors.

If the company employs an external firm to undertake its internal audit work and that firm is qualified to carry out external audits under law, then it is possible that the company could use the same external firm to provide it with internal and external audit services.

Chapter 2

Answer 2.1

Under the Companies Act 1985, a person is **ineligible** for appointment as a company auditor if he or she is one out of:

(a) An **officer** or **employee** of the company

(b) A **partner** or **employee** of such a person

(c) Any partner in **partnership** in which such a person is a partner

(d) **Ineligible** by virtue of (a), (b) or (c) for appointment as auditor of any parent or subsidiary undertaking or a subsidiary undertaking of any parent undertaking of the company

Hence Anton and any other employees of AJ (Paper) Ltd would be ineligible.

Answer 2.2

SASs contain the following types of guidance.

(a) Basic principles and essential procedures ('Auditing Standards') with which auditors must comply when carrying out an audit of financial statements

(b) General auditing standards which apply to other types of audits and related services

(c) Auditing Standards which apply to the audits of certain types of entity such as clients within specialist industries

(d) Explanatory and other material designed to assist auditors in interpreting and applying Auditing Standards

Answer 2.3

Due to the auditor's position of trust in relation to a company, he has a professional duty of confidentiality. This means that he has a duty to keep company information private.

In limited circumstances, the auditor is permitted or required to disclose company information. Examples of such instances include:

- When the client authorises it

- When the law requires disclosure (for example, when the auditor suspects the client of a criminal offence such as drug-trafficking)

- When it is necessary to protect the auditor's interests, (for example, as evidence during a trial)

- When it is in the public interest to make disclosure

Chapter 3

Answer 3.1

(a)   Auditors should send out an engagement letter for the following reasons.

Defining responsibilities

An engagement letter defines the extent of auditors' and directors' responsibilities. For auditors the engagement letter states that their duties are governed by the Companies Act, not the wishes of the directors. It should also state that auditors report to the members (not the directors). For directors, the engagement letter states they are responsible for safeguarding assets, maintaining a proper system of internal control and preventing fraud. The letter should thus minimise the possibility of misunderstanding between auditors and directors.

Documenting acceptance

The engagement letter also provides confirmation in writing of the auditors' acceptance of appointment, the objective and scope of the audit and the form of the audit report.

Other matters

The letter should also lay out the basis on which fees are charged and hence minimise the possibility of arguments about fees.

The letter also sets down what the client should do if he is unhappy with the service he has been given.

(b)   The main contents and form of the engagement letter will be as follows.

(i)   It will be addressed to the directors and on the audit firm's letterhead.

(ii)   It will lay out the responsibilities of the directors of the company.

- Maintaining proper accounting records
- Ensuring the accounts show a true and fair view
- Preparing accounts in accordance with CA 1985
- Making all records/accounts available to the auditors

(iii)   It should also lay out the duties of the auditors, comprising mainly a statutory duty to report to the members their opinion on whether the accounts show a true and fair view and are prepared in accordance with CA 1985.

(iv)   It should state that the audit will be conducted according to auditing standards.

(v)   It should state that the accounts should normally comply with accounting standards (SSAPs and FRSs) and the auditors will report if they do not.

(vi)   It should state that it is the directors' responsibility to detect fraud and error, but that audit procedures are designed so that there is a reasonable expectation of detecting material misstatements.

Other matters which might be covered include the following.

- Fees and billing arrangements

- Procedures where the client has a complaint about the service
- Arrangements to be made with the predecessor auditors, in the case of an initial audit
- A reference to any further agreements between the auditors and the client
- A proposed timetable for the engagement
- Any agreement about further services (tax, preparing accounts etc)

The letter should end by stating that it will remain effective from one audit appointment to another, until it is replaced. The directors should confirm acceptance in writing.

Answer 3.2

In English law, persons may be found guilty of an act called negligence. There are three criteria which need to have been met for a person to be found guilty of negligence:

- They must have owed the other party a duty of care
- They must have breached that duty of care
- The other party must have suffered loss as a result

The key issue in negligence claims against auditors is whether the auditors owed the injured party a duty of care.

Auditors always owe their client (the company) a duty of care as in English law a duty of care is implied into any contract such as the one between auditor and company, and the auditors cannot avoid this duty.

It is less likely that auditors owe a duty of care to other parties such as a bank who lends to the company they have audited. This is because the auditors do not have a contractual relationship with them, so no duty of care is implied. Judges have ruled in the past that a duty of care does not arise in any other way, unless the auditor has been made aware that the specific third party exists and that it intends to rely on the audited financial statements. If this is the case, the auditors may be found to owe the established third party a duty of care.

Chapter 4

Answer 4.1

Auditors have a responsibility under SAS 110 to plan procedures that give reasonable assurance of detecting fraud that has a material effect on the company's financial statements. The indications are that the amounts involved are material, and the auditor has also been warned by the managing director that there may be potential problems. An auditor therefore investigate the allegations as part of the audit.

(a) He would discreetly try and check if the branch manager had a lifestyle that appeared to be unduly lavish. There may be legitimate reasons for expensive purchases, for example a legacy or lottery win.

He would also consider the general behaviour of the manager during the audit. Signs of particular concern would include a lack of co-operation, evidence that the branch's staff were cowed, and general evidence of limited central control of the branch, as well as lack of the specific controls outlined below.

Travel expenses

He would review travel expenses to see how they compared with previous years and also with the levels of expenses at other branches. He would investigate any significant variations, although there may be legitimate reasons for these, for example special sales promotions.

He would also consider the controls operated by head office over the expenses. Strong controls would include head office booking of tickets or hotel accommodation, and approval of other travel expenses.

He would also examine the documentation for individual expenses, considering whether the amounts claimed appeared reasonable, and checking with other evidence that the travel had been undertaken, for example evidence of sales arising.

Purchases

He would compare levels of purchases with previous years and other branches, and would also consider profit margins, and attempt to reconcile amounts purchased with amounts sold and in stock.

He would consider internal controls over purchases, assessing the strength of the system, for example whether suppliers were chosen from an approved list, and whether payments to suppliers could be made without being supported by a valid purchase invoice or purchase order. He would also ascertain the degree of involvement of the branch manager in the purchasing process, whether he chose suppliers, or whether there were any suppliers that he handled directly outside the normal purchase system.

He would also scrutinise the records of suppliers to see if any appeared to have unusual addresses such as box numbers or an address which was the same as the home address of the branch manager. He would examine individual invoices to see if they had unusual features such as missing addresses or phone numbers, incomplete or inadequate product descriptions or were photocopies. He would also be alert for different suppliers with the same address or with similar business stationery.

(b) **Stock**

He would scrutinise the records of stock written off and ascertain the reasons for write-off. If the company had a policy for scrapping stock, he would ascertain whether the write-offs fulfilled that policy. If stock had to be written off for reasons such as deterioration due to damp, he would check whether the problem had been remedied. He would also consider whether stock write-offs had to be authorised; he would gain comfort if write-offs had to be authorised by someone who was independent of stores.

He would also review stock write-offs, considering the amounts written off and the proportion of stock held that was written off. He would compare these figures with write-offs for previous years and write-offs for other branches. He would also consider whether stock orders appeared to be in excess of requirements, as some stock might be ordered just to be stolen.

He would review the records of internal stock-counts carried out during the year. He would check whether they were carried out by staff who were independent of the stock section, and whether they identified particular problems at the branch with obsolete or slow-moving stock.

Chapter 5

Answer 5.1

When planning an audit auditors need to know:

- How general economic factors affect the client's business
- How conditions in the industry affect the client's business
- The client's directors, management and ownership; their involvement, knowledge and integrity
- Details of the client's business, its products, markets, supplies etc
- Other factors which affect the client's financial environment
- Reporting requirements which affect the accounts

Answer 5.2

It is the responsibility of directors and management to implement an appropriate system of financial and non-financial controls. Good management is itself an internal control, but other procedures must be in place as directors and senior managers cannot supervise everything, particularly in large companies. Hence overseeing an effective internal control system is how senior management discharge their responsibilities.

SAS 300 emphasises the importance of the general objective of internal controls ensuing the orderly and efficient conduct of a company's business. Clearly with the cost pressures many businesses face, they are seeking to maximise efficiency, and well-designed internal controls should be an aid, not a hindrance towards that end. Orderliness is related to efficiency, and it is also necessary so that a company fulfils its various legal obligations.

SAS 300 lists a number of further specific objectives.

Adherence to internal policies

In order for management to be able to implement their decisions, there have to be policies in place to ensure management directives are followed.

Safeguarding of assets

Safeguarding of assets is a vital objective of internal control, since directors have the responsibility of stewardship over a company's assets. Safeguarding means not only physical protection of assets but also their proper recording.

Prevention and detection of fraud and error

This objective is related to the safeguarding of assets. If the company's internal control systems cannot prevent or detect fraud or error, there would be serious legal consequences if frauds are allowed to continue, or if the company publishes inaccurate information.

Accuracy and completeness of accounting records

Directors are required by the Companies Act to maintain proper accounting records. As we have stated, this objective also relates to safeguarding of assets.

Timely preparation of financial information

Directors have a statutory responsibility to prepare accounts which show a true and fair view within time limits set by statute. Internal financial information such as management accounts and budgets also helps directors monitor what is going on, and if any areas of the business are causing concern.

Answer 5.3

Control	Control objective
Goods returned should be recorded on goods returned notes, which should be sequentially numbered. Credit notes should not be issued for returned stock until the goods return note has been checked to the original invoice	To ensure that credits are only given for valid reasons
All invoices received by the company should be given a sequential number also filed under a supplier's reference. Goods received notes should be reviewed frequently to establish if an item does not appear to have been invoiced or an invoice has gone missing.	To ensure that the company only recognises genuine liabilities to the company, but also does not understate its liabilities.
Pay increases should be authorised and the details of the pay rise kept on employees files	To ensure that employees are not paid too much or too little for their work
Employees starting and leaving dates should be agreed in writing and details kept on employees' files.	To ensure that employees are not wrongly paid when they have left or not paid once they have started.

Answer 5.4

The questions to be asked in order to review the computer controls in existence over purchases and creditors must cover controls over input, processing, access, files and output. The following questions could be asked of the accountant responsible for the creditors section.

(a) What systematic action is taken to ensure the completeness, accuracy and authorisation of input of purchase invoices, credit notes, journal entries, cash and so on? For example, batch totalling, sequence checking, programmed matching of input to control files containing details of expected input, and authorisation limits and reasonableness checks.

(b) By what methods is it established that all input is fully and accurately processed? Examples are batch reconciliation after records update, summary totals, programmed validity checks.

(c) What controls are in place to prevent or detect unauthorised amendments to programs and data files (for example, restrictions of access to programs and to users of the on-line terminals)?

(d) What controls exist over the work done by computer operators (for example, division of duties, job scheduling, computer logs, cross-checks to input control, authorisation of file issue)?

(e) What procedures are in operation to ensure the continuing correctness of master files and the standing data they contain? For example, record counts or hash totals for the files, produced and checked each time they are used, regular checks of all contents, run-to-run control totals.

(f) Are there procedures for the review and despatch of output by the computer operators? Examples are: comparison of output with prelist totals of input, checking all queries have been properly dealt with, distribution list for all output and close control over exception reports, audit totals and so on.

(g) Is the reasonableness of output tested? For example, is output tested against file totals after update, and compared with manually prepared totals and balances on individual debtors accounts?

(h) Is there an adequate management (audit) trail of generated data and regular listing of ledger balances and creditor analysis?

(i) Is there an accounting manual in existence, detailing all procedures and clerical processes relating to the purchases and creditors system, and is it up to date?

Answer 5.5

The following general controls should be exercised to prevent unauthorised access to the computer system from the terminals.

(a) There should be physical security over the system by keeping terminals, or the room in which they are located, locked. Such physical security should prevent access by staff who do not ordinarily have reason to use the computer system in the course of their work.

(b) If practicable, access to the main computer could be restricted to the usual working hours of the company. Any person requiring access outside these hours would be required to obtain special authorisation.

(c) Each terminal should be set up to provide only those services which the users of that terminal need to use. For example, the terminal sited in the payroll department will be able to provide access to the payroll system, but not to the purchases, sales or nominal ledger systems. The computer should log terminals and users and this log should be checked regularly for unusual access times etc.

(d) Individual users should only be able to gain access to those facilities which he or she needs to use in the course of his or her normal job. This form of restriction may be implemented by the use of passwords, so that the system identifies for each valid password the range of facilities which the person having that password may use.

(e) Passwords should be unique to the individual. This uniqueness reduces the risk of passwords becoming commonly known. Passwords should also be changed periodically. Computer users should be instructed to memorise their passwords rather than to write them down. The system should have a facility for issuing a new password, following appropriate authorisation, if one becomes forgotten. Passwords should not be displayed on screens when they are being keyed in by users.

(f) As an alternative to, or in addition to, passwords users could be issued with plastic cards or infra-red keys which can be inserted at the terminal to identify the user. There is a risk that people may lose cards or keys.

(g) Controls over the programs used to process accounting data should be very strict. Amendments should only be allowed when authorised by a senior official (eg the Data Processing Manager) and after testing by another department in order to iron out any problems. Such changes should only be enacted on entry of a secret code and all changes should be logged and checked.

Chapter 6

Answer 6.1

Audit risks at AJ (Paper) Ltd

Selling paper and paper-related products appears to be low-risk. There is unlikely to be substantial additional regulation of this company and the market is unlikely to be volatile. The plans to diversify represent a business risk and may also impact on the audit in terms of going concern, if the plans do not work out and the business fails as a result of its attempted expansion.

The fact that the company has one or two major suppliers could have a serious impact on the going concern assumption if one or either of them were to stop supplying AJ (Paper) Ltd for any reason. However, provided that these suppliers issue suppliers' statements, creditors should be a low risk area of the audit as testing two or three suppliers will give good coverage of the total trade creditors balance.

Conversely, debtors will be a more difficult part of the audit, with a high sample required to give good coverage of the total debtors balance as there are a large number of small value customers.

If the bank intends to rely on the audited accounts, this increases the risk of the audit as the bank may become a third party to whom the auditors owe a duty of care.

Answer 6.2

(a) Because the business is stable, auditors are likely to base overall materiality on a % of turnover or gross assets, or possibly an average of both. Profit before tax is unlikely to be used overall as its fluctuation does not appear to be significant. However a different materiality level may be set when considering the one-off expense, since it may be particularly significant to readers of the accounts.

(b) Auditors are likely here to pay some attention to the level of profit when setting materiality, because the outside members regard profit as significant. However the auditors are also likely to take into account gross and net assets. Low profits will be of less significance if the business has a strong asset base, but of more significance if the business is in long-term financial difficulty.

Chapter 7

Answer 7.1

Shahid must put together an audit plan which covers the following elements:

- Knowledge of the business
- Risk and materiality
- Nature, timing and extent of procedures
- Co-ordination, direction, supervision and review
- Other matters (such as any regulatory, going concern and reporting issues)

Shahid should obtain the knowledge of the business he requires from notes made by Tariq and the audit team who visited AJ (Paper) Ltd on pre-planning visits in order to obtain knowledge of the business. This should include a summary of the accounting systems and organisational chart of the key personnel.

From the above knowledge of the business and any draft financial statements that the company can provide, or latest management accounts if no draft financial statements are available, Shahid should be able to make preliminary assessments of inherent risk. He may also be able to make initial assessments of control risk from the notes made about the accounting systems. If he is able to assess inherent and control risk, he will be able to draw some conclusions about detection risk. This will be linked to an assessment of materiality, which he should also be able to draw preliminary conclusions about from any draft financial statements he has been given. If he has not already been given draft financial statements, after checking with Tariq that he has not already made arrangements with Anton, Shahid should telephone Anton and request such information to enable him to put the plan together.

The audit plan should contain details of who is on the audit team. It would make reference to whether the audit team intended to use the work of the internal audit team or an external expert. Neither is likely to be the case in the audit of AJ (Paper) Ltd. There are no specific regulatory or other matters which the audit plan should refer to. The plan should note that the terms of the engagement set out that a report on control weakness will be submitted if any major control weaknesses are observed as part of the audit.

When Shahid has completed the audit plan, he should pass it to the audit supervisor for review. The audit plan will have to be approved by Tariq Hussain before the audit commences. Tariq Hussain should also call an audit planning meeting to brief the audit team about the key issues in the audit of AJ (Paper) Ltd.

Chapter 8

Answer 8.1

(a) Working papers should be headed with:

- The name of the client
- The balance sheet date
- The file reference of the working paper
- The name of the person preparing the working paper
- The date the working paper was prepared
- The subject of the working paper
- The name of the person reviewing the working paper
- The date of the review

(b) Working papers should also show:

- The objective of the work done
- The source of information
- How any sample was selected and the sample size determined
- The work done
- A key to any audit ticks or symbols
- The results obtained
- Analysis of errors or other significant observations
- The conclusions drawn
- The key points highlighted

Chapter 9

Answer 9.1

(a) The physical inspection of an asset by auditors is inherently strong audit evidence since it is evidence obtained directly by auditors rather than from the client.

The physical inspection of an asset gives auditors the strongest possible evidence concerning its existence.

It also may give auditors some evidence as to valuation if for example machines appear to be obsolete or buildings appear to be derelict. More likely however auditors will require specialist assistance to value very material assets.

Inspection also gives auditors some assurance that assets have been completely recorded. Auditors can check that all assets inspected have been recorded.

However ownership of assets cannot be verified solely by physical inspection. Auditors will need to inspect documents of title, vehicle registration documents and so forth depending on the assets being verified.

(b) Debtor confirmation of balances owed is inherently strong audit evidence since it is written confirmation by a third party.

The evidence is particularly relevant to the assertions of existence (the debtor exists) and rights and obligations (the debtor owes the client money).

Further evidence however is likely to be needed of valuation because although the debtor has acknowledged money is owed, that does not mean that the money will be paid.

(c) Oral representations from clients about what is owed at the year-end are inherently weak evidence since they are not in writing and do not come from an independent source. Auditors should seek written confirmation of the representations, and seek confirmation from other audit evidence, for example suppliers' statements, post year-end accounting records and invoices received after the year-end.

The representations do give some comfort on the completeness of creditors, and also the obligations of the client.

Answer 9.2

(a) Loss of audit trail means that auditors do not have full details of the accounting process that goes on within the computer, and cannot therefore check that process for accuracy. In addition auditors cannot be sure that the output of the computer is complete. Certain procedures may also take place entirely within the computer without any visible evidence.

(b) Auditors can overcome the loss of audit trail in the following ways.

   (i) Placing reliance on controls. Controls such as check digit verification or record counts can give assurance on the completeness and accuracy of processing. Other controls can give assurance that the programs run have been developed properly and access to those programs is limited.

(ii) Audit interrogation software can be used to reperform reconciliations, analyse accounts and identify items which do not fulfil criteria set down by the auditors and may therefore be subject to fraud.

(iii) Test data can be used to see whether the system produces the results expected.

(iv) Likewise an integrated test facility, involving the creation of a fictitious department, can be used to test the operation of processes.

(v) The results of processing can be subject to analytical review, comparisons with previous years, budgets etc.

(vi) Similarly the results of processing can be compared with other audit evidence, for example computer stock balances being compared with actual stock counts.

(vii) Procedures can be reperformed manually but this is very time-consuming.

Answer 9.3

Sample selection

(a) Aspects of Ping's approach which are inconsistent with sampling

A key criterion of sampling is that all items in the population could have been picked. In **not selecting accounts <£100 or government accounts**, you have not taken the right approach.

Choosing the **two highest accounts** is not really sampling either. The choice of those accounts was not random, haphazard or statistical.

(b) **Alternative means of sampling material balances**

You could **stratify the sample**. This would involve splitting the sample into sub-populations, on the basis of size, or alphabetically, for example. In this instance, size would be logical because it is a relevant factor as a high proportion of the value of debtors is likely to be in a small proportion of debtors.

If you did this on the basis of size, then you would be able to 100% test the material balances and then sample (by one of the methods above – random, haphazard or statistical) in the other populations.

(c) **Comparison of methods of sample selection**

- **Random**. This is where a sample is chosen on standard basis, such as mathematical tables.

- **Systematic**. This is where a sample is chosen by selecting the nth one when reading through the list of debtors or the ledger in order.

- **Haphazard**. This is where there is no method of any kind to the sample selection.

While haphazard to the layman appears to be random selection, this is not the case. The first two forms of sample selection are more mathematical than the last one. Haphazard is far more prone to bias than the other two as it can be influenced by such factors as ease of selection.

Chapter 10

Answer 10.1

(a) Controls over the file containing suppliers' details will include the following. These should prevent fraud by the creation of a fictitious supplier.

   (i) All amendments/additions/deletions to the data should be authorised by a responsible official. A standard form should be used for such changes.

   (ii) The amendment forms should be input in batches (with different types of change in different batches), sequentially numbered and recorded in a batch control book so that any gaps in the batch numbers can be investigated. The output produced by the computer should be checked to the input.

   (iii) A listing of all such adjustments should automatically be produced by the computer and reviewed by a responsible official, who should also check authorisation.

   (iv) A listing of suppliers' accounts on which there has been no movement for a specified period (6 months, 12 months) should be produced to allow decisions to be made about possible deletions, thus ensuring that the data is current. The buying department manager might also recommend account closures on a periodic basis.

   (v) Users should be controlled by use of passwords. This can also be used as a method of controlling those who can amend data.

   (vi) Periodic listings of data should be produced in order to verify details (for example addresses) with suppliers' documents (invoices/ statements).

(b) The input of authorised purchase invoices and credit notes should be controlled in the following ways.

   (i) Authorisation should be evidenced by the signature of the responsible official (say the Chief Accountant). In addition, the invoice or credit note should show initials to demonstrate that the details have been agreed: to a signed GRN; to a purchase order; to a price list; for additions and extensions.

   (ii) There should be adequate segregation of responsibilities between the posting function, stock custody and receipt, payment of suppliers and changes to data.

   (iii) Input should be restricted by use of passwords linked to the relevant site number.

   (iv) A batch control book should be maintained, recording batches in number sequence. Invoices should be input in batches using pre-numbered batch control sheets. The manually produced invoice total on the batch control sheet should be agreed to the computer generated total. Credit notes and invoices should be input in separate batches to avoid one being posted as the other.

   (v) A program should check calculation of VAT at standard rate and total (net + VAT = gross) of invoice. Non-standard VAT rates should be highlighted.

   (vi) The input of the supplier code should bring up the supplier name for checking by the operator against the invoice.

PROFESSIONAL EDUCATION

(vii) Invoices for suppliers which do not have an account should be prevented from being input. Any sundry suppliers account should be very tightly controlled and all entries reviewed in full each month.

(viii) An exception report showing unusual expense allocation (by size or account) should be produced and reviewed by a responsible official. Expenses should be compared to budget and previous years.

(ix) There should be monthly reconciliations of purchase ledger balances to suppliers' statements by someone outside the purchasing (accounting) function.

Answer 10.2

(a) The most important controls over the safe custody of stock are as follows.

(i) **Physical**

Access to the stock-rooms should be restricted to authorised staff. Outside working hours, the stock area should be locked.

(ii) **Segregation of duties**

Stock movements should be recorded by different staff from those responsible for ensuring the safe custody of stocks.

(iii) **Stock records**

Appropriate documentation should be maintained including stores ledger accounts giving details of movements, quantities held and pricing of stock lines, bin cards giving details of movements and quantities held, and materials requisitions and return notes.

(iv) **Controls over movements**

(1) Stock being delivered should be logged in by goods received notes and goods inwards records, which should be reconciled with supplier delivery notes and purchase orders.

(2) All internal movements of stock should be authorised.

(3) Stock should only be despatched if a sales order has been received, and should only be despatched to authorised customers. Stock despatches should be recorded on despatch notes and in goods outwards records, and these should subsequently be reconciled to sales order and invoices.

(v) **Stocktakes**

Regular stocktakes should be carried out by someone who is independent of the stores department. All stock should be counted at least once a year. Stock counted should be compared with stock records, and differences investigated.

(b) The most important controls over the custody of tangible fixed assets are as follows.

(i) **Physical**

As with stock, fixed assets, particularly portable ones, should be locked away when not in use or outside business hours. Companies may also mark fixed assets with identification codes.

(ii) **Segregation of duties**

There should be segregation of duties between the people responsible for authorising fixed asset purchases and disposals, those responsible for custody and those responsible for recording fixed assets.

(iii) **Fixed asset register**

Fixed assets held should be recorded in a fixed asset register, maintained separately from the company's general ledger and cash systems.

(iv) **Purchases and disposals**

All fixed asset purchases, disposals and scrappings should be authorised by staff of appropriate seniority. Major purchases and disposals should be authorised by the board.

(v) **Reconciliations**

The fixed asset register should be reconciled to the general ledger on a regular basis by someone other than the staff member who maintains the fixed asset register. There should also be comparisons made by independent staff to check if fixed assets recorded in the fixed asset register are actually held, and to check that assets held are recorded in the fixed asset register.

Answer 10.3

	ICQ question	Internal control objective	Audit tests	Consequences of lack of control
1	Does an appropriate official authorise rates of pay?	Employees are paid amounts authorised	Test rates of pay from payroll to schedule of authorised pay rates (personnel files, board minutes etc)	Incorrect rates of pay could lead to over/under statement of profit
2	Are written notices required for employing and terminating employment?	All employees paid through payroll exist	Check a sample of employees from payroll files for authorisation of employment or termination Check details for cheque or credit transfer salary payments to personnel files	Payroll may include fictitious employees
3	Are formal records such as time cards used for time keeping?	Employees are only paid for work done	Review time records to ensure they are properly completed and controlled Observe procedures for time recording Check time records where absences are recorded to payroll to ensure they have been accounted for Review the wages account and investigate any large or unusual amounts	Overstatement of payroll costs. Employees over/under paid
4	Does anyone verify rates of pay, overtime hours and computation of gross pay before wage payments are made?	Employees are paid the correct amount	Examine payroll for evidence of verification Recompute gross pay (including overtime) Check wage rates to authorised schedule	Misstatement of payroll costs
5	Does the accounting system ensure the proper recording of payroll costs in the financial records?	Payroll costs are properly recorded	Check posting of payroll costs to the nominal ledger	Misstatement of payroll costs

Chapter 11

Answer 11.1

Audit objective	Typical audit tests
Completeness	(1) Review of post balance sheet items
	(2) Cut off
	(3) Analytical review
	(4) Confirmations
	(5) Reconciliations to control account
	(6) Sequence checks
Rights and obligations	(1) Checking invoices for proof that item belongs to the company
	(2) Confirmations with third parties
Valuation	(1) Checking to invoices
	(2) Recalculation
	(3) Accounting policy consistent and reasonable
	(4) Review of post balance sheet payments and invoices
Existence	(1) Physical verification
	(2) Third party confirmations
	(3) Cut off testing
Disclosure	(1) Check compliance with CA 1985 and SSAPs and FRSs
	(2) True and fair override invoked

Answer 11.2

Client: AJ (Paper) Ltd	Reviewed by:	Ref
Subject: Analytical review (P and L)	Date:	17.2
Prepared by: SA		
Date: 12.2.01		
Accounting reference date: 31.12.00		

Objective: To identify areas of risk which necessitate additional investigation on the audit.

Work done: Review of the draft profit and loss account and key ratios within it (see 17.3).

Results and
conclusions:
There has been a massive increase in turnover and general activity in the year since the additional investment in the company and the expansion in activities. We should investigate the nature of these increases and identify whether the growth is entirely due to the new product or whether there has been growth in the traditional product and market as well. As cost of sales does not appear to have risen the same amount as turnover, we should also ensure that turnover is not overstated, for example, by the inclusion of January 2001 sales or that some costs have been excluded, or that closing stock has not been overstated. The increase in the growth profit margin could indicate that costs have been left out/turnover overstated or it could indicate that the new products result in better contribution for the company.

The company's expenses have similarly increased substantially. Many of these are still comparatively small despite the significant increase and so are not material for our audit purposes. However, the following matters should be investigated:

Salaries: These are material and have increased substantially. We can check whether these have been stated fairly by carrying out further analytical techniques such as comparing cost of staff to numbers on the payroll at the beginning and end of the year. If there has been a significant increase in staff we should ensure controls over staff joining are strong, as if not, there is increased risk of a payroll fraud.

Audit: There appears to be audit expenses despite the fact that an audit has not yet been carried out. Disclosure of audit expenses is a statutory requirement, so it will be important that we check whether this amount is correct. We should be able to verify this to our own records.

Bank charges: These have increased by a round £1,000 which seems high and possibly odd. We should identify what this is, in case it is has not been disclosed properly. If some of the additional funding in the year was from the bank, loan charges should have increased, and this £1,000 could be a misanalysis.

Travelling and advertising costs: These have both risen dramatically. This may be explained by the launch of new products, but these codes should be examined to ensure that the costs they include are all business related amounts.

The significant increase in turnover and the disparity between the increase in turnover and cost of sales should be mentioned to the audit supervisor at an early stage as an important matter of interest relating to the audit which could indicate audit problems.

Client: AJ (Paper) Ltd				
Subject: Analytical review (P and L)				
Prepared by: SA				
Date: 12.2.01				
Accounting reference date: 31.12.00				

Reviewed by:
Date:

Ref
17.3

		2000 £	% inc	1999 £	
Turnover		1,536,088	57	978,045	
Cost of sales		(1,245,930)	38	(903,487)	
Gross profit	18.8%	290,158		74,558	7.6%
Administration and establishment charges					
Salaries and wages		103,279	77	58,224	
Computer charges		602		598	
Incidental expenses		54		20	
Insurance		4,725		3,928	
Legal and other professional fees		24,949	3,966	629	
Printing, postage and stationery		10,430	373	2,794	
Repairs and renewals		2,226	80	1,237	
Telephone		4,829	511	944	
Depreciation		4,836	765	632	
		155,930		69,006	
Finance charges					
Audit		468			
Accountancy		2,049	98	1,031	
Bank charges		1,625	260	625	
Loan interest		2,495		2,495	
Bad debts		967		62	
		7,604		4,213	
Selling and distribution charges					
Travelling and entertainment expenses		5,327	1,296	411	
Motor expenses		927		317	
Advertising		6,417	2,160	297	
		12,671		1,025	
		113,953		314	

Answer 11.3

Under SAS 450 auditors have a responsibility to obtain sufficient appropriate audit evidence that amounts derived from preceding period's accounts have been properly brought forward and included in this year's accounts.

Opening balances

For opening balances, this means obtaining appropriate audit evidence that:

- Opening balances have been appropriately brought forward.

- Opening balances do not contain material misstatements which affect the current year's accounts.

- Accounting policies are consistently applied or changes in accounting policies are appropriate and fully disclosed.

Auditors' procedures should include consultations with management. They should check that balances in last year's trial balance have been brought forward to this year's accounting records, and should consider whether the accounting policies which affect the opening balances are appropriate.

They should review the accounting records, accounting procedures and internal controls that were in operation during the last accounting period.

Often these procedures will suffice since auditors can gain assurance on the correctness of opening balances by obtaining assurance on this year's closing balances and transactions during the year. However audit verification work may be required on opening balances if the review procedures mentioned above do not provide sufficient evidence. SAS 450 suggests that verification procedures are more likely when, as here, the previous year's accounts were not audited.

If additional verification procedures are required, auditors should concentrate on those areas which are material to this year's accounts, particularly areas where there have been significant changes as compared with last year.

Comparatives

SAS 450 requires auditors to obtain sufficient appropriate audit evidence that:

- Accounting policies used for comparatives are consistent with those used for the current period, or appropriate adjustments and disclosures have been made.

- The comparatives agree with the accounts and other disclosures presented in the previous periods and are free from errors.

- Where comparatives have been adjusted, appropriate disclosures have been made.

Unlike with opening balances, it should not be necessary to carry out verification work on comparatives. Auditors should ensure comparatives have been correctly brought forward and appropriately classified for Fluff Ltd, and they should check that the comparatives are clearly disclosed in the accounts as being unaudited.

If the auditors become aware that the comparatives have been materially misstated, they should encourage the directors either to restate the comparatives or reissue last year's accounts. If the comparatives are re-stated in this year's accounts, auditors should ensure the re-statement is adequately disclosed. If the comparatives are not re-stated, the audit opinion is likely to have to be qualified.

Chapter 12

Answer 12.1

Before the stocktake

Chantal should:

(a) Read the planning papers/talk to the audit manager

(b) Review last year's stock section

(c) Understand the nature of the business and stock, for example manufacturing process, conditions of storage, shelf-life/obsolescence, range/types of stock, relative value of different types of stock, nature of WIP and how the percentage complete is assessed, need for specialists

(d) Review and evaluate the client's procedures, for example

    (i) How many items are to be counted? too few counted fails to give adequate assurance, too many creates excessive follow-up work

    (ii) Which items are to be counted?

    (iii) Location(s), date(s), time, client contact

Common problems include:

- Going to the wrong location or getting lost

- Arriving after the count has finished

- Having no idea of the value of the stock so that the number of test counts may be inappropriate or major items are not covered

- The count overrunning by hours or even days

- Wearing inappropriate clothes

During the stocktake

Chantal should:

- Agree test counts to client counts before leaving the premises
- Obtain details of last/first goods movements before/after count
- Be prepared to extend the sample if unusual or unexpected items are noticed
- Obtain sequence of numbers of stock-sheets and perform sequence check
- Obtain copies of stock sheets where possible
- Identify any third party stocks
- Be aware and note down details of any old, obsolete and damaged stock
- Review the area being counted to ensure all stock has been included in the count

Common problems (and their solutions) include the following.

(a) Differences found on test count from client figures

    (i) Get the client to recount.

(ii)   Perform more test counts in that area.

(b)   Goods moving during the stock count

(i)   Stop the goods being moved.
(ii)   Note down details (serial numbers etc).
(iii)   Find out why they were moving.
(iv)   Recount to make sure they are not being double-counted or omitted.

(c)   Count takes longer than expected.

(d)   Stock value is much greater than anticipated (say due to a late delivery).

(e)   GRNs and other documents are not accessible during stock count (find out when they will first be available and look at them then).

After the stocktake

Chantal should write the results up immediately and pass the working papers for review by Ping or Andrew.

Since the company anticipates that production will continue whilst the counting of stock takes place and that there will also be movements of goods (in and out) up to noon on 30 December, there could be a major problem in relation to cut-off, unless very strict controls are instituted in this area. To minimise the possibility of cut-off errors, the following additional stocktaking instructions should be issued:

(a)   **Acceptance of deliveries from suppliers**

To avoid the risk of goods inwards delivered on 29 and 30 December being counted twice, they should be held in the goods received area, until noon on 30 December (normal procedures for checking quantity and quality and raising GRNs should be applied).

If any of these goods are required for Friday's production, then they should only be released on the signed authority of Mr Wells. Care should be taken to ensure that they are properly recorded (ie according to normal procedures) in the stores records and on issue to production.

At noon on Saturday, careful note should be taken of the last GRN number in order to facilitate the subsequent matching of invoices relating to the period ended 31 December (an essential part of the cut-off procedures).

(b)   **Issues from stores to production**

In order to avoid cut-off and counting problems that would ensue if piecemeal issues were to be made from stores to production throughout Friday, it will be necessary for production department heads to estimate their requirements for Friday production by (at the latest) 5.00 pm on 27 December.

During 28 December stores staff should make up all production requisitions for the following day. The stocks in question should be separately stored and labelled so that on the Friday, production requests can be met without there being any necessity for movement of the goods to be counted.

As before, if it turns out that, because of underestimation of production requirements, issues have to be made, then this should only be permitted on the signed authority of Mr Wells. Careful note should be made of the requisitions in question so that the appropriate adjustments may be made to the count records.

(c) **Transfer of finished goods from production to warehouse**

All completed production for 29 December should be passed through to the warehouse in accordance with normal procedures (re documentation etc). Upon receipt in the warehouse, this production should be stored in a separate area. This area should not be counted until the morning of 30 December.

(d) **Despatch of finished goods**

The procedure here will be the reverse of what is required in relation to acceptance of deliveries from suppliers. Sales orders due for despatch on Friday and Saturday morning should be determined by the evening of 27 December. These orders should be made up on 28 December and stored in a separate area of the warehouse, in order that a full count of the finished goods may be started on 29 December.

As before, if any urgent orders are required to be despatched on Friday or Saturday this should only be permitted on the basis of written authorisation from Mr Wells.

To facilitate proper matching of sales to the relevant period (another essential part of the cut-off procedure) a note should be made of the last despatch note number at 12 noon on 30 December for subsequent agreement with invoices per the sales department.

Five recommendations, with reasons, which it is felt will require action by management, if the company's stock count is to be effective, may be seen as:

(a) Mr Khanna should take more direct responsibility for the detailed organisation of the count.

(b) The pre-printed stock sheets should not show the balance of each stock item on hand as shown on the stock records held independently of the warehouse.

(c) The teams of counters should be instructed that in the event of their independent counts of the stock quantities not agreeing a further count should take place. If they are still unable to agree then a note of this fact should be made on the stock count tag (see (d) below) so that a further check may be made by the inspection team (see (d) below).

(d) A number of teams of checkers (2 or 3) should be appointed to go around after the counters. The task of these checkers would be to:

    (i) Carry out sample tests on the accuracy of the original counters
    (ii) Ensure that stock count completion tags have been left by the counters at each stock location.

(e) Where the count teams come across any goods that appear to be in poor condition, they should not, as instructed to do at present, deduct these from the quantities recorded on the stock sheets, but merely note the quantity of 'damaged etc' stocks in the comments column provided on the stock sheets. The value, if any, to be attributed to such items should then be determined at a later by Mr Khanna in consultation with Mr Wells.

Chapter 13

Answer 13.1

(a) **Printer**

  (i) Verify authorisation of purchase to minutes of board meeting.

  (ii) Inspect the asset, checking that its serial number agrees to the purchase documentation.

  (iii) Verify the cost of the asset to its purchase invoice, ensuring that any installation costs are treated as capital expenditure.

  (iv) Ensure that the company has an appropriate depreciation policy. (As manufacturing has not yet commenced, no depreciation may have been charged.)

  Leased van and lacing machine

  (i), (ii) and (iii) as above.

  (iv) Inspect the terms of the lease, and consider whether the lease should be classified as an operating lease or a finance lease. If the lease is an operating lease, the assets should not be treated as fixed assets. The lease rentals should be treated as revenue expenditure in the profit and loss account. If the leases are finance leases, the assets may be capitalised at fair value. Correct disclosure of the commitment to the leasing company will also need to be checked.

(b) The key tests are to investigate the content of the training course and assess the reasons why the workshop technician was sent on the course. If the training was essential for the new machinery to be brought into operation, the costs may be capitalised. If however the training was of a more general nature, the costs should be treated as revenue expenditure.

  If the training costs are to be treated as revenue expenditure, they should be removed from fixed assets and included under the appropriate revenue expense heading. Depreciation will also need to be adjusted.

(c) We should carry out the following work on the depreciation charge.

  • Check whether the depreciation charge is consistent with charges for previous years, and consistent with the company's accounting policies relating to depreciation.

  • Check the calculation of the depreciation charge for individual vehicles/in total.

  • Review the profits or losses on disposals of motor vehicles during the year to ensure that the charge is not excessive.

  • Check that depreciation rates appear reasonable in the light of vehicle usage and replacement policy.

  • Check that all vehicles are being depreciated.

  • Check that no further depreciation is being charged on fully depreciated vehicles.

  • Check that the client's depreciation policy and depreciation charge are disclosed in the accounts.

Answer 13.2

(a) Alternative means of obtaining evidence of the existence of vehicles include the following.

- Insurance policies

- Evidence of repair and maintenance expenditure

- MOT certificate

- Correspondence with the salesmen, including acknowledgement by the salesmen that they have the cars

(b) Audit work should include:

- Inspect the machine to confirm its condition and the fact that it is still being used.

- Check the invoices which detail the expenditure on the machine.

- If the client has used internal labour in bringing the machine back into use, check labour costs to wage records.

- Check the insurance policy on the machine for evidence of valuation.

If any further problems arise obtaining audit evidence in relation to these matters, I should mention them to Ping as this could represent a limitation on the scope of the fixed asset audit.

Chapter 14

Answer 14.1

(a) The debtors' circularisation should normally take place immediately after the year-end covering balances outstanding at the year-end. When planning the debtors' circularisation, auditors should obtain a list of debtor balances, reconciled to the total in the sales ledger control account. The auditors should review the list for any obvious omissions or misstatements (customers where large balances were expected).

The auditors should then select a sample from the list, concentrating on the following accounts:

- Overdue accounts
- Accounts written off in the period under review
- Accounts with credit balances
- Accounts settled by round-sum payments

The sample should also include:

- Accounts with nil balances
- Accounts that had been paid since the year-end

The auditors should ensure a letter is prepared for each debtor sampled. The letter should be on the client's headed notepaper and should be signed by the client. It should authorise the debtor to contact the auditors about the amount owed. A pre-paid envelope addressed to the auditors should be provided for this purpose. The letter would normally state that if the debtor agrees with the amount, they should sign the letter to indicate agreement. If they do not agree with the amount, they should notify the auditors directly of the amount they believe is owed, and if possible give full details of the difference.

The letter should be accompanied by a debtors' statement which should be prepared by the client at the year-end.

Auditors should check the letters and statements to the debtors' listing prior to despatch, and should supervise despatch themselves.

(b) The audit work required on the various replies to a debtors' circularisation would be as follows.

(i) **Balances agreed by debtor**

Where the balance has been agreed by the debtor all that is required would be to ensure that the debt does appear to be collectable. This would be achieved by reviewing cash received after date or considering the adequacy of any provision made for a long outstanding debt.

(ii) **Balances not agreed by debtor**

All balance disagreements must be followed up and their effect on total debtors evaluated. Differences arising that merely represent invoices or cash in transit (which are normal timing differences) generally do not require adjustment, but disputed amounts, and errors by the client, may indicate that further substantive work is necessary to determine whether material adjustments are required.

(iii) **Debtor is unable to confirm the balance because of the form of records he or she maintains**

Certain companies, often computerised, operate systems which make it impossible for them to confirm the balance on their account. Typically in these circumstances their purchase ledger is merely a list of unpaid invoices. However, given sufficient information the debtor will be able to confirm that any given invoice is outstanding. Hence the auditors can circularise such enterprises successfully, but they will need to break down the total on the account into its constituent outstanding invoices.

(iv) **Debtor does not reply to circularisation**

When the positive request method is used the auditors must follow up by all practicable means those debtors who fail to respond. Second requests should be sent out in the event of no reply being received within two or three weeks and if necessary this may be followed by telephoning the customer with the client's permission.

If no reply has been received a list of the outstanding items will normally be passed to a responsible company official, preferably independent of the sales department, who will arrange for them to be investigated.

Other auditing tests that can establish that there existed a valid debt from a genuine customer at the date of the verification are as follows.

- Check receipt of cash after date.
- Verify valid purchase orders, if any.
- Examine the account to see if the balance represents specific outstanding invoices.
- Obtain explanations for invoices remaining unpaid after subsequent ones have been paid.
- See if the balance on the account is growing, and if so, why.
- Test the company's control over the issue of credit notes and the write-off of bad debts.

Answer 14.2

Chantal should carry out the following tests on the bad debt provision.

- Check that the basis used is consistent with previous years.

- Consider whether the basis was reasonable, reviewing recent years to see the provision made had been adequate but not excessive.

- Review the sales ledger for this year, checking the ageing of debtors, and considering whether the pattern of debtors had changed in terms of amounts owed and collection period.

- Review the sales ledger for all large debts against which specific provision might be required.

- Check the calculation of the provision.

- Confirm that the debtors' balances used agreed with the adjusted control account provision.

- Confirm that the provision had been posted to the accounting records.

Answer 14.3

(a) The main elements of a standard bank letter are as follows.

   (i) Titles, numbers and balances on all bank accounts including loans

   (ii) Details of accounts where the customer's name is joined with that of other parties or where the account is in a trade name

   (iii) Account details and date of closure for accounts closed during the twelve months up to the audit confirmation date

   (iv) Details of loans, overdrafts and associated guarantees and indemnities

- Term
- Repayment frequency and/or review date
- Detail of period of availability of agreed finance ie finance remaining undrawn
- The facility limit

   (v) In relation to the facilities:

- Details of any supporting security formally charged
- Details if a security is limited in amount or to a specific borrowing, or if there is another charge

   (vi) Set-off arrangements

   (vii) Additional relationships with other branches or subsidiaries of the bank

(b) The following tests should be carried out on the bank reconciliation.

   (i) Check the arithmetic of the bank reconciliation.

   (ii) Trace cheques shown as unpresented on the bank reconciliation to the cash book before the year-end and the bank statement after the year-end.

   (iii) Check uncleared bankings per the bank reconciliation to paying-in-slips to confirm that they have been paid in prior to the year-end, and check they appear on bank statements soon after the year-end.

   (iv) Investigate other reconciling items.

   (v) Verify balance per cash book on reconciliation with cash book and general ledger.

   (vi) Verify balance per bank on reconciliation with bank statements and bank letter.

   (vii) Scrutinise cash book and bank statements before and after the year-end for unusual items which may materially affect the bank balance.

Answer 14.4

The following key considerations relate to the count itself:

(a) All cash/petty cash books should be written up to date in ink (or other permanent form at the time of the count.

(b) All balances must be counted at the same time.

(c) All negotiable securities must be available and counted at the time the cash balances are counted.

(d) At no time should the auditors be left alone with the cash and negotiable securities.

(e) All cash and securities counted must be recorded on working papers subsequently filed on the current audit file. Reconciliations should be prepared where applicable (for example imprest petty cash float).

After the cash count, you should ensure that:

(a) Certificates of cash-in-hand are obtained as appropriate

(b) Unbanked cheques/cash receipts have subsequently been paid in and agree to the bank reconciliation

(c) IOUs and cheques cashed for employees have been reimbursed

(d) IOUs or cashed cheques outstanding for unreasonable periods of time have been provided for

(e) The balances as counted are reflected in the accounts (subject to any agreed amendments because of shortages and so on)

Chapter 15

Answer 15.1

(a) The audit work I would carry out to verify that purchases cut off has been correctly carried out at the year end is as follows.

    (i) From the notes taken at the stocktake I will have the number of the last GRN that was issued before the year end.

    (ii) I will then select a sample of GRNs issued in the period immediately before and immediately after the year end. The period to be covered would be at least two weeks either side of the year end.

    (iii) I will concentrate my sample on high value items, and more on those GRNs from before the year end as these represent the greatest risk of cut-off error.

    (iv) I will check that the GRNs have a correct number, according to the last GRN issued in the year and whether the goods were received before or after the year end.

    (v) For GRNs issued before the year end I will ensure that the stock has been included in the year end stock total. In addition, I will ensure that the creditor is either included in trade creditors or purchase accruals.

    (vi) For GRNs issued after the year end, I will need to ensure that the stock is only included in the stock records after the year end balance has been extracted. In addition, I will need to check to the purchase ledger to ensure that the relevant invoice has been posted to the supplier account after the year end.

(b) The audit work I will carry out to check balances on the purchase ledger is as follows.

I will select a sample of creditors and compare suppliers' statements with purchase ledger balances. The extent of the sample will depend on the results of my tests of controls and my assessment of the effectiveness of controls within the purchases system (ie if the system of control is strong I will check fewer items).

I will select the sample on a random basis. Selection of only large balances or those with many transactions will not yield an appropriate sample as I am looking for understatement of liabilities. Nil and negative balances will also need to be included in the sample.

If no statement is available for any supplier, I will ask for confirmation of the balance from the creditor.

If the balance agrees exactly, no further work needs to be carried out.

Where differences arise these need to be categorised as either in transit items or other (including disputed) items.

In-transit items will be either goods or cash.

If the difference relates to goods in transit, I would ascertain whether the goods were received before the year end by reference to the GRN and that they are included in year end stock and purchase accruals. If the goods were received after the year end, the difference with the suppliers' accounts is correct. If not, a cut-off error has occurred and should be investigated.

Similarly, cash in transit would arise where the payment to the supplier was made by cheque before the year end but was not received by him until after the year end. The date the cheque was raised and its subsequent clearing through the bank account after the year end should be verified by checking the cash book and the post year end bank statements.

However, if the cheque clears some while after the year end date, it may indicate that the cheque, though raised before the year end was not sent to the supplier until after the year end, and the relevant amount should be added back to year end creditors and to the end of year bank balance.

Differences which do not arise from in-transit items need to be investigated and appropriate adjustments made where necessary. These differences may have arisen due to disputed invoices, where for example the client is demanding credit against an invoice which the supplier is not willing to agree to. The client may decide not to post the invoice to the supplier account as he does not consider it to be a liability of the company. However, differences may also arise because invoices have been held back in order to reduce the level of year-end creditors.

If significant unexplained differences are discovered it may be necessary to extend my testing. There may also be a problem if sufficient suppliers' statements are not available. Alternative procedures, eg a circularisation may then need to be required.

(c)   The audit work I will carry out to ensure that accruals are correctly stated is as follows.

   (i)   I will assess the system of control instituted by management to identify and quantify accruals and creditors. Where controls are strong, I will perform fewer substantive procedures, taking the materiality of the amounts into consideration.

   (ii)   From the client's sundry creditors and accruals listing I will check that accruals are calculated correctly and verify them by reference to subsequent payments. I will check that all time apportionments have been made correctly (eg for electricity).

   (iii)   **PAYE and VAT balance**

      (1)   I will check the amount paid to the Inland Revenue for PAYE and NI. The balance at the year end would normally represent one month's deductions and can be verified to the payroll records. The payment should be traced from the cash book to the PAYE payment book (if used) and subsequent bank statements.

      (2)   For the VAT balance I will review for reasonableness to the next VAT return. I would also ensure that the payment for the previous return was for the correct amount and had cleared through the bank.

   (iv)   I will review the profit and loss account and prior year figures (for any accruals which have not appeared this year or which did not appear last year) and consider liabilities inherent in the trade (eg weekly wages) to ensure that all likely accruals have been provided.

   (v)   I will scrutinise payments made after the year end to ascertain whether any payments made should be accrued. This will include consideration of any payments relating to the current year which are made a long time after the year-end.

   (vi)   I will consider and document the basis for round sum accruals and ensure it is consistent with prior years.

(vii)   I will ascertain why any payments on account are being made and ensure that the full liability is provided.

(viii)   Accrued interest and basic charges on loans or overdrafts can be agreed to the bank letter received for audit purposes.

Answer 15.2

Client: AJ (Paper) Ltd
Subject: Creditors
Prepared by: AW
Date: 2 March 03
Accounting reference date: 31.12.02

Reviewed by:
Date: E2

Objective   To obtain evidence that purchase ledger balances are fairly stated.

Work done   Selected a sample of trade creditors as at 31 December and reconciled the supplier's statement to the year end purchase ledger balance. Vouched any reconciling items to source documentation.

Results   **Suppliers' statement reconciliations at 31/12/X3**

			£
Forestguard	Balance per supplier's statement		39,315.82
Paper	Less: invoice 128604003 – 27/12/02		6,952.48
	Less: £20 error on statement re invoice 126200741		
	(£16,885.86 – £16,865.86) – not material		20.00
	Balance per purchase ledger		32,343.34
Terry's Paper	Balance per supplier's statement		42,510.88
	Less: payment on 26/11/02 not on statement		19,654.62
	Balance per purchase ledger		22,856.26
Woodcutter Ltd	Balance per supplier's statement		89,655.68
	Add: Credit note 00071483 not on purchase ledger	(Note)	4,975.46
	Balance per purchase ledger		94,631.14

Note. This credit note has not been accounted for in the books of AJ (Paper) and therefore an adjustment is required.

Adjustment   DEBIT   Trade creditors   £4,975
required   CREDIT   Purchases   £4,975

One other error was found, which was immaterial, and which was the fault of the supplier. In view of the error found, however, we should recommend that the client management checks supplier statement reconciliations at least on the larger accounts – management letter point.

Conclusion   After making the adjustment noted above, purchase ledger balances are fairly stated as at 31 December 2002.

Chapter 16

Answer 16.1

(a) The purpose of a letter of representation is to obtain evidence about matters which are critical to the audit where that evidence is not available by other means.

SAS 440 suggests that matters where representations are obtained will mainly be where knowledge of the facts is confined to management, or where the directors have used judgement or opinion in the preparation of the accounts.

The fundamental weakness of representations is that they are not a substitute for stronger, independent evidence. Therefore representations will be insufficient if other stronger evidence is expected to be available.

If other evidence would not be expected to be available, auditors will consider the following:

(i) The fact that making misleading representations to auditors is an offence under the Companies Act

(ii) Whether other evidence that the auditors have sought to corroborate the representations, does do so

(iii) Whether the representations are consistent with other evidence obtained during the course of audit

(iv) Whether those making the representations are able to do so knowledgeably

(b) (i) Since the year-end, we have been assured that the cash flows of Y Limited have improved significantly, and some small progress payments have been made. As a result we believe that amounts of £200,000 which have been owed since WW will be fully recoverable.

Answer 16.2

(a) Auditors should carry out the following procedures as part of their post balance sheet events review.

(i) Consider the procedures management has established in order to ensure post balance sheet events are correctly treated. Auditors will be concerned with how post balance sheet events have been identified, considered and properly evaluated as to their effect on the financial statements.

(ii) Review post year-end accounting records which contain further evidence of conditions existing at the balance sheet date. This review will include review of debtors for evidence of receipt from cash from debtors, and review of bank and cash for evidence of clearance of cheques which were uncleared at the year-end.

(iii) Review budgets, profit forecasts, cash flow projections and management accounts. These may indicate significant income or expenditure which needs to be disclosed, and will also give general indications about the company's trading position.

(iv) Search for evidence about known risk areas and contingencies. This includes a review of documentation relating to legal matters.

(v)   Read the minutes of directors' meetings which took place after the year-end. These may provide evidence of significant decisions which may need to be disclosed. Auditors should find out details of what has happened at meetings for which minutes are not yet available.

(vi)   Review relevant sources of evidence that are external to the client, such as knowledge of competitors, suppliers and customers and industry trends.

(vii)   Discuss with management whether any events have occurred that may affect the accounts. Examples include new commitments, changes in assets or events which bring into question the accounting policies or estimates used in the accounts.

(b)   (i)   The main use of after-date evidence in stock is to determine the client's ability to sell its stock and hence to determine what net realisable value should be. The following information may be relevant:

- After-date sales made or orders received
- Details of planned reductions in sales prices
- Industry trends and details, particularly prices and performance of competitors
- Details of increases in average age of stock
- Details of stock scrapped

(ii)   The main uses of information on trade creditors and accruals are:

- Trade creditors and accruals have been completely recorded
- Stock cut-off has been correctly applied

Relevant information includes:

- Information received after the year-end for goods or services received prior to the year-end
- Credit notes received after the year-end for goods returned before the year-end
- Suppliers' statements received after the year-end relating to periods prior to the year-end
- Payments made after the year-end relating to goods or services received before the year-end

(c)   Auditors should carry out the following procedures to obtain evidence about legal actions.

- Discuss with management the arrangements for instructing solicitors or barristers.

- Examine board minutes for indications of legal actions.

- Examine correspondence with, and bills rendered by, solicitors and obtain confirmation that no bills are outstanding.

- Obtain a list of matters referred to solicitors.

- Obtain written assurances that directors or other officials are not aware of any outstanding matters other than those disclosed.

- If appropriate (due to problems with other evidence), obtain confirmation from solicitors about the directors' assessment of likely outcomes of legal actions, and of whether the information provided by the directors is complete.

Answer 16.3

Report to partner

Stock

Review of the stocktaking instructions revealed weaknesses in the system to prevent cut off errors. Additional testing was carried out to ensure that cut off was correct in the financial statements. However, this point should be raised in a management letter.

Fixed assets

Alternative audit work to that which had been planned had to be carried out on some areas of fixed assets as it did not prove possible to physically verify all the motor cars. However, different evidence proved satisfactory.

The client had brought a previously written off machine back into use in the business. The valuation was agreed as reasonable by checking labour costs and insurance cover arrangements.

Debtors

There is one significant old debt owing, from Y Limited. The directors have represented to us that the company is emerging from cash flow difficulties and that they expect the debt to be paid in full. Some recent, regular progress payments give further evidence to this belief. No other issues arose on the debtors audit.

Bank and cash

The client asked us to undertake a cash count due to recent problems with an employee defrauding the company. The employee has been sacked and the problems appear to have been isolated. The cash count undertaken revealed no issues. Cash controls were reinforced after the issue and it appears that they are now operating effectively.

Creditors

Creditors testing revealed some minor errors, but the overall balance appears fairly stated.

We should recommend in a management letter that the client carries out regular reconciliations between the purchase ledger balance and supplier statements for the major creditors.

Note: As an audit senior, you need to recognise all the issues around information you are given. For example, in activity 14.4, you were asked to carry out a cash count due to a recent fraud. As audit senior you should also consider the implications that this has for the auditors' consideration of internal controls, for example.

In the above answer, some audit work carried out has been assumed for the purposes of completeness.

Chapter 18

Answer 18.1

Khan Associates
Certified Accountants
20 East Road
Westnorth
Southshire
WN1 2NW

The Director
AJ (Paper) Ltd
24/26 Arthur Road
Newcastle Upon Tyne
NT1 4LJ

23 April 2003

Members of the board,

Financial statements for the year ended 31 December 2002

In accordance with our normal practice we set out in this letter certain matters which arose as a result of our review of the accounting systems and procedures operated by your company during our recent audit.

We would point out that the matters dealt with in this letter came to our notice during the conduct of our normal audit procedures which are designed primarily for the purpose of expressing our opinion on the financial statements of your company. In consequence our work did not encompass a detailed review of all aspects of the system and cannot be relied on necessarily to disclose defalcations or other irregularities or to include all possible improvements in internal control.

Segregation of duties in administration department

Weakness

Segregation of duties in the administration department is **inadequate**, as the administration manager is responsible for all the tasks involved in purchasing goods.

Implication

Unauthorised purchases may be made and posted to the purchase ledger.

Recommendation

Different members of staff should perform the tasks of ordering, recording and payment.

Reconciliation of despatch to order

Weakness

Finished goods are **not checked** to **customer orders** prior to being despatched.

Implication

If **queries** are **raised** about the quantity or quality of goods received by customers, the **company** will be **unable** to **confirm** that the **goods ordered** were **despatched**.

Recommendation

When **goods** are **loaded**, they **should** be **checked** to the **customer order** and the check evidenced in writing.

Wages of production staff

Weakness

Timesheets completed by production department workers are **submitted** to the payroll department **without being checked**.

Implication

Staff in the production department could **complete** their **timesheets incorrectly** and hence be **paid** the **wrong amounts**.

Recommendation

The **production department supervisor** should **check** all **timesheets** before they are submitted to the payroll department. The company should also consider introducing a **computerised clock in system**.

Salaries of office staff

Weakness

Changes to **staff salaries** in the office department are **notified verbally** to the payroll department.

Implication

Incorrect amendments could be made to staff salaries in the office department by the payroll department, and hence **staff** in the office department could be **paid the wrong amounts**.

Recommendation

Salary changes should be **recorded** in **writing** by the personnel department and **authorised in writing** by the personnel department manager before being sent to the payroll department.

Our comments have been discussed with the chief accountant, Mr Khanna, and these matters will be considered again by us during future audits. We look forward to receiving your comments on the points made. Should you require any further information or explanations please do not hesitate to contact us.

This letter has been produced for the sole use of your company. It must not be disclosed to a third party, or quoted or referred to, without our written consent. No responsibility is assumed by us to any other person.

We should like to take this opportunity of thanking your staff for their co-operation and assistance during the course of our audit.

Yours faithfully

Khan Associates

PROFESSIONAL EDUCATION

Chapter 19

Answer 19.1

(a) '...the financial statements on pages ... to ...'

Purpose

The purpose of this phrase is to make it clear to the reader of an audit report the part of a company's annual report upon which the auditors are reporting their opinion.

Meaning

An annual report may include documents such as a chairman's report, employee report, five year summary and other voluntary information. However, under the Companies Act, only the profit and loss account, balance sheet and associated notes are required to be audited in true and fair terms. Thus the page references (for instance, 8 to 20) cover only the profit and loss account, balance sheet, notes to the accounts, cash flow statement and statement of total recognised gains and losses. The directors' report, although examined and reported on by exception if it contains inconsistencies, is not included in these page references.

(b) '...in accordance with Auditing Standards...'

Purpose

This phrase is included in order to confirm to the reader that best practice, as laid down in Auditing Standards, has been adopted by the auditors in both carrying out their audit and in drafting their audit opinion. This means that the reader can be assured that the audit has been properly conducted, and that should he or she wish to discover what such standards are, or what certain key phrases mean, he or she can have recourse to Auditing Standards to explain such matters.

Meaning

Auditing Standards are those auditing standards prepared by the Auditing Practices Board.

These prescribe the principles and practices to be followed by auditors in the planning, designing and carrying out various aspects of their audit work, the content of audit reports, both qualified and unqualified and so on. Members are expected to follow all of these standards.

(c) 'In our opinion ...'

Purpose

Under the Companies Act, auditors are required to report on every balance sheet, profit and loss account or group accounts laid before members. In reporting, they are required to state their opinion on those accounts. Thus, the purpose of this phrase is to comply with the statutory requirement to report an opinion.

Meaning

An audit report is an expression of opinion by suitably qualified auditors as to whether the financial statements give a true and fair view, and have been properly prepared in accordance with the Companies

Act. **It is not a certificate**; rather it is a statement of whether or not, in the professional judgement of the auditors, the financial statements give a true and fair view.

Answer 19.2

(a) The auditing guideline on stocktaking states that auditors should attend the stock-taking where stocks are material in the company's financial statements, and the auditor is placing reliance upon management's stocktake in order to provide evidence of existence.

There appears to have been therefore a material limitation of scope on the audit.

The basis of opinion section of the audit report should state that the evidence available to us, as auditors, was limited because we could not attend the stock-take and (presumably) were unable to carry out alternative procedures necessary to give sufficient assurance. The paragraph should state the amount of stock involved.

The opinion section of the audit report should be headed up as an opinion qualified due to limitation of scope. The section should state that the accounts give a true and fair view except for any adjustments that may have been necessary had we been able to obtain sufficient assurance concerning stock.

The opinion section also should state in a separate paragraph that in respect of the limitation on the work relating to stock, we did not obtain all the information and explanations that we considered necessary for the purpose of our audit, and we were unable to determine whether proper accounting records had been kept.

(b) It appears that there is no prospect that the monies owed will be recovered.

The audit opinion should therefore be qualified on the grounds of disagreement. The opinion section should be headed up as qualified opinion arising from disagreement about provision for debtor.

Details of the disagreement should be given in a paragraph above the opinion paragraph. We should state that the debtor has ceased trading and is unlikely to make any payment. We should also specific the amount of the provision that we believe should be made.

The opinion paragraph should state that the accounts give a true and fair view except for the failure to provide against the debtor.

(c) We need to decide whether the legal claim is a material matter and whether it is fundamental to the view given by the financial statements. Because of the importance of the customer, it may be that an adverse judgement will have serious consequences for the whole of the company's business, and thus the matter is fundamental.

If we agree that the disclosure is adequate, and on balance, we believe no provision is required, the impact on the audit report will depend on whether the inherent uncertainty involved is material or fundamental. If it is material, we do not need to mention it in the audit report. If it is fundamental, the audit report should include a separate paragraph, headed fundamental uncertainty. This should give details of the circumstances and amounts involved, and make reference to the note in which further details are given. The paragraph should also state that the audit report is not qualified in respect of this matter.

No reference to the claim should be made in the opinion section of the audit report.

Answer 19.3

Going concern

In forming our opinion, we have considered the adequacy of the disclosures made in note X of the financial statements concerning the uncertainty over the changes in the company's customer base. In view of the significance of the uncertainty we consider that it should be drawn to your attention, but our opinion is not qualified in this respect.

Glossary

Analytical procedures The analysis of relationships between items of financial data and non-financial data deriving from the same period, or, between comparable financial information deriving from different periods to identify consistencies and predicted patterns or significant fluctuations and unexpected relationships and the results of investigation thereof.

Audit An exercise whose objective is to enable auditors to express an opinion whether the financial statements give a true and fair view of the entity's affairs at the period end and of its profit and loss for the period then ended and have been properly prepared in accordance with the applicable reporting framework.

Audit plan The formulation of the general strategy for the audit, which sets the direction for the audit, describes the expected scope and conduct of the audit and provides guidance for the development of the audit programme.

Audit programme A set of instructions to the audit team that sets out the audit procedures the auditors intend to adopt and may include references to other matters such as the audit objectives, timing, sample size and basis of selection for each area. It also serves as a means to control and record the proper execution of the work.

Audit risk The risk that the auditors may give an inappropriate opinion on the financial statements.

Current audit file The audit file in which auditors maintain working papers relevant to the current year audit.

Control environment The overall attitude, awareness and actions of directors and managers regarding internal controls and their importance in the entity.

Control procedures Those policies and procedures in addition to the control environment which are established to achieve the entity's specific objectives.

Control risk The risk that a misstatement could occur in an account balance or class of transactions, could be material, either individually or when aggregated with misstatements in other balances or classes and would not be prevented, or detected and corrected on a timely basis by the accounting and internal control systems.

Detection risk The risk that the auditors' substantive procedures do not detect a misstatement that exists in an account balance or class of transactions that could be material, either individually or when aggregated with misstatements in other balances or classes.

Error Unintentional mistake in financial statements.

Fair When information is free from discrimination and bias and in compliance with the expected standards and rules. The accounts should reflect the commercial substance of the company's underlying transactions.

Fraud Comprises both the use of deception to obtain an unjust or illegal financial advantage and intentional misrepresentation by management, employees or third parties.

Financial statement assertions Assertions made by the directors about assets, liabilities, expenses and income in the financial statements they prepare. Includes: completeness, existence, rights and obligations, occurrence, valuation, measurement and presentation.

Going concern The assumption that the business will continue to operate in the foreseeable future.

Internal control systems Comprise the control environment and control procedures adopted by the directors and management of an entity to ensure, as far as practicable, the orderly and efficient conduct of its business.

Inherent risk The susceptibility of an account balance or class of transactions to material misstatement, either individually or when aggregated with misstatements in other balances or classes, irrespective of related internal controls.

Materiality An expression of the relative significance or importance of a particular matter in the context of financial statements as a whole.

Permanent audit file Audit file where the audit team maintains working papers and documents of ongoing significance to the audit.

Segregation of duties A system of internal check where a number of people are involved in the accounting process.

Substantive procedures Tests to obtain audit evidence to detect material misstatements in the financial statements.

Tests of control Tests to obtain audit evidence about the effective operation of the accounting and internal control systems, that is, that properly designed controls identified in preliminary assessment of control risk exist in fact and have operated effectively throughout the relevant period.

True Information is factual and conforms with reality, not false. In addition the information conforms with required standards and law. The accounts have been correctly extracted from the books and records.

Index

AAT Guidelines on Professional Ethics	27
Accounting and control systems	68
Accounting estimates	182
Accounting for stock	193
Accounting records	6
Accruals	249
Analysis of errors	144
Analytical procedures	103, 175, 271
Association of Accounting Technicians (AAT)	22
Audit	7, 12
Audit appointment	8
Audit evidence	132
Audit exemptions	7
Audit files	125
Audit interrogation software	136
Audit programme	96
Audit requirement	7
Audit team	110
Auditing standards	24
Auditor rights	10
Auditors' opinion	323
Auditors' report	8
Bad debts	230
Bank	234
Borrowing facilities	273
Bulletins	24
Cash	237
Chartered Institute of Management Accountants (CIMA)	22
Chartered Institute of Public Finance and Accountancy (CIPFA)	22
Client staff	111
Companies Act 1985	5, 193
Companies Act 1989	6
Comparatives	185
Completeness	134
Completion checklists	284
Compliance with accounting regulations	271
Computer assisted audit techniques (CAATs)	136
Confidentiality	26, 124
Confirmation of the system	155
Contingencies	281
Continuing auditors	184
Contract law	40
Control environment	68
Control procedures	69
Control risk	98, 141
Cost	194
Cost of conversion	194
Current audit files	125
Current liabilities	246
Cut-off	233, 236, 248
Debtors	226
Debtors' circularisation	227
Design of the sample	139
Designing substantive tests	174
Detection risk	99, 141
Development costs	216
Direction	112
Directors' emoluments	264
Directors' report	49
Disagreement	327, 329
Disagreements	329
Distributions	261
Dormant companies	7
Duty of reasonable care	40
Embedded audit facilities	137
Engagement letter	35
Engagement partner review	114
Estimates	182
Evaluation of sample results	144
Existence	134
Expected error	142
Expert	114
Expression of opinion	323
Final assessment of control risk	150
Financial records	6
Financial statement assertions	134
Financial statements	10
Finished goods	193
First in first out (FIFO)	193

Fixed asset register   211
Flowcharts   76
Fraud and error   49
Fundamental uncertainty   331

Going concern   53, 271
Goods on sale or return   233
Goodwill   216

Haphazard selection   143

Incoming auditors   184
Independence   25
Ineligible for appointment   343
Inherent risk   98, 141
Inherent uncertainty   331
Intangible fixed assets   215
Inter-company indebtedness   231
Internal audit   86
Internal audit   16
Internal Control Evaluation Questionnaires
   (ICEQs)   82, 83
Internal Control Questionnaires (ICQs)   82
Internal control systems   16, 50, 68
Investments   217

Judgmental sampling   143

Law and regulations   52
Limitation in scope   327
Limitations in the scope of the audit   327
Limitations of control systems   70
Long term liabilities   260

Management   308
Management representation letter   278
Management representations   276
Manager review   114
Material misstatement   100
Materiality   100
Measurement   134

Narrative notes   76
Negligence   40
Net realisable value   194

Objectives of internal control systems   71
Occurrence   134
Oral representations   276
Overall audit risk   96
Overall review of financial statements   270

Payments on account   193
Permanent audit files   125
Planning meeting   111
Practice Notes   24
Prepayments   232
Presentation and disclosure   134
Principal auditors   296
Professional ethics   25
Projected population error   144
Purchases   247
Purchases cut-off   248
Purchases system   73, 159

Qualified audit reports   326

Random selection   142
Raw materials   193
Reasonable care   40
Recognised Qualifying Bodies   23
Recognised Supervisory Bodies (RSBs)   23
Recording internal control systems   76
Registrar of Companies   6
Related parties   55
Report to partner   283
Reporting inherent uncertainty   331
Reports by exception   320
Reports to management   310
Representation letter   276
Reserves   261
Review   112, 283
Review of audit working papers   113
Rights and obligations   134
Risk-based approach   96

Sales 232
Sales system 72
Sales system 156
Sample size 140
Sampling risk 141
SAS 110 *Fraud and error* 50
SAS 120 *Consideration of law and regulations* 26, 52
SAS 130 *Going concern basis in financial statements* 271
SAS 140 *Engagement letters* 35
SAS 160 *Other information in documents containing financial statements* 48
SAS 200 *Planning* 94
SAS 210 *Knowledge of the business* 65, 121
SAS 220 *Materiality and the audit* 100
SAS 230 *Working papers* 121
SAS 240 *Quality control for audit work* 110
SAS 300 *Accounting and internal control systems* 156
SAS 400 *Audit evidence* 133
SAS 410 *Analytical procedures* 103, 176
SAS 420 *Audits of accounting estimates* 182
SAS 430 *Audit sampling* 139
SAS 440 *Management representations* 276
SAS 450 *Opening balances and comparatives* 183
SAS 460 *Related parties* 55
SAS 470 *Overall review of financial statements* 270
SAS 510 *The relationship between principal auditors and other auditors* 296
SAS 520 *Using the work of an expert* 114
SAS 600 *Auditors' report on financial statements* 320
SAS 610 *Communication of audit matters to those charged with governance* 308
Security 26
Segregation of duties 69
Selection by value 143
Selection of the sample 142
Sequence sampling 143
Share capital 261
Small charities 7
Small companies 7
Specimen management letter 311
SSAP 9 Stocks and long term contracts 193
Standardised working papers 121

Statement of directors' responsibilities 47
Statements of Auditing Standards (SASs) 24
Statements of responsibility 322
Statistical sampling 143
Statutory books 261, 263
Stock cut-off 198
Stocktake 194
Stocktaking procedures 195
Subsequent events 54, 279
Substantive procedures 134
Sufficient appropriate audit evidence 133
Summarising errors 283
Supervision 112
Suppliers' statements 247
Systematic selection 142

Tangible fixed assets 211
Tender 11
Test data 136
Tests of control 133, 155
Third parties interested in reports to directors or management 311
Those charged with governance 308
Tolerable error 142

Unadjusted errors 284
Uncertainty 331
Unqualified reports 321

Valuation 134
Valuation of stock 200

Wages and salaries 250
Wages system 75, 164
Walk-through test 155
Work in progress 193
Working papers 121
Written confirmation 276

See overleaf for information on other
BPP products and how to order

AAT Order

To BPP Professional Education, Aldine Place, London W12 8AW
Tel: 020 8740 2211. Fax: 020 8740 1184
E-mail: Publishing@bpp.com Web:www.bpp.com

Mr/Mrs/Ms (Full name) _____

Daytime delivery address _____

Postcode _____

Daytime Tel _____ E-mail _____

OTHER MATERIAL FOR AAT STUDENTS	8/03 Texts	3/03 Text
FOUNDATION (£5.95)		
Basic Mathematics	☐	
INTERMEDIATE (£5.95)		
Basic Bookkeeping (for students exempt from Foundation)	☐	
FOR ALL STUDENTS (£5.95)		
Building Your Portfolio (old standards)	☐	
Building Your Portfolio (new standards)	☐	☐

£ ☐   £ ☐

TOTAL FOR PRODUCTS   £ ☐

POSTAGE & PACKING

Texts/Kits	First	Each extra	
UK	£3.00	£3.00	£ ☐
Europe*	£6.00	£4.00	£ ☐
Rest of world	£20.00	£10.00	£ ☐
Passcards			
UK	£2.00	£1.00	£ ☐
Europe*	£3.00	£2.00	£ ☐
Rest of world	£8.00	£8.00	£ ☐
Tapes			
UK	£2.00	£1.00	£ ☐
Europe*	£3.00	£2.00	£ ☐
Rest of world	£8.00	£8.00	£ ☐

TOTAL FOR POSTAGE & PACKING £ ☐
(Max £12 Texts/Kits/Passcards - deliveries in UK)

Grand Total (Cheques to *BPP Professional Education*)

I enclose a cheque for (incl. Postage) **£** ☐

Or charge to Access/Visa/Switch

Card Number ☐☐☐☐☐☐☐☐☐☐☐☐

Expiry date _____ Start Date _____

Issue Number (Switch Only) _____

Signature _____

We aim to deliver to all UK addresses inside 5 working days; a signature will be required. Orders to all EU addresses should be delivered within 6 working days. All other orders to overseas addresses should be delivered within 8 working days. * Europe includes the Republic of Ireland and the Channel Islands.

Review Form & Free Prize Draw – Building your portfolio

All original review forms from the entire BPP range, completed with genuine comments, will be entered into one of two draws on 31 July 2003 and 31 January 2004. The names on the first four forms picked out on each occasion will be sent a cheque for £50.

Name: _____ **Address:** _____

_____

_____

How have you used this Interactive Text?
(Tick one box only)

☐ Home study (book only)

☐ On a course: college _____

☐ With 'correspondence' package

☐ Other _____

Why did you decide to purchase this Interactive Text? *(Tick one box only)*

☐ Have used BPP Texts in the past

☐ Recommendation by friend/colleague

☐ Recommendation by a lecturer at college

☐ Saw advertising

☐ Other _____

During the past six months do you recall seeing/receiving any of the following?
(Tick as many boxes as are relevant)

☐ Our advertisement in *Accounting Technician* magazine

☐ Our advertisement in *Pass*

☐ Our brochure with a letter through the post

Which (if any) aspects of our advertising do you find useful?
(Tick as many boxes as are relevant)

☐ Prices and publication dates of new editions

☐ Information on Interactive Text content

☐ Facility to order books off-the-page

☐ None of the above

Have you used the companion Assessment Kit for this subject?   ☐ Yes   ☐ No

Your ratings, comments and suggestions would be appreciated on the following areas

	Very useful	Useful	Not useful
Chapter topic lists	☐	☐	☐
Examples	☐	☐	☐
Activities and answers	☐	☐	☐

	Excellent	Good	Adequate	Poor
Overall opinion of this Text	☐	☐	☐	☐

Do you intend to continue using BPP Interactive Texts/Assessment Kits?   ☐ Yes   ☐ No

Please note any further comments and suggestions/errors on the reverse of this page.

The BPP author of this edition can be e-mailed at: Catherinewatton@bpp.com

Review Form & Free Prize Draw (continued)

Please note any further comments and suggestions/errors below

Free Prize Draw Rules

1   Closing date for 31 July 2003 draw is 30 June 2003. Closing date for 31 January 2004 draw is 31 December 2003.

2   Restricted to entries with UK and Eire addresses only. BPP employees, their families and business associates are excluded.

3   No purchase necessary. Entry forms are available upon request from BPP Publishing. No more than one entry per title, per person. Draw restricted to persons aged 16 and over.

4   Winners will be notified by post and receive their cheques not later than 6 weeks after the relevant draw date.

5   The decision of the promoter in all matters is final and binding. No correspondence will be entered into.